Opium and Empire

By the same author:

Prince of Pirates: The Temenggongs and the Development of Johor and Singapore, 1784–1885

Opium and Empire

Chinese Society in Colonial Singapore, 1800–1910

CARL A. TROCKI

Cornell University Press

ITHACA AND LONDON

First published 1990 by Cornell University Press.

International Standard Book Number 0-8014-2390-2
Library of Congress Catalog Card Number 90-55123
Printed in the United States of America
Librarians: Library of Congress cataloging information
appears on the last page of the book.

♾ The paper in this book meets the minimum requirements
of the American National Standard for Information Sciences—
Permanence of Paper for Printed Library Materials, ANSI Z39.48-1984.

Contents

Illustrations

Maps

Tables

Figures

Acknowledgments

This reinterpretation of the history of Singapore is based on much used but misunderstood data. It relies heavily on the works of the colonial historians who have created the standard accounts of this period. The most useful primary sources have been the English-language *Straits Settlements Records* (*SSR*) for the period 1800–1867 and the Colonial Office Records (CO 273) for the years thereafter. These have been supplemented by the English-language newspapers of the period and by the standard published works of the nineteenth century. Chinese-language sources are scarce but necessary, and my access to them has been through secondary published works. These have been supplemented by the Malay-language sources of the Johor Archives, which I used for my earlier studies. The Johor records have proven an invaluable resource, and it is doubtful that the history of Singapore can be properly understood without them.

Although I have raised questions about the assumptions of the colonialist historians who have produced the substantial literature on the Chinese and the secret societies, I could not have begun this work without their contributions. I have also attempted to test the theories of more recent scholars, Maurice Freedman and G. William Skinner, who have been responsible for pointing the study of the overseas Chinese in a new direction. I have also benefited from the important work many Malaysians and Singaporeans are doing as they take charge of their own history. This group includes Wong Lin Ken, Wang Gungwu, Khoo Kay Kim, Lee Poh Ping, Wang Tai Peng, Hong Lysa, Mak Lau Fong, and Ng Chin-keong. Finally, I see this as only a part of the much larger effort being undertaken by other students of opium and the imperial process. These are my colleagues and contemporaries in this effort who are presently reinterpreting the history of the entire region.

Much of the research for this book was supported by grants from the Social Science Research Council and the American Council of Learned Societies in 1981 and by a Fulbright Grant from the Council for International Exchange of Scholars in 1985. The first permitted me to spend three months in London, where I used the collections at the India Office, the Public Record Office, and the Library of the School of Oriental and African Studies, University of London. I am most grateful for the assistance and support of the staffs of all these archives. The Fulbright award allowed me to spend eight months in Singapore, where I benefited from the sponsorship of the Institute of Southeast Asian Studies (ISEAS) and its director, Dr. Kernial Sandhu. My work in Singapore was aided by the active assistance of the staffs of the National Library, the National Archives, the Library of the National University of Singapore, and the library of ISEAS. In particular I thank Dr. Patricia Lim, formerly of the ISEAS Library, and David K. Y. Chng of the National Library for their many acts of personal assistance on my behalf.

I made several other less sustained research forays to collections in the United States, the most important of which were the John M. Echols Collection and the Wason Collection at Cornell University. I also made significant use of the special collections of the Cleveland Public Library and of the Southeast Asian collections of the Ohio University Library. I also acknowledge material support from the academic institutions that employed me while I worked on this project. Both Thomas More College in Crestview Hills, Kentucky, and Georgetown University, Washington, D.C., have provided the institutional foundations without which this sort of scholarly endeavor cannot be undertaken. In particular, I am grateful to my friends Raymond G. Hebert; Sr. Mary Philip Trauth, S.N.D.; Howard Spendelow, and Matthew Gardner. I also acknowledge the support of Hans and Lisa Jacobson. The interest and assistance of my friends in Johor Bahru was an important contribution to my understanding of this material. I am especially thankful to Dato Kuek Ho Yao, Dato Wong Peng Long, Chern Yen Ming, and Cheng Chean Chiang.

Numerous colleagues read all or parts of this manuscript and, through their kind criticism and comments, saved me from many glaring errors. Their time and interest has resulted in the substantial improvement of this work. In particular I am indebted to Ruth McVey, George and Audrey Kahin, James R. Rush, Jennifer Cushman, Dian

Murray, Leonard and Barbara Andaya, Jeya Kathirithamby-Wells, John Butcher, Sharon Carstens, Wong Lin Ken, Hong Lysa, and Mary Somers Heidhues. Others have shared with me, at some point in this project, their insights on opium, secret societies, kongsis, revenue farms, and British imperialism in general. These include Mary Turnbull, Mak Lau Fong, Ng Chin Keong, Lim How Seng, Ernest Chew, Diane Lewis, Anthony Reid, Khoo Kay Kim, Lee Poh Ping, Robert Taylor, Helen Chauncey, Vivienne Wee, and Geoffrey Benjamin. Finally, I make special mention of the unflagging support, both material and intellectual, of my good friend Benedict Anderson, who not only provided hospitality during my many trips to Ithaca but also read, discussed, criticized, and encouraged this work in ways too numerous to mention.

My family, who have stood by me and often suffered neglect while I pursued this project, I also acknowledge: most important, my wife, Orrawin; my children, Rebecca and Carl; my mother, Helen Trocki; and my brothers and sisters. Finally, I am grateful for the companionship of my many friends in Singapore, London, Johor, and elsewhere.

CARL A. TROCKI

Washington, D.C.

Abbreviations

BMOC	British Malayan Opium Commission (Report of the Opium Commission)
CO	Colonial Office (Great Britain)
CPL	Cleveland Public Library
CSSH	*Comparative Studies in Society and History*
EIC	East India Company (English)
Exco	Executive Council (Straits Settlements)
G.D.	Governor's Despatch
IOR	India Office Records
ISEAS	Institute for Southeast Asian Studies (Singapore)
JIAEA	*Journal of the Indian Archipelago and East Asia*
JLB	Johor *Letterbook (1 and 2)*
JMBRAS	*Journal of the Malaysian (Malayan) Branch of the Royal Asiatic Society*
JRAS	*Journal of the Royal Asiatic Society (of Northern Ireland and England)*
JSBRAS	*Journal of the Straits Branch of the Royal Asiatic Society*
JSEAH	*Journal of Southeast Asian History*
JSEAS	*Journal of Southeast Asian Studies*
JSSS	*Journal of the South Seas Society*
KSSSU	*Kumpulan Surat2 yang di-Simpan oleh Setia Usaha Kerajaan* (Johor)
Legco	*(Straits Settlements) Legislative Council Proceedings* (Singapore)
Roycom	*First Report of the Royal Commission on Opium: With Minutes of Evidence and Appendices . . . etc.*
SC	*Singapore Chronicle*
SCD	*Straits Calendar and Directory* (see *SSD*)
SFP	*Singapore Free Press*
SRP	Separate Revenue Proceedings (India)
SSADR	*Straits Settlements Annual Departmental Reports*
SSD	*Straits Settlements Directory* (various titles)

SSFR	*Straits Settlements Factory Records*
SSGG	*Straits Settlements Government Gazette*
SSOT	Society for the Suppression of the Opium Trade
SSR	*Straits Settlements Records* (Singapore)
SSTP	*Surat2 Titah Perentah* (Johor)
ST	*Straits Times* (Singapore)
STOJ	*Straits Times Overland Journal* (Singapore)
STWI	*Straits Times Weekly Intelligence* (Singapore)

Opium and Empire

Opium Smoking

Chinese opium den in nineteenth-century Singapore (National Archives, Singapore)

Introduction

For European observers, one of the most enduring nineteenth-century images of the Chinese, whether in China or in Southeast Asia, was that of the opium "wreck." The hollow-eyed, emaciated Oriental stretched out on his pallet, pipe in hand, stood as the stereotype of Asiatic decadence and indulgence. He was the icon of all that was beyond the pale of Christian morality and human decency. Even if we went beyond the picture to learn that it was Westerners, really English and Americans, who were most actively involved in selling the drug in Asia, the association between the "Chinaman" and his pipe was fixed. The victim had come to stand for the crime, and the image has acquired an extraordinary historical durability.

The irony of this perception so far as Singapore is concerned is that the average Chinese coolie had probably never tasted opium before coming to the British settlement. Thomas Stamford Raffles, who established the East India Company settlement on Singapore Island in 1819, actually had a great deal to do with creating the system that led to the addiction of millions of Chinese laborers. British colonial historians have neglected this aspect of their countrymen's historical role in Asia. Instead they have presented the history of Singapore as a tribute to the enlightened liberalism that pushed back the night of barbarism, abolished slavery, and opened Asia to free trade and the rule of law. One might come away with the impression that Raffles worked for the liberation of Chinese opium wrecks.

Determining moral responsibility for the opium trade and for the long-term effects of colonial rule involves very complex issues. Raffles was part of a system that was in place before he came to Asia and that

1

continued after he had returned home. Perhaps, if we are placing blame, the British administrators and merchants who succeeded him should also bear a share of the onus. But thousands of Chinese, both in Singapore and in China, actively participated in the enthrallment and exploitation of their fellows. The questions of blame, credit, and responsibility are difficult ones for the historian since the moral standards of the past seem so different from those of the present. Nevertheless, Raffles claimed responsibility for founding the British free port, and his successors have regularly found reason to praise his noble purpose. At the same time, voices of criticism were in fact raised against the opium trade even in the nineteenth century. So, perhaps modern standards applied to the drug traffic would not be entirely alien to the age in question.

My purpose in writing about Singapore and opium is not simply to cast blame; it is to grasp the factors of historical causation, which may seem to be the same thing. It is impossible to read the archival records of nineteenth-century Singapore without encountering opium over and over. The statistics and the facts show it to have been ubiquitous throughout the century. The weight of such a factor cannot be ignored if we are to understand the forces that shaped the social, political, and economic order of the British colony.

For the early decades of Singapore's existence as a British port, the major item of trade was opium. It was carried to the Company's free port of Singapore by British free traders from British India, where it had been grown under an East India Company monopoly by debt-ridden Bengali ryots. In Singapore, there were no taxes on trade, no port duties, and the port was open to the ships, peoples, and products of all nations. Opium in particular was traded freely, but only as a wholesale commodity for export. Smokable opium, known as *chandu*, was retailed under a strict government-sanctioned monopoly called the opium farm. For the first century of the colony's existence, this privately held concession was responsible for the lion's share of the state's locally collected revenue. It rarely accounted for less than 40 percent and often made up over 60 percent. In other words, Raffles's liberal, capitalist Singapore not only created the opium-smoking Chinese coolie; it literally lived on his back. He paid for free trade.

This intimate connection linking the Singapore Chinese, opium, and British imperialism is the subject of this book. The relationship was crucial to guiding the forces that created Chinese society in nineteenth-century Singapore. My first book, *Prince of Pirates*, brought me to the edge of this inquiry. It became clear to me that the story of Johor and of

Chinese pepper and gambier planters who settled the state was simply a peripheral repercussion of the expansion of influences from Singapore. Singapore was the source and center of Johor's people, of its economy, and of its history. In this book, I have emulated the Japanese, who in 1942 successfully invaded Singapore through its back door, from Johor. In *Prince of Pirates*, I traced the migration of the Chinese pepper and gambier agriculture from Singapore to Johor; here, I retrace my steps to examine the evolution of Chinese society at its center by approaching from the periphery. I try to make sense of the social, political, and economic institutions the Chinese themselves used to organize their activities in Southeast Asia and of the conflict among Chinese, European, and indigenous social institutions, political entities, and economic systems in colonial Singapore.

There have been several previous attempts to explain the outbreaks of violence among the Chinese in nineteenth-century Singapore. Normally, colonialist writers have treated outbreaks of "secret society" wars as indicative of "inherent" Chinese divisiveness. Lee Poh Ping, though, views these conflicts as evidence of "class" conflict between the "pepper and gambier society" of Singapore's interior and the "free trade society" of the colonial port. Lee offers an important insight; I also believe the conflict was deep seated and went beyond mere ethnicity and clan loyalties.

In this book, I attempt to chart a sort of institutional history of the Chinese migration to Southeast Asia. The Chinese planters who came to Singapore brought with them an economic and political system with deep roots. The pepper and gambier society, to borrow Lee's term, was based on a shareholding partnership of planters, capitalists, and laborers known as a *kongsi*. It was organized to pool labor and capital to produce commodities for shipment back to China. Its political structure and ideology were derived from the *triad* societies of southern China, which were secret societies that bound members by blood oaths to ties of brotherhood. The kongsis thus were more than mere economic partnerships; they constituted a ritual community of single men who had ventured from their homelands to seek their fortunes among the "barbarians" of the South Seas, the Nanyang.

In Singapore the Chinese kongsis came into contact and conflict with the entrepôt society of European free traders and a colonial state possessed of a technological and economic strength hitherto unknown in the region. Both operated according to an economic ethic that stood in significant contrast to the fair-shares ethic of the kongsis. The Europeans found ready allies in the community of Straits Chinese, a group of creole and mestizo Chinese who had inhabited the port cities of Southeast Asia for centuries and often married into local societies but who continued to retain important aspects of their Chinese identity. They came to Singapore from Melaka and Pinang.

The nineteenth century saw a progression of conflicts and compromises, growth and decay, in this confluence of systems. The two societies were founded on radically different assumptions about the value of labor, the nature of property, the sanctity of contracts, and the rights of the individual as against those of the social group. One drew its strength from control of labor and production, the other from its control of capital, weapons, and long-distance communications. Each possessed economic factors the other lacked, and each sought to exploit opportunities the presence of the other offered: Chinese needed access to European capital, and Europeans sought to gain access to Chinese labor.

The Chinese kongsis were organized to share the wealth among the workers and investors, who generally repatriated their products and profits to China. The kongsis were, however, commercial enterprises and had always been associated with a special group of Chinese merchants, or *taukehs,* who also joined the kongsis and swore oaths of brotherhood and received a share of the profits. These merchants, by necessity, lived and worked in the world of the ports and thus came into regular contact with the European merchants and Straits Chinese traders. The pivotal relationship of the pepper and gambier taukehs with both the Straits Chinese and the kongsis lies at the heart of the economic struggles that raged in Singapore during the nineteenth century.

The field of conflict was the whole pepper and gambier economy, which in fact was not limited to Singapore but also included the Dutch settlements in the Riau-Lingga Archipelago, where it had originated; Sumatra; the Malay state of Johor; and the other British-controlled territories of Negri Sembilan, Melaka, and even Sarawak. This economic system, which came to center at Singapore, included a Chinese population that numbered close to one million by the end of the century. The economy was characterized by a combination of monopolies and free enterprise in an atmosphere of unrestricted expansion. A large and increasing supply of Chinese labor was flowing into a mostly uninhabited and undeveloped region. This was the "dragon" the British lion had to ride if it wished to control Malaya.

Within this "free" economy, the opium farm lent itself to monopoly control. The connection between the British colonial state and Chinese labor was forged by the Chinese opium farmers. The farmers purchased the right to sell opium to the population of Singapore. The most important market was the large population of agricultural coolies on the pepper and gambier plantations. This connection between the market and the consumers was vital to both the financial and political success of the British colony. Financially, opium capital underwrote both the state and the producing economy. Politically, it established a system of social control upon which the British administrative structure was based. The workings of the farm and its relationship to the economy, to the colonial state, and to the developing Chinese social order are thus central to this book. The farm brought colonial governors, Straits Chinese merchants, Teochew pepper and gambier traders, secret society chiefs, and the masses of Chinese labor into the same arena. The fight for the farm was really the fight for Singapore, and it is the century-long struggle for control of that institution that I have attempted to reconstruct here.

This is not just an account of conflict between a few financial cliques; it is an important and hitherto neglected part of the history of European colonialism and of Chinese social and economic development. The opium farmers built a chain of indebtedness which connected the European economy of the entrepôt with the kongsi economies of the jungles while at the same time extending the power of the colonial state. Furthermore, the process by which this system of indebtedness and control was constructed actually lay at the roots of most of the secret society fights, riots, or conflicts that marked the history of Chinese Singapore. This account refutes standard European accounts that blame these disruptions on some inherently instable element in the "Oriental mind." Conflict was essentially economic. It took place between the forces of labor and capital for control of the means of production and of the surplus product. The means of production were Chinese labor and British opium capital. This was the essence of the colonial class struggle. The result was clear. In the end, the only viable political structure in Singapore was the authoritarian apparatus of the colonial state. All other indigenous political institutions had been rendered incapable of reproducing themselves. This unfortunate result is the continuing inheritance of the people of Singapore.

The story of the opium trade and its role in the entire imperial century has been almost totally neglected. Understandably, British colonial historians have not been eager to probe deeply into what must now seem an entirely shameful aspect of their imperial adventure. For reasons that are less clear, Asian historians of every ideological persuasion, even the Marxists, have failed to approach the opium question seriously. In any case, the story is not simply one of European expansion but of the construction of economic, social, and political systems. The impact of opium cannot be gauged by simply looking at the bases of production in India and at the import figures on the China coast. It is necessary to understand how opium was related to the day-to-day functioning of colonial economic and social systems. The history of the farms and their associated economic systems is only one example of this process. I believe there are many others that remain to be explored.

The history of the Singapore opium farm, as an institution, unwholesome or not, is also important for other reasons. It spanned an entire century. It is really the only accessible thread of continuity in the history of the Singapore Chinese community. It may be the only overseas Chinese economic institution that can be said to have a history. As such, it provides a series of benchmarks and some further information on the identities of the cast of characters who created the social system of the present community. The events of the farm have made it possible to put the secret society conflicts in the correct context and at the same time highlight several important areas of European colonial administrative history. Recent studies in a similar vein, in other parts of Southeast Asia, show that opium farms and farmers played similarly important roles as agents of the colonial process. The farms provided a central core around which families, dynasties, and even classes were created. It is one thing to speak glibly of class conflict; it is quite another to show it. I believe I have done that here.

1 The Kongsi and the History
of the Singapore Chinese

On one of the low hills rising behind the town of Johor Baru (map 1) there is a grave in a desolate Chinese cemetery. No sign along the paved road, Jalan Ngee Heng, indicates that this is a place of interment. There is only a pair of rutted dirt tracks going off into the wasteland of scrub and lallang. We parked along the pavement and followed the tracks for about fifty meters before the first graves appeared, and then we searched around for this monument. The lallang grass had been freshly chopped away, perhaps for the benefit of our group.

The grave is large and imposing, and in the typical fashion of these graves it is backed into the side of a low hill with two concentric stone rings arching behind it on the top of the knoll. The central face of the grave is about ten feet wide and maybe five feet high. It is flanked by low walls that extend another twenty feet on each side. In front is a large, square platform about thirty feet wide. The tomb and platform are faced with yellow, brown, white, and green ceramic tiles.

The grave does not commemorate any particular person, and there is no body beneath the stone. There is no certainty about what is there, perhaps only a box of tablets, perhaps more. No one admits to knowing. In the center is a white marble slab incised with two Chinese characters painted in gold. They read 明墓 , or "Ming Tomb," nothing more. This is the "grave" of the Ngee Heng Kongsi, perhaps the oldest and most formidable of all the Chinese secret societies in Malaya during the nineteenth century.[1]

1. Wynne, *Triad and Tabut* (1941), pp. 9–10.

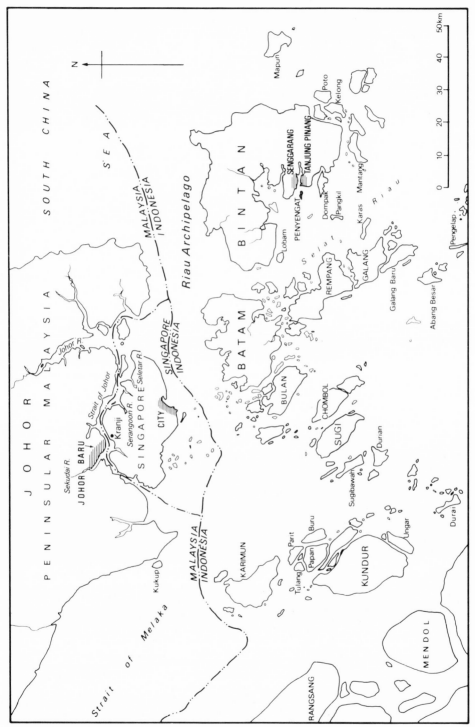

1. The gambier-producing areas of Singapore, Riau, and South Johor.

How the Ngee Heng[2] came to end its days in this forlorn spot in Johor is a part of my story. It seems to have been one of the earliest Chinese organizations in the Malay Peninsula and may have been founded sometime in the eighteenth century. Initially it was associated with Chinese pepper and gambier planters. It came to Johor from Singapore in the 1840s along with those planters and, for a variety of reasons, continued in Johor long after it had been suppressed else-where. In 1915, when triads had been proscribed throughout the Malay states, the Johor Ngee Heng remained the only legal Chinese triad society in British Malaya. According to A. E. Coope, the kongsi abolished itself after some pressure from the British, who had finally succeeded in placing a general advisor in the state in 1912. According to my informants, it was reasoned that the society's purpose had been fulfilled with the overthrow of the Qing dynasty in China. The members of the Ngee Heng gathered up its ancestral tablets, its records, sacred symbols, and regalia. Then, after a procession and a formal ceremony, the objects were buried. The treasury of the society was turned over to a committee and became the initial endowment for what is today the Foon Yew School, the largest Chinese school in the federation.[3]

On this day in March of 1985, I stood together with fifteen or twenty Chinese gentlemen. They included some of the most prominent Chinese businessmen and community leaders of Johor Baru. Among them were the Foon Yew School Committee, which was made up of representatives of the entire Chinese community (the "five kinds of Chinese": Teochew, Hokkien, Hakka, Cantonese, and Hainanese) as well as the head of the Johor Baru Chinese Association. So far as I knew, none of them were members of current secret societies. We gathered for what my host referred to as a "semiannual function." For as long as anyone can remember, the ceremony has been held on the occasion of both the vernal and autumnal equinoxes. Respects are paid at the Ming Tomb and also, since 1946, at the memorial to the Johor Chinese killed by the Japanese during the Occupation. At both sites there was a simple ceremony in which the committee lined up in

2. In Mandarin also pronounced "Yi Hsing." Generally, most authors refer to this society by the Hokkien pronunciation, "Ghee Hin," but since the Johor Chinese were primarily Teochew, I have followed the romanization based on the Teochew pronunciation. The name has generally been translated as "righteous rising society," or the "justice arousal society" or some similar title.

3. Coope, "Kangchu System in Johore" (1936), p. 253. Coope notes that a school, known in the 1930s as the Ngi Hin School, had been built on the site of the old Ngee Heng Society Lodge. This school was later renamed the Foon Yew School.

front of the memorial and the person officiating tendered offerings of "joss, fruit, and flowers." When each official had done likewise, the items were placed in front of the stone. Then the clerk recited an elegy. Finally, all present bowed three times, and that was it. We stood around for a few minutes and made sure everyone had a ride home and then left.

Although my host and some of the company were diffident about the ceremony and its meaning, some even suggesting it is outdated and should be abandoned, the fact that the memorial ceremony continues to be held implies a seriousness of purpose and a significant sense of piety. Other remarks confirmed a commitment to the concept of brotherhood as well as to a sense of Chinese identity, which both the monuments and the ceremonies represent. The Johor Baru Chinese are particularly proud that they, alone among the Malaysian Chinese, have broken down the barriers of speech group and provincial origin to support an all-Chinese school and a unified Chinese community. In modern Singapore, just fifteen minutes away across the causeway, such a ceremony would be unheard of, and the issue of Chinese identity is a rather different matter. There, the much grander monument to the victims of the Japanese massacres is only the object of private respects, and there are no public or community observances. An observance commemorating a secret society would probably be illegal.

The Johor Baru ceremony at the Ming Tomb, the grave of the Ngee Heng Kongsi, seems a contradiction. There is a paradox in the general disrepute that surrounds the topic of secret societies and the obvious respectability of the company present which demands an explanation. What is it that continues to draw wealthy and prosaic businessmen to this unlikely spot on a weekday morning? What is their link to the old kongsi? Do they see the memorial not only as a symbol of community identity, but also as one of secret, sworn brotherhood between people who would otherwise be strangers in a foreign land? Do they see its links going back to the oath first sworn in the peach orchard between the heroes of *San Guo*, in the last days of the Han dynasty?[4] Certainly the men did not express themselves to me in those terms. But, the fact that they find in the memory of the kongsi a sense of community is something that has not been fully explored by students of their history. Their presence at the ceremony shows that the old kongsi, though dead, still commands reverence as an ancestor and benefactor.

This abiding respect suggests that it is important to look more

---

4. Triad rituals recall the oath of brotherhood sworn in a peach orchard between the three third-century heroes of the Chinese epic *San Guo:* Liu Pei, Chang Fei, and Kuan Yu. See Lo, *Three Kingdoms* (1976), pp. 1–13.

closely at the so-called secret societies of the nineteenth century. Although the official view of these groups was, and remains today, that they were criminal gangs of thieves and extortionists, it is clear that beneath the surface disapproval, most Chinese regard them as something more respectable and honorable than the nineteenth-century version of organized crime. Their historical criminalization by unfriendly colonial and postcolonial governments has obscured an important key to understanding the history of the Singapore and Malaysian Chinese.

The Problem of Overseas Chinese History

What I do here is approach the study of Chinese society through its institutions. It seems sensible to seek the "carriers" of Chinese history in the social and economic institutions the immigrants brought with them and adapted in Southeast Asia. Every society is composed of structured patterns of association. These underlie the social organism and facilitate joint action by its members. Likewise, the process of social change is reflected in the growth and evolution of a society's fundamental institutions. These institutions made it possible for the Chinese to leave their home country in fairly large groups; to occupy territory in foreign lands; to set up functioning communities; to establish viable economic systems; and to maintain an organized social structure. The institution that allowed the Chinese to do these things was the kongsi.[5]

Kongsi is a generic Chinese term for a range of social and economic configurations that includes everything from business partnerships to clan and regional associations to secret triad societies. It signifies a kind of corporation or, most correctly, a "company" in which a group of individuals pooled economic resources and thus received a share in the enterprise. The term has as many variant meanings in Chinese as does the word *company* in English, but not all of them are parallel. Moreover, it appears that, like any word, its meanings and usages have changed over time. For instance, today the term is used in Southeast Asia and Hong Kong to designate a small business. The sources show that eighteenth- and nineteenth-century kongsis were quite different.

The term once covered a much broader range of social and eco-

5. *Kung sze*, literally, "public management," but in most dictionaries it is given as company, firm, or partnership. The most complete explication of the term is Wang, "Word *Kongsi*" (1979), and much of the following discussion is based on Wang's insights, research, and conclusions about the term and its origins. See also O'Brien, "Correspondence" (1977).

nomic groupings, and such groups were not so functionally defined then as they are today. Current ideas of classifying groups by activity and function would probably have been quite alien to nineteenth-century Chinese coolies. It is doubtful they would have drawn fine distinctions between groups engaged economic, political, family, clan, business, or "criminal" activities. Moreover, since very few Chinese coolies left records of themselves, we know very little about how they viewed their own social and economic environment. The most abundant sources we have about them are the results of their activities and the written comments of foreigners. The latter often do as much to confuse as they do to enlighten, thus they must be used with care.

My hypothesis is that in nineteenth-century Singapore, Chinese kongsis were organized for economic purposes. Some of them, certainly the most famous, were also characterized by some form of triad ritual and could thus be considered as "secret" societies. My argument draws on the work of Wang Tai Peng,[6] who argues that the kongsis which appeared in Southeast Asia were unique in their combination of Chinese brotherhood traditions within an economic partnership. He argues that the laborers' kongsis of Southeast Asia were different from the "secret" societies of China:

> Chinese *kongsi* that emerged in Southeast Asia in the 18th century, rooted as they were in both Chinese partnership and brotherhood traditions, were only new in the region. Their origins, unlike the Chinese brotherhood in an attempt to overthrow the Ch'ing dynasty, were entirely connected with the rise of the overseas Chinese mining industry. But although some of the Chinese *kongsi* in Southeast Asia may have carried over the ritual oath-taking ceremony and even the name of T'ien-T'i Hui, they generally evolved from a small partnership, either in commerce or mining.[7]

His conclusion is that despite structural and cultural similarities between kongsi organizations in Southeast Asia and the triads, guilds, and other business groupings in China, the kongsis of Southeast Asia were a distinct variation on the theme. Moreover, there does not seem to have been any direct institutional connection between a China-based triad and any of the Southeast Asian groups.[8] What distin-

6. Wang, "Origins of Chinese *Kongsi*" (1977).
7. Wang, 1979, p. 103.
8. The one possible exception to this might be the Xiao Dao Hui, variously known as the "Small Sword Society," the "Dagger Society," and the "Small Knife Society." But here the connection went the *other* way; that is, the society was founded in China by a Chinese who had returned from Singapore. Wynne, pp. 92–93.

guished most of the major kongsi organizations in Southeast Asia was not the use of triad oaths in their rituals and initiations and their acceptance of the classic ideas of brotherhood expressed in the Chinese epics *Romance of the Three Kingdoms* (*San Guo*) and *Watermargin*. The distinction between the Southeast Asian triads and the China-based groups was in the economic orientation of the organizations in the Nanyang.

The triad was endemic among the southern Chinese, and its main role was to form the "alternative" structure within the rural world of southern China. When the normal order of the world was disturbed, or when the formal hierarchy of the state (e.g., the Confucian system) failed to provide the peasant with justice, the triad was his recourse. For overseas Chinese, however, the "normal" order of the world was inverted. They were in "barbarian" lands, and family and Confucian relationships had been left behind. The only relationship remaining was the last of the "Five Relationships," that between friend and friend, or in Chinese terms, sworn brotherhood. It thus seems useful to treat the laborers' kongsis and the Southeast Asian triads as aspects of the same impulse to form brotherhoods in order to achieve economic ends. It is this "impulse" that I suggest is a peculiar trait and primary characteristic of the overseas Chinese laborers.

When the British arrived in the Malay world, everywhere they found the Chinese, they were grouped in kongsis. As one period source explains,

> It is not unreasonable to infer that the Chinese colonists at Malacca, in Java, Borneo and other parts of the Indian Archipelago at an early period after emigration would find the advantages of binding themselves to-gether as a means of defence and self-protection in a foreign land. Many of them had probably been members . . . in their native land. Henceforth numerous "Kongsees" or public clubs with which we find them invariably linked particularly at the mines and plantations in the interior.[9]

Chinese merchants who had settled in the towns also formed kongsis, but these were often based on surnames, such as the Khoo Kongsi of Pinang.[10] Because the founders of such kongsis were well established, they were able to attract clansmen from China as their clients. The basis of organization was less problematic for the surname kongsis than for those organized by miners or planters who were much

---

9. Newbold, "Chinese Secret Society of the Tien-Ti-Huih" (1841), p. 130.
10. Wong, *A Gallery of Chinese Kapitans* (1963), pp. 23–26. Wong discusses the Khoo family of Pinang and the history of the Leong San Teong Khoo Kongsi established in 1835.

more numerous and who could not count on finding clansmen. They could not rely on any of the other corporate groups that traditionally would have sustained them. To survive economically and socially, these migrants needed to create large-scale organizations that would unite rather than divide the Chinese in any given area, so that they could deal more effectively with organized Europeans, Malay political entities, and even other Chinese. For them, the basis of solidarity had to be something that most Chinese understood and could identify with. At the same time, it needed the potential to overcome the natural divisions of family, region, and language. The basis of solidarity, in addition to the economic enterprise itself, was the triad ritual, which elevated sworn blood brotherhood above other relationships. And, since all Chinese had come to Southeast Asia to trade, work, or otherwise seek their fortunes, all triad oaths, as well as oaths to clan kongsis, were inevitably made in an economic context.

Still other kongsis were pure business partnerships. The element that bound these kongsis to the brotherhood and surname kongsis appears to have been the shareholding aspect. Most kongsis were institutions within which individuals could pool resources, either labor or capital, toward the accomplishment of some economic objective such as the success of a mine, a plantation, a trading voyage, or any kind of business venture. Each participant received a share of the profits. Taking the kongsi as the primal social unit of the overseas Chinese provides a device for placing a range of Chinese social and economic groupings on the same footing and treating them as parts of the same process. Thus, this history of the Singapore Chinese begins with the earliest kongsis established in the Malay world in the eighteenth century and continues with the secret societies in Singapore.

One note of caution in putting forward Wang's hypothesis as the basis for my argument is that no other researcher supports Wang's contention that the kongsi was a prevalent organization in the maritime world of the south China coast before the eighteenth century. Ng Chin-keong, in his reconstruction of the "Amoy network," does not mention the term *kongsi*.[11] He does, however, make it clear that the Fujian merchant shippers who pioneered the commodity trade, first to Taiwan and then to Southeast Asia, were organized in guilds (*hang*) and also in *hui*. While some of these were *hui guan*, or place-of-origin associations, others were fund-pooling cooperatives and still others were organized around temples and cults. It seems that some of these

11. Ng, *Trade and Society* (1983), pp. 89–102.

huis obviously had a ritual aspect and that many of them were seen as subversive by the Qing government; also, the term *hui* was often used interchangeably with *kongsi* in documents relating to the history of Singapore. The evidence suggests that the kongsi, as it emerged in the eighteenth century within the Chinese settlements in Southeast Asia, was primarily a *workers'* organization.

The kongsi, at its heart, was an *economic* brotherhood. Every mining venture was capitalized by a kongsi, in which each member was a shareholder entitled to a specific share of profits according to his contribution. Roderick O'Brien makes the point that the original meaning attached to the term *kongsi* was probably "fair shares" rather than the modern "public shares."[12] Each mine was run by its own kongsi, and the overall community was governed by the collective membership of all the smaller kongsis. This form of organization was initially based on the principle of equality, and new members who lacked capital could eventually earn shares in a mine after working for a year. According to Wang, the guiding principle was the idea that, as all men were brothers, all men were shareholders. In addition to making it possible for members to pool resources and share profits, the kongsi also regulated social relations among its members and provided for various aspects of the general welfare. Its ritual of brotherhood bound the miners to the Chinese tradition of sworn brotherhood.

These Chinese went to Southeast Asia to produce raw materials and agricultural commodities for a market back in China. So far as we can tell, their migration does not appear to have been the result of actions taken, or conditions created, by European trade or settlement; rather, it seems to have arisen largely as a result of internal conditions in China itself—those created by the Manchu takeover in the South as well as general economic ones. This, in fact, is probably one reason why European sources take little note of it: the initial movement originated from an economic system that the Europeans had no part in. Chinese mining technology and the organization of labor and financing had followed its own course of evolution and development within China. Joint ventures in which a capitalist and a group of laborers formed a "company" to develop mines in Yunnan and other frontier areas within China were a relatively common occurrence.[13]

12. O'Brien, p. 171.
13. Balasz, *Chinese Civilization and Bureaucracy* (1964), p. 48. For his description of the Yunnan mining companies, Balasz quotes Wang Ming-lun, "Ya-pien chan-cheng ch'ien Yunnan t'ung-kuang-yeh ti tzu-pen chu-i meng-ya," in *Chung-kuo tzu-pen chu-i meng-ya wen-ti tao-lun chi* (symposium) (Peking, 1957) 2:277–84.

Chinese miners were migratory by necessity, and it would seem that the expansion into the Nanyang was just one more step. They simply followed the junk trade.

Wang Tai Peng has mapped out a history of the kongsi that takes it from the anti-Manchu navy of Cheng Zheng-gong to the goldfields of Borneo. It seems appropriate to seek the origins of Singapore's history within the structure of Wang's analysis, that is, in the first kongsi established by Hakka gold miners in the interior of western Borneo around the beginning of the eighteenth century. It is possible, I believe, to string together a succession of kongsi settlements that lead from Borneo to Singapore. These include those of the miners in Bangka and Phuket as well as the pepper and gambier planters in Riau (map 2).

According to Wang and most other scholars and observers, the Borneo kongsis were virtually self-governing communities. They had been settled with little more than a by-your-leave to the local Malay chief, who was at the mouth of the river and seems never to have been strong enough to exercise effective control over the Chinese miners in the interior. For nearly a century, the kongsi was the only government that the Borneo Chinese knew, and from all reports, it was a reasonably effective one. Territory was divided, disputes were settled, taxes were collected, public services such as roads and water supplies were constructed and maintained. Officers were elected by all inhabitants of the kongsis, and security was also provided for. Decisions affecting the communities were reached after open and public discussion. The kongsis were, as Wang Tai Peng has suggested, a form of native Chinese "democracy," rooted in the ancient concept of brotherhood.[14] Most important, the communities replicated and perpetuated themselves with new immigrants and expanded into new territories within Borneo.

Different circumstances did, however, lead to different kongsi configurations. In certain situations, ties based on kinship or speech group or regional origin cut across oaths of brotherhood. Kongsis could fragment along lines based on speech group affiliation or kinship. Being economic in function, kongsis grew up around certain occupations and industries. In different places and different times, kongsis maintained a variety of relations with external political structures. Likewise, whether or not a kongsi was a "secret" society was largely a function of its situation. Rituals were probably always private, but in situations where the kongsi was not a forbidden organization, secrecy was probably only a formality.

14. Wang, 1977, chap. 5.

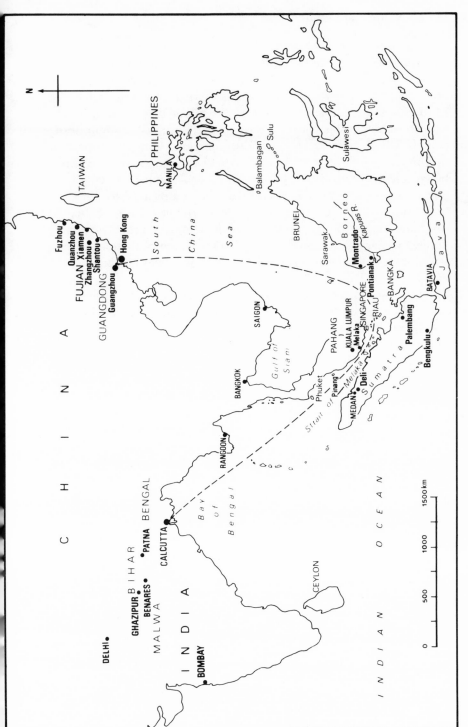

2. India, Southeast Asia, and China, showing the British trade route from Bengal to Guangdong and important areas of Chinese settlement in the Malay world.

Thomas Horsfield reported that the tin-mining settlements on the island of Bangka were first settled by migrants from Borneo.[15] There is no indication, however, that the Bangka settlements were recognized as autonomous. It appears that the Malay sultan of Palembang and the Chinese settled at his court exercised a certain measure of authority over the Bangka miners. Horsfield does mention a kongsi, but it is clear that the kongsi did not constitute itself as an autonomous governing body, at least not initially.[16] Generally, it seems that if an effective local government was already in power, whether Southeast Asian or colonial, kongsis did not form self-governing communities to the extent that they sought to displace the original state structures. The mining kongsis in Bangka were subordinate to the sultan of Palembang, and the Chinese in Riau were likewise subject to the Malay and Bugis chiefs at Riau.[17]

The kongsis were thus economic organizations that assumed the functions of government when necessary. The triad concept of brotherhood, the "heaven-earth-man" society, seems to have formed the umbrella, particularly in frontier situations. In Borneo, the triad linked together the smaller mining kongsis. Clearly something quite similar had happened with the pepper and gambier kongsis of Riau and later of Singapore. Thus, the political and military aspects of the kongsis

15. Horsfield, "Report on the Island of Banka" (1848), p. 310. There is some confusion in the sources about the precedence of Borneo over Bangka. The Dutch sources report Chinese gold miners first appearing in Borneo around 1740 or even later (James C. Jackson, *Chinese in the West Borneo Goldfields* [1970], p. 20). Jackson even suggests that the Bangka settlements were earlier than the Borneo ones and dated from 1720, but Horsfield says the Chinese founder of the Bangka settlement, one "Assing," "introduced from China and Borneo persons acquainted with the processes of collecting the ore and refining the metal as they are conducted in those countries." Wang Tai Peng suggests that the original Chinese in Bangka came, not from Sambas or Pontianak, but from Brunei (1977, p. 55), but I have seen no record of a Chinese mining settlement in Brunei at this time.

16. It is also clear that Horsfield did not exactly understand the meaning of the word. A reading of his remarks suggests that he assumed the kongsi was a person, rather than an organization; see Horsfield, p. 800: "The Kongsy or chief of Belinyu obtained the permission of the Sultan for opening the ground shortly before Banka became a British possession," and p. 808: "I shall add a few documents which were afforded me by the books of the Kongsies (or chiefs of the mines)." Elsewhere (p. 811) Horsfield indicates that a "fellowship" existed among the miners: "There is, in general, no difference of rank or condition among the workmen at one mine; its work is undertaken in fellowship and they share equally in the produce; the labour connected with the process is performed by all indiscriminately." These remarks suggest the presence of a brotherhood kongsi similar to the ones described by Wang and others in Borneo. Also, so far as Bangka is concerned, I am deeply grateful for information in personal communications from Mary F. Somers Heidhues and Barbara W. Andaya.

17. Trocki, "Origins of the Kangchu System" (1976), pp. 134–38. From the 1720s the Malay court of Riau was dominated by a family of Bugis adventurers and their descendants. These chiefs from southwest Sulawesi were largely responsible for the first settlements of Chinese in Riau. *See* Trocki, *Prince of Pirates* (1979).

cannot be ignored. There seem to have been links between the rebel privateers of Cheng Zheng-gong's forces and the Borneo gold miners, the Bangka tin miners, and the Riau pepper and gambier planters. These early settlements of overseas Chinese were an extension of the maritime world dominated by the anti-Manchu rebels. The settlers came in ships or as groups perhaps already organized as kongsis. Another reason for the maintenance of the military-political functions was that these overseas settlements had to provide for their own defense in a relatively hostile and unsettled environment. Even where a reliable local government provided security, the Chinese were generally left to manage their own internal affairs. These were undertaken by the kongsis.

Those who know Singapore today understand that it is essentially a Chinese city. As a Chinese center, the argument can be made that its history should also be seen as a continuation of the history of the Chinese in Southeast Asia. It seems logical, therefore, that Singapore's Chinese history must begin with something other than the story of Thomas Stamford Raffles and the Temenggong of Johor. To a certain extent, I made a start on this sort of history in the first chapter of *Prince of Pirates,* with an examination of the fortunes of the Chinese pepper and gambier planters who had established themselves at Riau in the eighteenth century.[18] This community was, in some respects, a forerunner of the Singapore Chinese settlement. They brought with them the Ngee Heng and the kongsis I have described in earlier studies and identified with the kangchu system. They also brought some of the economic structures that had already been the foundations of Chinese life in the area for nearly a century.

The History of Singapore and the Chinese Triads

Studies of the Chinese migration to Southeast Asia, particularly to the Malay world, have hitherto been too narrowly focused. Victor Purcell, in his pioneering work on the Chinese of Southeast Asia, structured his approach by location.[19] But for him, as to most Europeans, the political boundaries drawn by the colonial powers have delineated his geographic categories. He offers a series of separate chapters dealing with the Chinese of Malaya, Indonesia, Burma, Indo-

18. Trocki, 1979; Trocki, 1976, pp. 132–40.
19. Purcell, *Chinese in Southeast Asia* (1965).

china, and so on. Despite its inadequacies, this was the only practical approach to the investigation in its initial stages. It has, for good or ill, typified most of the succeeding work. Thus, the best studies have been on the Chinese of Thailand, of the Philippines, of Malaya, of Indonesia, . . . The flaw in this approach is that it obscures connections that spread beyond these boundaries. This gives the history of the overseas Chinese an appearance of discontinuity, and in the nineteenth century at least, it forces Chinese history into a colonial format.

A student bound by this structure would perhaps even object to the idea of beginning a history of the Singapore Chinese in Johor, and yet, as I have already made abundantly clear in earlier studies,[20] that is exactly where the Chinese history of Singapore did begin—or perhaps to add to the confusion, it began in Riau. This puzzle is only a mirage caused by colonialist categories. It disappears when we recall that before the British settlement in Singapore in 1819, the Johor mainland, Singapore Island, and the Riau-Lingga Archipelago were all a part of the same Malay state. My point is that the history of the Singapore Chinese cannot be treated in isolation from the history of the Malay state of Johor-Riau, nor can it be separated from the history of British Malaya; at the same time, however, it does have its own continuity. That continuity is in the history of its primary economic and social institutions, the kongsis.

This history is difficult to trace because most of our sources are of European origin. Aside from the geographic bias, other problems arise from these sources, because of their tendency to see the triads and kongsis of Southeast Asia as identical with the triads of China. This has meant that all the Chinese government assumptions about domestic triads have been simply transposed to the triads of Southeast Asia and Malaya in particular. Wang Tai Peng's insistence on drawing a distinction between the domestic Chinese triads and the overseas kongsis is meant to combat those assumptions, largely because the European view tends to downplay the economic functions of the kongsis. Furthermore, the adoption of the domestic Chinese concept has made it possible to portray the overseas kongsis as criminal organizations.

The European literature on secret societies began with T. J. Newbold's article in the *Journal of the Royal Asiatic Society* in 1841. Newbold at least saw the kongsis as laboring groups, but he also saw them as a threat to British power; thus his attitude was distinctly unfavorable. The China-based bias really became established with the

---

20. Trocki, 1979, chap. 1; Trocki, 1976.

publication of Gustav Schlegel's *Thian Ti Hwui: The Hung League or Heaven and Earth League* of 1861, which relied heavily on Chinese sources stressing the ritual and mythical history of the organization. The Chinese themselves did stress these aspects of the group in their formal accounts of it.

This view was reinforced by William Pickering, who almost single-handedly created the Chinese Protectorate and began the policy of suppression.[21] As a result, most of the early European writings on secret societies see the origin of the Chinese kongsis of Singapore in the mythical history of the Ngee Heng, or Heaven and Earth Society. Schlegel's influence is apparent in the most influential and complete account of the Malayan secret societies, that of M. L. Wynne.[22] Both focused on the China background of the Malayan triads and sought in that background the causes for conflict and the underlying continuities of these organizations. Although most writers have rejected Wynne's hypothesis that there were two ancient "stems" in China, the Han League and the Hung League, which were eternally locked in combat, most have continued to assume that the secrets of Chinese society were to be found in China.

Leon Comber and W. L. Blythe as well as many other colonialist commentators have glossed over the economic and contractual features that gave the kongsi much of its power and influence.[23] The "official" viewpoint has thus been that the kongsi was, at best, a revolutionary political organization whose actions were directed toward the situation inside of China. At worst, separated in Southeast Asia from its native political objective, it was treated as just a criminal

21. Pickering, "Chinese Secret Societies and Their Origin" (1878).

22. It is unfortunate that Wynne's *Triad and Tabut*, which is an invaluable compilation of data formerly available in colonial government sources, much of which was destroyed during the Japanese occupation, has as yet not been published in a way that would make it available to even the scholarly community, let alone the general public. It remains the standard work for all studies of secret societies and for Chinese social and political history in the Malay world during the colonial era. The few copies that exist are in research libraries in the United Kingdom (e.g., the School of Oriental and African Studies of the University of London, the Public Record Office, and the British Museum), Malaysia, and Singapore. These two latter countries, which have apparently inherited the copyright, have taken political decisions to continue the application of censorship restrictions to this particular publication. There are also a few microfilm copies available in some research libraries in the United States and Australia, but generally speaking, access to this work is highly restricted.

23. Comber, *Chinese Secret Societies in Malaya* (1959). This work, which relies heavily on Wynne's research, is considered less authoritative than others. Blythe, *Impact of Chinese Secret Societies in Malaya* (1969), is generally considered more authoritative, but it too suffers from the same myopic approach, limiting itself to "British Malaya" and seeing the societies strictly as a "problem" of law and order. It is, in fact, a history of the British suppression of the societies and is in no way a systematic study of Chinese secret societies.

gang with no proper role or legitimacy in territories under the "enlight-ened" direction of European powers. According to Pickering, "As there are no patriotic aims to be attained under our gentle and liberal Government, the only objects for which they can strive, are those lower interests which are only too dear to the average Celestial mind, such as intrigue, assistance in petty feuds, combination to extort money and to interfere with the course of justice."[24] To Pickering and to many modern observers, the societies were and remain merely a police "problem."

The Europeans saw the kongsis as a threat to their authority, so the tendency to treat them as illegitimate was natural; but to reinforce the taint of criminality it was necessary for them to link the Southeast Asian kongsis to the triads in China and to attack them on that ground. As Wynne explains, however, colonial governments, in order to exercise some powers over the Chinese in their areas, often gave tacit legitimization to the triad by recognizing its leader as the *kapitan China*:

> Whatever justification and political objective . . . the [Hung] league might have had in China . . . , there was no good reason why its revolu-tionary aims and secret ritual should have been fostered in overseas lodges under a stable non-Chinese government, except on grounds of the natural exclusiveness of the Chinese and the fact that the secret and self-contained organisation of the league provided a ready instrument where-by Chinese settlers . . . could govern themselves . . . as an *imperium in imperio,* thus avoiding interference or friction with the local authorities, who welcomed these industrious settlers and were glad to appoint their leader, usually the headman of the local Hung lodge, to be "Kapitan China," to rule his own community "according to Chinese law and customs" (usually those of the league) and to be answerable always to the local authorities for crimes committed by, or questions affecting the members of the local Chinese community.[25]

The question of kongsi legitimacy clouds much of the literature. Ob-viously, defenders of European imperialism have raised the issue in their studies, and many others, less critical of these assumptions, have followed them. By focusing on the "natural exclusiveness" of the Chinese and other such racist perceptions, British administrators like Wynne found it easy to ignore the economic foundations of the kongsi and thus did not acknowledge that their settlers were so "industrious" *because* of the kongsi.

24. Pickering, p. 66.
25. Wynne, p. 14.

The comments of Wynne and the other colonial administrators I have quoted reflect a paradox and a tension in British policy toward the Chinese. On the one hand, the administrators felt threatened by the *imperium in imperio* they saw in the triads and kongsis. On the other hand, if they were to control the populations they sought to rule, they needed to acknowledge the community leadership that already existed. If they wished to profit from the "industry" of the Chinese, they also had to allow the kongsis to function; for the kongsi was in fact the goose that was laying the golden eggs. The long-term management of this contradiction is one of the recurrent themes in this book.

British reports reveal a certain confusion about the use of the term *kongsi*. Wynne, for instance, attempts to draw a distinction between the triads and the economic kongsis and offers the following quotation from L. A. Mills:

> The genuine Hue riots in Singapore were of two kinds, those between rival branches of the Thian Tai Hue [i.e., Tien-di hui, or the Heaven and Earth Society] and the quarrels of the Kongsis, or associations. These were mutual benefit societies intended to assist needy members, carry out various religious rites, give aid in all disputes, etc. . . . the Kongsis cut across the lines of other secret societies, the branches of the Thian Tai Hue, which accepted members from every part of China. Many Chinese belonged to both organizations, so that those who were brothers in the Thian Tai Society cut one anothers' throats with great zest as members of rival provincial Kongsis.[26]

Much of the actual comment on secret societies, kongsis, and other forms of Chinese organization during this period seems to be contradictory, but it may be that the contradictions were mostly in the minds of the European observers. According to John Patullo, a Straits Settlements' magistrate in 1829, the kongsis were "secret combinations": "Indeed the very formation of such societies indicate secret combinations, and amongst such an intriguing race as the Chinese, opposition to law and good Government and the protection of their brethren under any circumstances. The jealousy which also exists between many of the Kongsees frequently leads to breaches of the public peace."[27]

One difficulty is in the exact meaning of the two terms Wynne uses, *hui* and *kongsi*. A reading of nineteenth-century materials suggests that there was little substantive distinction between the old concept of a kongsi and most of the nineteenth-century secret societies. Indeed,

26. Wynne, p. 67.
27. Patullo to Anderson, "Report on the Hoeys" (1829), *SSR*, X 5, p. 173.

the Ngee Heng was indiscriminately termed a "kongsi" or a "hui."
While I have never seen the Tien-di hui referred to as the "Tien-di
Kongsi," an important nineteenth-century source identifies the Ngee
Heng Kongsi with the Tien-di hui.[28] J. D. Vaughan, one of Singapore's
most knowledgeable individuals on the Chinese, shows the collection
of labels heaped on the Ngee Heng: "Secret societies abound in the
Straits. They are the offspring of the famous Triad society of China;
meaning 'the society of the three united, Heaven, Earth and Man,'
which according to Chinese philosophy . . . imply the three depart-
ments of nature. The Triad society . . . is known in the Straits Settlements, as the 'Ghi Hin or Tian Tay Hoey or Kongsi' literally, 'The
Heaven and Earth Society.' "[29]

On the surface, however, there seems to be little of significance that
separated the two. Perhaps some of the confusion stems from the
assumption that all secret societies were triads, which is probably not
true; or that no kongsis were secret, again probably untrue. In the early
nineteenth century, British observers certainly saw at least some kongsis as secret. The reason for this is not entirely clear; it may have been
because they *were* triads or simply because the British did not understand Chinese. Moreover, it appears that the "mutual aid" societies
Mills referred to were in fact the *pang*, or speech group organizations,
most of which were under the leadership of merchants such as Tan
Tock Seng and Seah Eu Chin.[30]

Perhaps because European writers have seen the organizations and
activities of Chinese merchants, laborers, and other migrants in Southeast Asia during the eighteenth and nineteenth centuries as less than
legitimate, they have missed the rhythm of Chinese history. In fact, so
little real thought has been given to these questions that the very idea
of Chinese history in Southeast Asia having a pattern and process of its
own is not very well developed.

An alternative analysis, initially proposed by Maurice Freedman,
has been to view the societies as simply one facet of Chinese social
organization. This approach has been less judgmental and perhaps
more "objective" than the official view. Freedman's approach has been
guided by social science methods and academic concerns rather than
by the urge to establish control. From his work, a considerable body of

28. *SFP*, 7 April 1846: "The Hoes [huis] in Singapore are numerous, the principal being
the Tan Tae Hoe (Heaven and Earth Society) otherwise called the Ghee Hin Hoe (Justice
Exalted Society) . . . [which] is said to number from 10 to 20,000 members."
29. Vaughan, *Manners and Customs of the Chinese* (1879), p. 95.
30. Yen Ching-hwang, *A Social History of the Chinese* (1986), pp. 181–95.

analysis has emerged. A major breakthrough in the historical treatment of a Chinese community was G. William Skinner's *Chinese Society in Thailand*. Until Skinner's work was published, there was little solid historical research that would support an attempt to apply Freedman's insights to the history of the Malayan Chinese.[31]

I made a beginning on reinterpreting that history with my work on the Chinese in Johor. The Johor Archives contains a collection of *surat sungai*, or "river letters." These were documents that licensed a Chinese to open up a river valley for pepper and gambier plantations. The settlement this Chinese and his followers would then establish was called a *chukang*, or a *kangkar*. The term *kang* literally means "port," but in this case, it referred to a small settlement with the residence of the leader of the place, the *kangchu*, a few shops, an opium and gambling den, a temple, a meeting house, and perhaps a pig farm.

The surat sungai collection in the Johor Archives shows that each settlement was actually owned and organized by a kongsi made up of the kangchu, several of the planters in his settlement, and usually a shopkeeper from Singapore or Johor Baru. The shopkeeper was the capitalist, the kangchu was the organizer, and the planters ran the pepper and gambier bangsals together with crews of coolies, or laborers. Usually each planter had one share in the kongsi; the kangchu and the shopkeeper may have had more. Sometimes Malay officials of the Johor government held shares in these kongsis. The coolies were probably not members. The surat sungais in the Johor Archives recorded the names and numbers of shares held by each member of the kongsi. Thus, the plantations of Johor were organized around a kongsi framework. There are also records showing that mines in Johor were organized in the same manner.

In both Riau and Singapore, pepper and gambier planters were organized in a similar fashion. Virtually all rural settlements in Singapore were known as some kind of kang; for example, Yio Chukang, Lim Chukang, and Choa Chukang are place names that continue in use to this very day. Begbie reports settlements called Pitchukang and Sinkang in early nineteenth-century Riau. The so-called Kangchu system was the pepper and gambier version of tin-mining kongsis that flourished in Borneo and Bangka at this time. I have shown that it existed but that there was little evidence of it in contemporary Euro-

---

31. Freedman, *Study of Chinese Society* (1979), especially "Immigrants and Associations: Chinese in Nineteenth-Century Singapore," pp. 61–83. Skinner, *Chinese Society in Thailand* (1957).

Boat Quay in the nineteenth century, showing pepper and gambier shops and tongkangs pulled up along shore (National Archives, Singapore)

pean sources. Only the very rudimentary state apparatus of the first rulers of Johor found it worthwhile to record such matters. Both the Dutch in Riau and the British of Singapore were apparently unconscious of an entire complex of such arrangements in their own territories. There were no surat sungais, but there were still kangchus, kangkars, and chukangs, and there were surely kongsis. While it is probable that the affairs of each kangkar were managed locally, there obviously was an overarching political structure that existed among the Chinese pepper and gambier planters and kangchus and included the pepper and gambier dealers whose shops lined Boat Quay. This was the Ngee Heng, or the Tien-di hui, and for a time, it seems clear that it functioned as the Chinese government of the pepper and gambier kongsis. The Ngee Heng Kongsi was the grand kongsi of all the little kongsis. The secret society brought the planters to Singapore from Riau and later, as I have shown, led them from Singapore to Johor.[32]

32. Trocki, 1979, chap. 4; Trocki, 1976. See also Begbie, *Malayan Peninsula* (1967), p. 305.

At the time I wrote about Johor, I was unaware that others were working on related questions that would add considerably to our knowledge of the Chinese migration. Happily, a number of recent studies have provided a significant body of essentially new information that has made possible a reexamination of that history. The appearance of studies such as those by Ng Chin-keong and by Jennifer Cushman, both based largely on Chinese sources, have radically altered our picture of Chinese activities in Southeast Asia before 1800.[33]

The eighteenth and nineteenth centuries saw the meeting of two waves of migrants in Southeast Asia, the Europeans from the west and the Chinese from the east. The vehicles of European migration or expansion, were the joint-stock trading companies, the Dutch and English East India Companies, together with the military establishments of their respective nation-states. Within these institutional frameworks Europeans were able to establish an environment that supported and made possible the activities of private European traders, missionaries, and other settlers. Analagously, the kongsi was the vehicle of Chinese immigration. Kongsis undertook social, economic, military, and even religious functions for the immigrants. They were armed, organized brotherhoods of economic adventurers and, in that respect, not so very different from the Europeans they encountered in the region, except that the Chinese had no state apparatus behind them. Both the European and Chinese institutions were adaptations of ones in their native countries. As adaptations, both forms of organization were hybrids; institutions exactly like them did not in fact exist in the home countries.

The history of Chinese society in Singapore, and probably in most of the Malay world, can be understood as the history of the kongsis. In this context, it is important to understand the division of overseas Chinese society into opposing classes. The dynamic of that history appears as groups of laborers, usually represented by the so-called secret societies, engaged in struggle with groups of merchants, bound together in their own kongsis. This long-term struggle was the underlying cause of much of the conflict colonial observers have labeled "secret society wars" or "clan fights." Over the course of Singapore's first century, the laborers' kongsis were increasingly circumscribed by the colonial state and ultimately criminalized and forbidden under the Societies Ordinance. At the same time, the business organizations of

---

33. Ng, 1983; Cushman, "Fields from the Sea" (1975). These two studies offer a view of trade and commerce in Southeast Asia that, while certainly important to our understanding of contemporary developments, has been largely unknown until now.

the merchants evolved toward the form of European-style corporations, although they never quite duplicated the European institutional form. Concurrently, to maintain their positions within colonial society, the merchants also developed more exclusive social groups, their hui guans, based on kinship and lineages.[34] The merchants allied themselves with the colonial power and accepted positions of responsibility within the official administration, thus betraying the principles of brotherhood in exchange for personal power and profit within an alien system. By the end of the nineteenth century, the leaders of the merchant kongsis, initially formed around the opium revenue syndicates, had come to compose the core of the Chinese social and business elite that ultimately inherited political and economic power in Singapore and Malaysia from the colonial rulers.

While it may be ironic that some members of this same business elite have now taken upon themselves the responsibility for maintaining the "ancestral" rites of the deceased brotherhood in modern Johor, it may also be so that they fully understand the importance of keeping its spirit at rest. Alternatively, the continuing ambiguity and insecurity of the Chinese position in Malaysia may underline the importance of the ethnic solidarity the brotherhood has, despite its many reincarnations, always represented. This book is my attempt to trace the evolution of the Chinese kongsis in the Malay world, from worker-brotherhood to merchant "corporation." Despite the checkered history of the old kongsi, and its flirtation with respectability, it seems never to have lost the power to raise heroes. The Ngee Heng remains a potent symbol of Chinese solidarity in an alien world.

34. These organizations, based on surname or provincial origin, have generally been the only groups recognized under the Societies Ordinance. Lee Poh Ping (*Chinese Society in Nineteenth Century Singapore Analysis* [1978]) and other students show that the hui guans have always been closely aligned with the merchants and the official power structure.

2 Conflict and the Kongsis of Southeast Asia

To explain the process by which the histories of the Chinese migrants came to be intertwined with that of European imperialism and the global capitalist system, I must first propose a periodization of Chinese history in Southeast Asia and then offer some thoughts on the conflict among overseas Chinese. Periodization and explanations of conflict are interdependent. The time frame is the structure of crises and "great events" within which Chinese history occurred. Conflict is the dynamic of change within that structure; it provides the explanation for historical evolution and offers an understanding of Chinese society in the region. Both the periodization and the depiction of struggle are revisions and reinterpretations of earlier views of these events.

Periodization of Chinese History in Southeast Asia

There has not been, to my knowledge, a systematic periodization of the history of the Chinese migration to Southeast Asia—only the tendency to force it into the categories already established for European colonial history. This is only normal, since Europeans were intent on writing European history, and to them, the Chinese and the Southeast Asians were always on the periphery. Even the Chinese writers of Chinese history in China had little concern for the activities of the wandering denizens of the South Coast, most of whom were considered criminals and rebels. This history has been pretty well ignored. Chinese history in Southeast Asia moved according to its own rhythms.

29

I believe the history of the Chinese in Southeast Asia can be broken into five periods:

1. The growth of the Xiamen (Amoy) trading network with Nanyang bases at Batavia, Siam, and perhaps Manila (1630–1700).
2. The establishment of kongsi settlements throughout Southeast Asia and the expansion of the junk trade (1700–1800).
3. The growth of junk trade and increased Chinese migration in conjunction with the expansion of European commerce to Asia (1800–30).
4. The decline of the junk trade and the absorption of Chinese settlements in Southeast Asia by European colonies (1830–80).
5. The disempowerment of popular Chinese social and economic structures and the integration of the overseas Chinese into the global capitalism system (1880–1910).

Three trends stand out in this periodization. The first is the expansion and decline of the Chinese junk trade, that is, of commerce carried in Chinese ships. The second trend is the developing emigration of Chinese laborers to engage in mining and planting enterprises. The third is the interaction between the Chinese and the European colonial systems.

The studies I have already referred to by Skinner, Cushman, Ng, and Wang provide the basis for my reordering of the early periods. They offer views of Chinese activities in Southeast Asia that do not necessarily revolve around European activities. Skinner and Cushman do this by focusing primarily on the relationship between China and Siam; Ng, by directing his attention to the Fujian traders and their offshore activities; and Wang, by working within the context of the kongsi. All of them have made extensive use of Chinese language sources as well as indigenous Southeast Asian sources where applicable. Together they provide vistas of Chinese activities in the Nanyang that suggest the outlines of an independent scheme of periodization.[1]

Ng's work has provided the basis for the first period. Obviously, Chinese from these areas had been going to sea to trade for centuries, but the events he discusses seem to be a discrete phase in Chinese maritime history in that they involved the migration of labor. Ng has described the expansion of Chinese maritime activity that occurred during the late seventeenth and early eighteenth centuries with the

---

1. Cushman, 1975; Ng, 1983; Skinner; Wang, 1979.

creation of the "Amoy network," as he calls it. Not only did the traders of Xiamen (Amoy) expand their trading networks up and down the Chinese coast, but they also pioneered the development of commercial rice and sugar production on Taiwan. They financed the operations and transported the settlers and subsequently managed trade in the items produced and consumed by the Chinese migrants to Taiwan.

This trading network provided the foundation for the next step of Chinese maritime expansion in the years after 1700. The significant aspect of the Xiamen network was the creation of a system of off-shore production intended for consumption in China. The constellation of economic activities involved in this process were essentially commercial. Agriculturalists in Taiwan were engaged in cash-cropping and were not merely subsistence farmers. They were supplied with certain necessities from the outside and were supported by a financial and commercial network extending from the mainland.

Another aspect of this first period was the continuing conflict between the Manchu invaders and the southern Chinese. For a time in the seventeenth century, Cheng Zheng-gong ran a rebel movement based in Taiwan. His rebellion was supported by a coastal navy made up of "privateers" and "pirates," and these anti-Manchu forces were very much a part of the coastal trade and of the Xiamen network. One might suppose that they alternately functioned as traders and warriors. This militance was an important characteristic of the southern expansion.

In the second period, beginning about 1700, the network expanded to Southeast Asia and brought a significant change in the nature of the Chinese presence in the region: the appearance of settlements of Chinese laborers engaged in primary production. Before this time it appears that the only Chinese in Southeast Asia were merchants and sailors. Some time around 1700 the first settlements of Chinese miners and planters were established in the region. Determining the exact nature of their connection with the Xiamen network is problematic. There is no data to link them directly, but circumstances strongly indicate they were part of the same movement. Possibly, the Chinese merchants and sailors, particularly those from Xiamen, were in part responsible for the organization of these groups of laborers, though this has yet to be demonstrated.

In the much older Chinese settlements in Siam, Manila, and especially Batavia, the settlers were the so-called *peranakan*, some of whom had created hybrid cultures as they merged with local Southeast Asian cultures. Until about 1683, their settlements were primarily merchant centers. Leonard Blussé, however, reports the importation of Chinese coolies to dig the canals of Batavia in the 1620s; many stayed to engage in market gardening and sugar cultivation in subsequent years. By 1680, he suggests, the Chinese population of Batavia may have reached something over three thousand. He points to 1683, however, as the turning point:

> A new era of development opened when Krawang with its sizeable Javanese population was added to the Batavian jurisdiction (1677) and a lasting peace was concluded with Banten in 1683. These events combined with the official reopening of the Chinese trade with Southeast Asia—it had been banned by the Chinese government during the army campaigns to annex Formosa which was held by the Ch'eng family until 1683— created the ideal conditions for an increased immigration of Chinese labourers, who might plough new lands for the Company. They came in great numbers indeed. The number of junks from China that anchored each year at the Batavian roads burgeoned from three or four to more than twenty. Thousands of immigrants flooded the city. A new rush had started.[2]

While most migrants flowed into the area around Batavia, other Chinese settlements appeared about the same time in Siam and later in the Malay world. Evidence suggests that many of the settlements outside of Java were characterized by some form of kongsi organization. The settlements on Bangka and Borneo, which date from about 1720 and 1740 respectively, must have benefited by the flight of Chinese from Batavia after the massacre by the Dutch in 1740. Blussé presents a scenario of Chinese labor in Java dominated and exploited by a combination of Chinese merchants (presumably peranakans) in the town and Dutch officials. The Dutch massacre was a response to protests by an army of unemployed Chinese laborers. Thus the first round in the "class war" took place in Java. The memory of the massacre must have left a deep impression on the Chinese who fled to other settlements.

Wang Tai Peng suggests that the mining kongsis of Borneo owed little to the mercantile guilds and "business" groups, although he shows that the kongsis did originate from within the maritime community. There seems to have been a qualitative difference here in that the overseas kongsi settlements, even though essentially commercial, were politically and economically self-determined and dominated by the

2. Blussé, "Batavia, 1619–1740" (1981), p. 170.

forces of labor. Or, perhaps more correctly, by a nonmercantile, charismatic leadership that mobilized a power base among the China-born laborers, the *sinkeh*. This period may be characterized as that of independent kongsi migration. It continued throughout the eighteenth century and into the nineteenth, expanding with the Chinese junk trade.

Cushman has studied the expansion of the Chinese junk trade, particularly that with Siam during the late eighteenth and early nineteenth centuries. This traffic, based partly on cordial relations between Phya Taksin and the first three Chakri kings of Siam and the Qing emperors, attempted to fill Chinese needs for rice and "Straits" produce. Given their knowledge of the markets in China and their ability to deal with Southeast Asian rulers and chiefs in a knowledgeable and equitable fashion, the Chinese junk traders were able to block the entry of European shipping into the Siam-China trade until the mid-nineteenth century. Siamese trade with China was carried by Chinese junk traders and was thus not restricted to Canton. During this period, the junk trade flourished, not only in Siam, but throughout Southeast Asia. It was greatly enhanced by the traffic in goods produced by the Chinese kongsi settlements scattered throughout the region, particularly tin, gold, pepper, and gambier. The years after 1770 were distinct from earlier years in that an official tributary relationship existed between the Siamese and Chinese governments which was absent in the earlier days of the Qing dynasty.

The third period, 1800–30, was transitional. The junk trade and the number of kongsi settlements seemed to grow at a much more rapid rate. The reason was the massive expansion of the European, particularly British, trade and settlement. The Chinese traders and laborers benefited from the huge infusions of capital the British brought with them as well as from the fact that British traders provided a whole new market for the products of their trade. The growth of ports such as Singapore, Pinang, Bangkok, Saigon, Batavia, and Manila, not to mention hundreds of smaller places, was an important aspect of this period. The enormous "native trade" of Singapore described in the early nineteenth-century sources is an indication of this prosperity. Much of this affluence was the result of the enormous growth of the opium trade.

In the fourth period, after 1830, the junk trade went into abeyance throughout Southeast Asia. The expansion of the European presence, initially so beneficial to a growing Chinese economic community, ultimately forced the junk traders out of the China-Southeast Asia carrying trade. China's 1842 defeat in the Opium War with Great Britain and the opening of the treaty ports gave Europeans greater access to the China market. Another factor that made it possible for Europeans to take advantage of the new situation was the technological change that resulted in the increase in square-rigged trading vessels owned or operated by European and Chinese merchants, which offered a much more secure voyage than the junks. Before the end of the century, clippers and then steamers and steel ships would change the maritime world of Asia beyond recognition.

Another mark of growing European influence was the move by the colonial governments to achieve political domination of the Chinese kongsi settlements and the subsequent integration of the kongsi economies into the world capitalist market. This "capture" of the Chinese economy of Southeast Asia is a major part of my story. The Chinese history of Singapore is a microcosm of this process of envelopment of Chinese economic activity.

During the midnineteenth century, Europeans generally lacked the power to achieve control over their subject populations alone. They needed allies. Thus between about 1830 and the 1870s, colonial governments and European merchants and businessmen actively cultivated collaborators among certain groups of Chinese and Southeast Asians. These included the *temenggongs* of Johor, as I have shown in *Prince of Pirates,* as well as the peranakan Chinese merchants. Thus, a class of "respectable" Chinese came to enjoy great power in Singapore as well as in other colonial settlements. James Rush has noted a trend in Java that precisely mirrored events in Singapore.[3] The most important of this group were the opium revenue farmers. In Singapore, this fourth period came to a very abrupt end in 1880.

The fifth period, the years between 1880 and 1910, saw the final advance of European colonial power. European administrations embarked on programs of rationalization and centralization. Compromises that left certain political and social powers in Asian hands were no longer tolerable in governments that had come to see themselves as custodians of the "white man's burden." Having used Asian elites to dominate the Asian masses through the manipulation of traditional institutional frameworks, European rulers now sought to dispense with both the traditional institutions, like revenue farms, and the farmers themselves. In Singapore, the struggle to dominate the opium-

---

3. Rush, *Opium to Java* (1990).

farming kongsis took the full three decades. The Dutch seem to have been more successful in Java, where they eliminated most revenue farms between 1894 and 1897.[4]

The Causes of Secret Society Wars

With the period framework established, I can resume the historiographic critique of British writings on Chinese society, particularly secret society, that I began in chapter 1. My earlier discussion focused on the nature of the kongsi; here my subject is conflict between kongsis: the secret society wars that erupted in Singapore and Malaya during the nineteenth century. My contention is that the struggle arose as a result of conflicts inherent in the colonial economy, and most directly as a reaction to British attempts to exercise control over Chinese economic institutions. It is necessary to clear away misconceptions about these wars that have characterized European versions and to justify the economic explanation that underlies my hypothesis.

The political domination of the Chinese laborers in the kongsi settlements did not occur abruptly; it came about by fits and starts with many tentative advances and reverses. The kongsis, whatever their structure and status when they were founded, changed over time. There has been a tendency among scholars to view Chinese secret societies, and Chinese society in general, as static entities. Common sense alone suggests that this assumption is erroneous; every element of Chinese society was in a state of flux. It was this very instability, which increased as contacts between Chinese and Europeans intensified, that brought the Chinese into conflict with one another.

There have been several attempts to explain the periodic conflicts among different groups of Chinese, particularly in Singapore but also elsewhere on the Malay Peninsula. During the nineteenth century, there were in fact two schools of thought, each characterized by one of the two British "authorities" on the Chinese. The most durable has been that of William Pickering, who found the cause in the secret societies: "Every emigrant on leaving China carries with him, if nothing else, the prejudice of race or the remembrance of his clan or district feud; these are elements of discord in any mixed Chinese community, but small compared with the baneful influences of the Heaven and

4. Rush, pp. 353–55. The French had eliminated the farms in Indochina in 1881.

Earth societies for the interests of which the Chinese is obliged and willing to forget his family, clan and district."[5]

J. D. Vaughan, who published his *Manners and Customs of the Chinese in the Straits Settlements* in 1879, a year after Pickering wrote his article in the *Journal of the Straits Branch of the Royal Asiatic Society,* held almost the opposite view. He too felt that the grudges brought from China were important, but he laid stress upon the influences of clan, district, speech group, and religion. He saw the secret society as an agent of peace among a diverse population, "a society enfolding the whole of these discordant elements within its embrace, and binding these hereditary enemies together under the most solemn vows of brotherhood and kinship, much of the ill-feeling brought from China would be dissipated and expelled."[6] I feel Vaughan was perhaps closer to the truth; he clearly saw the problem in cultural divisions and believed that the division of the once-unified Ngee Heng into rival societies was the source of the problem. He did not place the cause of this division in Singapore, however, and he did not see the problem as economic.

The first major systematic attempt by a European to determine the root cause of conflict between the Chinese secret societies in Malaya, *Triad and Tabut* by M. L. Wynne, was based on the hypothesis that there was a deep-seated animosity between what he called the "Han League" and the "Hung League." This mutual opposition, which Wynne tried to demonstrate with a complex theoretical edifice, is now generally dismissed. There do not seem to have been two opposed societies locked in continuing ideological struggle for causes lost in the mists of time, as Wynne supposed.[7] Although many have found fault with Wynne's argument, few have challenged his belief that the causes of disputes among Chinese in the British colonies were to be found in China. This assumption was consistent with the nineteenth-century British reports about the societies.

The hypothesis offered here is that causes of individual outbreaks of violence were complex, immediate, and situational; but all were rooted in economic issues, and behind those issues was a deeper struggle between the proponents of the colonial sociopolitical order and the popular institutions of Chinese workers. That causes were

5. Quoted by Vaughan, pp. 98–99.
6. Vaughan, p. 99.
7. The 1957 edition of Wynne's book contains an introduction by Wilfred Blythe criticizing Wynne's hypothesis. Blythe's own work *Impact of Chinese Secret Societies in Malaya* offers no systematic or analytic hypothesis other than the "criminal" view implicit in most colonialist studies.

economic is also the conclusion reached by Mak Lau Fong and also by Michael Godley.[8] Even commentators such as Blythe acknowledge the economic motivation behind some conflicts, but no one has tried to link these "Chinese" economic conflicts to the structure of the colonial environment. The circumstances I present here that surrounded most of the secret society riots, fights, and disputes in and around Singapore during the nineteenth century were rooted in the pepper and gambier cultivation, the opium revenue farms, and the changing relations between these Chinese and the colonial power structure.

The failure of British observers to dwell on economic factors when dealing with the Chinese kongsis appears linked to the general tendency of the Europeans to criminalize kongsi activities. If the kongsis were essentially illegal organizations, then the possibility of their playing a necessary economic function in the British settlements was not at issue. If the causes of strife could be located in China or in some deviant characteristic of Chinese culture, rather than in the immediate economic environment of the colony, the British could easily deny the possibility that they themselves should bear responsibility for being a partial cause of the strife. After all, British intervention in Malaya in the 1860s was justified by their attempt to "pacify" the states of Selangor and Perak, then torn by wars between mining kongsis and different Malay chiefs.

If the strife had been understood as economic, however, it might have been necessary to treat the kongsis otherwise and to accept a very different view of the colonial economy than the ideal of free trade in a free port conducted under the rule of British law—an ideal fondly cherished by Europeans of that age. For the Europeans to have identified the colonial economy as the root of strife in the colony would have required them to question their own assumptions and seek the cause of violence in the very "progress" they had instituted. This blind spot underlies much of what has previously been written about Chinese secret societies in Malaya and Singapore. A related point is that although the British administrators and merchants, as well as other European colonial rulers in the region, were instinctively hostile to the Chinese kongsis because they represented organized labor, the fact is that kongsis really did pose the threat of an alternative and competing political order. Also, simply because of European ignorance of the Chinese language, much of what happened among the Chinese was perceived as secret and conspiratorial. Ultimately, the colonialists de-

8. Mak, *Sociology of Secret Societies* (1981), pp. 46–54. Godley, *Mandarin-Capitalists from Nanyang* (1981), p. 27.

veloped official policies to criminalize the kongsis and to smash popular Chinese institutions.

At the beginning of the nineteenth century, however, the Europeans needed the kongsis. The settlements of Chinese laborers in Sumatra, Borneo, the Malay Peninsula, and the other islands of the Indonesian archipelago were the major sources of wealth and trade goods. These Chinese produced the tin, pepper, gambier, sago, gold, tapioca, tobacco, sugar, and other commodities that fueled European trade in Southeast Asia. European writings of the period, when they do not complain of Chinese clannishness, are full of accolades for the industry of the Chinese:

> John Chinaman is willing and able to perform those inferior offices for the Europeans and other residents of Singapore at which other portions of the population would turn up their noses in supercilious disgust. Are coolies wanted to make a drain or clear out a cesspool? There are China coolies always at hand ready and willing to undertake the task. Are there three or four hundred to dig and tunnel for the waterworks, or five hundred to a thousand wanted for earthworks to a fort? They are immediately procurable in superabundance. Then see them at sunrise as they hurry forth in Indian file to their appointed labour with baskets and poles and ropes: there they hurry along in light marching order, grinning and chattering, in good humour and strong bodily health, the very *beau ideal* of the daily labourer.[9]

The Chinese kongsis that brought together and organized labor and capital to carry out these tasks were, in fact, the foundations of colonial prosperity. And both within and outside of the European settlements, it was the kongsis that created and maintained social order among the Chinese. As already noted in the quotation from Wynne, when the European colonial administrators appointed Chinese headmen, or kapitans to govern the Chinese, they chose the secret society leaders, whether they knew it or not. Leon Comber makes the point: "We may take it for granted that all or nearly all of the Chinese *Capitans* were secret society leaders. No aspersions are cast in saying this: they could not have held their position if they were not. But it was not until long afterwards the British authorities realized with something of a shock that the very headmen on whom they had been relying were none other than the secret society leaders themselves." Comber's

---

9. *ST*, 3 March 1866, quoted in Song, *One Hundred Years History* (1967), p. 137.

remarks seem naive. Nineteenth-century observers such as Vaughan and Pickering both made the same point in their writings of the 1870s. Even at the beginning of the nineteenth century, colonial officials in Pinang were aware that the kapitans and the holders of the revenue farms were secret society leaders, as observers such as Newbold and Patullo seem also to have been aware.[10] Not only were officials aware of these connections, but their policies show continuing attempts to manipulate kongsi leadership.

Nevertheless, there was conflict between kongsis. The problems of social order raised by those conflicts have provided the major field for European discussion of the kongsis or secret societies. In fact, most "histories" of Chinese secret societies are little more than a catalog of the "clan wars," faction fights, or secret society wars that disturbed the colony. It has been in the search for causes of conflict that much of the theory about these groups has originated. No one has really asked what the secret societies were doing, or thought they were doing, when they were *not* fighting.

Wynne's explanation and his evidence, despite flaws, cannot be discounted out of hand. It is true that his theory about a deep-seated ideological conflict between Han and Hung, between "Tokong" and Triad, between Red Flag and White Flag, verges on paranoid specula-tion. Nevertheless, the facts that drove him to this speculation remain compelling. There was, it seems, a pretty consistent two-sided conflict in Malaya. Whether it was between Ghee Hin and Hai San, as in Pinang and Perak; or between Ngee Heng and Ghee Hok, as in Singa-pore; or between Hokkien and Teochew; or between Catholics and "pagans"; or whatever titles the contending parties assumed, Wynne is correct that there was a long-term, endemic, dualistic tendency in Chinese society. We may disagree with his explanation of this dualism, but its existence seems indisputable.

Given that this dualism existed, Wynne was correct in seeking a comprehensive explanation, and his errors should not sidetrack the search. He also drew attention to the economic influence of the secret societies, which others have consistently ignored. For instance, his demonstration of the interconnections between mercantile factions in British Malaya cannot be rejected. Likewise, his contention that these

10. Comber, p. 65. Wong Lin Ken, in "Revenue Farms of Prince of Wales Island" (1964–65), pp. 78–79, in discussing collusion over the Pinang farms, shows that the colonial administrators were well aware that the heads of the farms were both the kapitans and the headmen of the local secret societies, or kongsis.

mercantile factions were inextricably bound up with competing revenue farming syndicates and rival secret societies seems eminently reasonable. The problem with Wynne's explanation was that he perceived the struggles as the result of an ideological conspiracy engineered by "the hidden hand of Triad and Tabut." Khoo Kay Kim, taking the evidence but rejecting the conspiracy theory, suggests that the Chinese mercantile factions were connected to European mercantile factions and to conflicting parties in the politics of the various Riau-Johor sultans and chiefs.[11]

There is, in fact, a tacit consensus among many scholars that the root causes of conflict were economic, or at least related to the economy. In perspective this is eminently sensible; after all, Chinese and British inhabitants of Malaya and Singapore were there for one reason: to make money. And, if their presence in Malaya can be explained by economic forces, it is probable that their rivalries, struggles, and conflicts can likewise be explained. This certainly is the opinion of the most comprehensive and recent discussion of secret societies in Malaya, that of Mak Lau Fong. He points out that the socioeconomic base of the secret societies was occupational monopolization. This was a natural cause for periodic conflict. The continuing flow of Chinese immigrants into Malaya and the Straits Settlements meant that there were always newcomers ready to challenge the preserves of earlier arrivals.

There are two problems with this approach. First, if the primary interest of economic competitors was making money, then compromise would seem more likely than a physical fight, and even if they should come into conflict, the chances should be better than average that they could ultimately find a way to resolve the matter for mutual profit. Mak tries to dispose of this problem by suggesting that economic conflict between secret societies was a zero-sum game and that the flow of immigrants put increasing pressure on a constant economic pie. If this argument shows why there was a reluctance to compromise, it explains neither the fact that there was frequent compromise nor the frequent breakdown of compromise. Second, if Mak's theory is correct, then most conflicts would have been between newcomers and those already established, between the disorganized outsiders and the organized insiders, and it is not clear that this was the case.

11. Wynne, 326–50; largely moving out of his discussion of the Perak and Selangor wars, Wynne attempts to show a dualism in the revenue farms, in conflicting parties in the wars, and in both Malay and Chinese secret societies based on the triad and Tokong rivalry; on p. 350 he offers a chart showing the factions in the Singapore revenue farming syndicates. Khoo, *Western Malay States*, (1972), pp. 115–18, 209–12.

Class Conflict in Chinese Society

While there is some validity in all of these explanations, it strikes me that they fall short. I believe that it is a mistake to look at the succession of secret society conflicts and then attempt to find some common explanation. So long as we are looking at economic factors, why not look at the Chinese migration as an economic factor and then seek explanations once we understand the ebb and flow of economic forces associated with the migration. I believe that the divisions we are trying to explain were a result of the development of capitalism, which was the major work of the colonial establishment. The established Chinese economy and the society that grew up with it were gradually rechanneled into the stream of this new economic system. It seems sensible to seek the causes of struggle in economically motivated class conflict. There was, of course, a cultural clash between Chinese and Europeans as well as between different groups of Chinese, but my argument is that the basic struggle was between the principles of capitalism upheld by the mercantile classes and those traditional economic principles that derived from what James Scott has termed the "moral economy" of the peasant.[12]

In his study of nineteenth-century Chinese society, Lee Poh Ping attempted to explain the conflicts among Singapore's Chinese as an economic struggle between what he called the "pepper and gambier" society and the "free trade" society. Despite the insights this approach offered, the attempt was flawed by a failure to support his hypothesis with firm evidence. Lee's critics correctly fault his efforts to prove the pre-Rafflesian existence of the "pepper and gambier" society; he incorrectly maintained that a significant number of these planters had established themselves on Singapore Island some decades before 1819. He chose to ignore my evidence that argues for the society's existence in nearby Riau; for Lee himself was caught in the historiographic trap of colonial territorial boundaries.[13] I think, however, that Lee, in what he labeled as the "pepper and gambier society," correctly identified the major kongsi brotherhood of the island colony. And it does seem that the brotherhood did, in fact, come into conflict with a group of wealthy Chinese merchants of Singapore town, who were allied with the colonial state and involved in the entrepôt economy. Lee's hypoth-

12. Scott, *Moral Economy of the Peasant* (1976).
13. Lee, 1978; Lee's book has been criticized severely, not only for lapses in fact, but also on what appear to be ideological grounds. The reviews, which perhaps say more about their authors than about Lee himself, are: Wong Lin Ken, "Review Article" (1980), and Khoo, "Review of Lee Poh Ping" (1978). Trocki, 1976, pp. 134–38.

esis may well be correct; the problem is in demonstrating it and in showing the elements of continuity in what was really a century-long pattern of struggle.

Recently, Lee's hypothesis has been criticized by Yen Ching-hwang, who has located the source of conflict within Singapore's Chinese social order in ethnic differences. He has pointed to the *pang*, or speech-group organizations. There is a clear record of different Hokkien, Teochew, Hakka, and other such groups during the nineteenth century. But Yen also shows that conflict was just as likely to take place within pang groups as it was among the larger ethnic divisions. In fact, it seems that all these were taukeh-led groups, and that conflict was largely among mercantile factions.[14] While this explanation makes perfect sense, it does not take into consideration the links with the triad organizations nor does it effectively tie specific outbreaks of violence and conflict to economic trends. Furthermore, Yen's model is a static one that does not account for the process of change, nor does it go outside the boundaries of British Malaya. Although Yen takes issue with the class-conflict model proposed by Lee, much of his evidence appears to support it.

Lee's hypothesis bears a strong resemblance to the one offered by Wang Tai Peng for the demise of the Borneo kongsis. Wang paints a picture of historical development within the Hakka communities in Borneo that resulted in what might be called a "class struggle." As I have shown, Wang maintains that the heart of the Hakka mining kongsis was the brotherhood of the laborers. Kongsi government had been established on this basis and flourished during the eighteenth century.[15] By the midnineteenth century, the independent Chinese capitalists, or taukehs, began to assume greater financial power. This was particularly true as the influence of the Dutch began to penetrate

14. Yen (1986), pp. 177–91. Tan Tock Seng and his son Tan Kim Ching led a powerful H'ai Ch'ang subgroup of the Hokkien pang. The Cheang family, a major revenue-farming dynasty including Cheang Sam Teo and Cheang Hong Lim, led the Ch'ang T'ai group. These divisions reflect a common territorial origin in China, however; all were intimately connected with the leadership of certain wealthy patrons. This is particularly clear with the Teochew group known as the Ngee Ann Kongsi (initially called the Ngee Ann Kun), which was closely identified with the family of Seah Eu Chin and his pepper and gambier interests.

15. Wang's discussion of the kongsi has been preceded by a considerable body of work, much of which arrives at somewhat different conclusions than does Wang. Wang, however, has been one of the first to attempt to integrate the history of the Borneo kongsis into the general fabric of Chinese history. A more standard work is James C. Jackson, 1970. Earlier and contemporary accounts of particular interest include Ward, "Hakka Kongsi in Borneo" (1954); "Lan Fang Kungsi Chronicle" (1885); Earl, "Narrative of a Journey" (1836); Dotty and Pohlman, "Tour in Borneo"; Chang, "Historical Geography of Chinese Settlement" (1954).

the fastness of the upper Kapuas River where the mining kongsis had been established.

Initially, the kongsis were democratic brotherhoods, according to Wang. While he may have idealized the egalitarianism of these groups, outside observers have confirmed his description:

> The interest of *kongsi* coolies lay entirely in the *kongsi*-house. Through distinction in war, coolies were rewarded with shares in the *kongsi* mines. A new member or *Hsin-k'o* could also become a share-holder after a year working in the *kongsi*-mine. The old coolies who had retired from work were given a share each for their long service to the *kongsi*. The profits of the *kongsi*-miners after setting part of it for the *kongsi* fund, were divided by the share-holders or mine workers. When the profit was huge, every-one of them could expect a bonus to be added to their dividend. The *kongsi*-house provided them a roof under the sky, meals, democratic life and brotherhood and a share in gain and loss.[16]

Wang attributes the demise of the kongsi republics of West Borneo to the rise of taukeh influence, the expansion of the Dutch, and, to a certain extent, the penetration of Western capitalism. In particular, the taukehs' wealth gave them the means to settle their own families in the Nanyang and to create, or re-create, institutions of social solidarity based on kinship and lineage. As the Dutch began to move into the upper Kapuas in the second half of the nineteenth century, they gradu-ally extended a form of indirect rule over the kongsis. They appointed a kapitan to head the various communities. Initially, these were the elected headmen of the kongsi, but as time passed, they were more likely to be wealthy taukehs who had no intention of sharing power with or paying taxes to the kongsi.

In the Montrado kongsi, Wang notes that decline began as a result of financial losses. Faced with bankruptcy, the kongsi members were forced to accept loans from wealthy taukehs who controlled the down-river markets. The Ta-Kang Kongsi of Montrado had to give member-ship and special privileges to the three clans the taukehs represented:[17]

16. Wang, 1977, p. 94.
17. The use of the term *clan* here is perhaps informal and not entirely accurate according to the anthropological definition of a proper clan. I believe that what Wang really means here is a surname group. In a real clan, all of the members are related and belong to various lineages. Chinese do have true clan organizations, but in the overseas communities there were rarely enough actual clan members to form a viable group; thus the Chinese tendency to assume a fictive kinship between all individuals bearing the same surname was enough of a relationship upon which to create social solidarity.

They were given privileges that members of their clans should be placed in the *kongsi* mines' administration. In a *kongsi* mine, one of the two mineheads or *huo-ch'ang*, one of the three treasurers or *ts'ai-ku* must come from the surname groups of Huang, Wu or Cheng. Again, out of the eight foremen or *ting-kung*, two were distributed to Wu, two to Huang, two to Cheng and only one left to any other surname groups. In a small mine there usually were four positions of foreman, of which Wu, Cheng, and Huang clans each owned one respectively and left one to minorities.[18]

The taukehs, using their own surname groups as power bases, undermined the "democratic" and popular foundations of the kongsis. In the end, Wang shows that the colonial regime extended its control over the Hakka mining communities, and the kongsi governments disappeared.

There was, however, resistance to this course of events. The poorer kongsi members, many of whom had married Dyak women or were the children of these mixed unions, attempted to oppose the taukeh takeover of the mines and fell back upon the secret brotherhoods based on the triad rituals. These preserved the concept of brotherhood and, according to Wang, continued to press for the return of the system of economic democracy that had prevailed in the early days of the kongsi.

Another student of the Borneo kongsis, geographer James C. Jackson, has explained the development of conflict among the various kongsis as a result both of the exhaustion of the gold deposits and of disputes over water rights. He also notes the significance of conflict arising over changes in leadership and questions of "succession"; but, he too points to policies enacted by the Dutch as having exacerbated the conflicts. Some of the kongsis, particularly the large Montrado federation, actively resisted the Dutch colonial advance and for a time were successful, but by the middle of the nineteenth century, the tide had generally turned against the kongsis.[19]

I agree with Lee that there is a correspondence between the events Wang described in Borneo and those that took place in Singapore during the nineteenth century. The process that occurred in Borneo between 1720 and 1860 was as follows: the founding of pioneering settlements under more-or-less egalitarian conditions; the organization of production and labor by kongsis; the primary role of triad rit-

18. Wang, 1977, p. 90.
19. James C. Jackson, 1970, pp. 53–63.

uals in providing social solidarity through sworn brotherhood among the kongsis; conflicts arising out of increasing scarcity of resources; the growth of taukeh influence; the alliance between taukehs and colonialist forces; and finally, the criminalization of the brotherhoods and the substitution for them of surname organizations under the control of the taukehs. This sequence seems identical in its major outlines to what occurred in Riau, Singapore, and Johor between 1740 and 1880. It was also repeated again and again, with local variations, throughout the Malay world during the eighteenth and nineteenth centuries.

This explanation of the causes of disorder among the Chinese stresses economic struggle created by the expanding colonial state and the global capitalist economy. It does not contradict the fact that, in some cases, the struggles took place between members of different speech groups, between certain secret societies, or between other such China-related or culturally defined divisions. The prize in the struggles was invariably the control of a particular economic resource or preserve, and one side or the other was usually backed by the colonial state or by a European mercantile faction.

The Foundations of Economic Struggle

Even if all Chinese migrants had been of the same speech group and had come from the same villages, the conditions of Chinese colonization and economic production would have led Chinese society into this dialectal struggle between capital and labor. Each side had its own more-or-less incompatible conditions. In the face of a changing economic environment and unstable political conditions, it was possible for first one, then the other, to insist upon the primacy of its requirements to the detriment of others. For labor, the prime requirements were usually security of person, survival, and a flexible calculus of debt. For capital, they were profit, security of property, and a strict interpretation of contracts. The strength of labor was in its ability to defend itself; of capital, in its access to the market. The weakness of labor was its need for other resources and provisions. The weakness of capital was its lack of access to the producers and production facilities in general.

Generally, as pioneers, laborers were in a position to insist upon their requirements in the initial stages of a venture. So long as they lived in the interior, they were a law unto themselves. Merchants and backers could lend them capital, but they really could not force repayment. Moreover, the kongsis in given regions were apparently able to cartelize the flow of produce, which was the usual means of repayment. Capitalists often did not have unlimited sources of supply; they could not afford to alienate the laborers' kongsis.

It was necessary, in fact, to attract workers because of the preexisting labor shortage in the region. There was an incentive for laborers, under the conditions of the kongsi brotherhoods, to earn themselves a share of the enterprise and become "partners" in a mine or a plantation. Such incentives proved absolutely necessary to bring young men to forsake their families, their villages, and a reasonably civilized life in China, whatever the level of poverty and violence in their homes, and to travel thousands of miles over the sea, go into the equatorial rain forest, clear the jungle, and plant crops or conduct mining operations. Under these conditions, only the brotherhoods were capable of mobilizing manpower on a scale adequate for profitable production. As a result, merchants often joined kongsis with planters and miners on a share basis in order to ensure their access to the supply of goods produced. Moreover, the brotherhoods were also capable of providing military protection against most illegitimate attempts at confiscation, and against "legitimate" attempts as well, if there were a real difference.

Periods of prosperity and peace were more favorable to merchant concerns. Taukehs could establish links with colonial powers and gain access to European capital and to alternative sources of trade goods. At the same time, they could establish political and military relations with Europeans which offered them status within the colonial power structure and gave them a lever of control over the kongsis. Likewise, peacetime conditions allowed for a process of social stratification to occur within kongsis as economic roles became increasingly crucial to the success of ventures.

I believe that Wang's interpretation of kongsi government was somewhat idealistic. Kongsis could become coercive and exploitative. My studies of the pepper and gambier agriculture in Singapore and Johor suggest that established planters, shopkeepers, kangchus, and coolie brokers quickly came to control the kongsis. Coolies were bought and sold and forced to labor and were probably cheated of their "fair" shares one way or another. For them, the kongsi could be an agency of repression.

In the long run, the merchants came to dominate many kongsis and were able to draw the laborers and their erstwhile partners into debtor relationships that destroyed the independence of the kongsi and fully absorbed the profits of the venture. They could count on the assistance of the colonial state in this matter; for neither the state nor the European mercantile communities had anything to gain from an independent Chinese labor movement, nor from autonomous Chinese political entities, which is what the kongsis often represented, despite their exploitative tendencies. Changing political conditions could cause the process to reverse, throwing real power into the hands of charismatic leaders, warriors, and ultimately, the laborers themselves. Such conditions made the kongsis a force to be reckoned with.

The history of the mining settlements on Bangka in the period between 1784 and 1805 and the story of the pepper and gambier planters of Riau during the same period show the periodic necessity of self-protection that only the armed brotherhoods could provide.[20] Until 1784, prosperity and political control from Malay and Dutch centers had tended to grow stronger. There is evidence that kongsi organization characterized the settlements in both areas, but the presence of reasonably effective indigenous governments in Palembang and Tanjung Pinang must have tipped the balance in favor of the market communities in the entrepôts. After the collapse of the Bugis entrepôt at Riau, however, conditions changed markedly. Indigenous governments fragmented under Dutch pressure, particularly after the sack of Riau in 1784. Malay, *orang laut,* Bugis, and Illanun "pirates" began conducting raids throughout the archipelago. A most tempting target were the Chinese mining settlements of Bangka and the pepper and gambier kangkars of Riau. Since neither the Dutch nor the local Malay chiefs had either the will or the capability to protect the Chinese, the miners and planters were essentially on their own, and only their own brotherhoods could protect them.

Times of chaos, frontiers beyond the reach of any constituted political authority: these were the times and places that fostered the growth of the triad brotherhoods. Indeed, without the brotherhoods and the laborers who comprised their membership, there would have been no settlements. Neither the Malay chiefs, the Chinese taukehs, nor the European colonialists possessed the means to control and direct Chinese labor. These elites could only wait until the kongsis had gone ahead, cleared the "dead" land, and brought it into production. It then required alliance or collusion between European colonial powers and local elite groups, both Chinese and indigenous, to make good their claims on the produce of the Chinese laborers.

20. I have discussed these events in *Prince of Pirates* (Trocki, 1979, pp. 30–34).

48 | Opium and Empire

Nonetheless, capital and its controllers also had a role to play from the beginning. Merchants supplied provisions, tools, and the necessary connections to markets for the products of the plantations and mines. Laborers, occupied with commercial production, had to rely on outside sources for food, equipment, and other necessities. The Borneo kongsis enjoyed their unprecedented autonomy, it seems, at least partly because they grew their own rice and thus enjoyed a degree of independence few such settlements attained.[21] Most laborers had to rely on the market; no matter how well they managed to finance their initial ventures, they would ultimately have a bad year and be forced to borrow. By the beginning of the nineteenth century, many Riau plantation owners were already dependent on loans from merchants in Tanjung Pinang.

Even before the founding of Singapore, struggles had broken out between the Hokkien merchant community located in Tanjung Pinang and the Teochew kampong across the harbor at Senggarang in about 1790. The latter settlement was the headquarters for the pepper and gambier chukangs scattered all over the interior and coast of Bintan Island. In the eighteenth century, the Dutch had found it necessary to appoint two headmen for the Riau Chinese, one "Amoy" to rule the Hokkien Chinese and one "Canton" for the Teochews, who actually controlled the agricultural system.[22] British sources indicate that trouble had erupted between Chinese factions in Pinang at about the same time. I suggest that the cause of these struggles was the attempt by the laborers' brotherhoods to reassert themselves over mercantile leadership within their ranks and against the kongsis controlled largely by merchants.

There was always a degree of equitability in the relationship between merchants and kongsis. So long as the kongsis' mines and plantations functioned as an extension of the Chinese economy and their primary market links were with the China coast, there was a balance of powers between borrowers and lenders. The laborers were usually far off in the jungle, where of necessity, the brotherhoods policed the area and provided whatever security there was. Because the police forces of the urban centers, where the taukehs lived, were usually incapable of penetrating the interior, the merchants had to depend on the goodwill of the planters of miners to collect their debts. Merchants found it necessary, even desirable, to cooperate with and

21. James C. Jackson, 1970, p. 67.
22. Trocki, 1979, pp. 32–33.

even become members of the triad kongsis that dominated the interior. In Singapore's early days, Vaughan maintains, Malays, Indians, and even Europeans joined the Heaven and Earth Society for protection.[23]

Even though laborers and merchants each had leverage over the other, neither group was in total control of its own economic environment. The laborers could not guarantee nature and the merchant could not guarantee future market conditions. Questions of who would pay for late or short deliveries or who would absorb the cost of market fluctuations were always being negotiated, and neither party was ever really in a position to enjoy more than a temporary advantage.

But as the European presence grew in the nineteenth century, the power equation changed. The Chinese economy became increasingly involved in the European economy of the entrepôts and, through them, with the global capitalist economy. Trading patterns changed during the 1830s, and the importance of the China market decreased in comparison to the European. Entrance into the world market, while it brought considerable profits initially, increased price instability. Singapore became subject to the boom-and-bust cycles typical of a developing capitalist economy. These changes, over the long run, tipped the balance against the laborers' organizations and gave greater leverage to the merchants. The British, at the same time, imposed their own idea of "private property" within their territories, thus creating a novel legal framework that naturally favored the capitalists.

Capitalist strength was backed up not only by superior firepower and technology but by an additional form of economic leverage. Europeans, the British in particular, were able ultimately to dominate the trade of Asia in the nineteenth century by virtue of their control of opium. It was through opium that the colonial system of economic domination and dependence was constructed. Opium provided the crucial link in the chain of dependency between the entrepôt economy and the more or less exclusively Chinese economy of the kongsis and junk traders that had existed in the Nanyang since the beginning of the eighteenth century. It was the growth of the opium economy of Asia that tied together the British and the Chinese at Singapore in 1819.

23. Vaughan, p. 95.

3 Opium and the Singapore Economy

The founding of Singapore was a peripheral result of the India-China opium trade.[1] That trade, portrayed in the works of David Edward Owen and Holden Furber, has been updated by Jonathan Spence, among others.[2] Its details and history are integral to the history of the Singapore Chinese. For a full century, Singapore was "Opium Central: Southeast Asia." Opium was so common in nineteenth-century Singapore that most writers seem to take it for granted.

If the kongsis were the pioneers of Chinese labor in Southeast Asia, then the British agency houses in Singapore were the pioneers of British colonial capitalism. The British came as merchants of opium, and in a very real sense we can best understand the British Empire east of Suez as of 1800 as essentially a drug cartel. The first British merchants in Singapore seem to have been private traders who had decided

---

1. Opium is derived from the sap of the green seed pod of the opium poppy (*Papaver somniferum*). The plant is native to south and southwest Asia and its narcotic and pain-killing properties have been recognized since prehistoric times. At the beginning of the eighteenth century, opium was being produced in areas scattered from Asia Minor to Bengal, usually as a commercial crop of moderate value, and under some sort of monopoly or government levy. The drug, in various forms, entered international commerce and was marketed as a medicine and also as a recreational drug throughout Asia, but only on a very limited scale until the 1750s. For a fairly comprehensive discussion of the chemistry and pre–twentieth-century history of the drug, see Watt, "Papaver somniferum" (1893).

2. Owen, *British Opium Policy in India and China* (1934), and Furber, *John Company at Work* (1935), offer comprehensive pictures of British trade in the eighteenth and nine-teenth centuries; Owen, in particular, provides what is generally accepted as the basic delineation of British economic policy in Asia. His bibliography is an important guide to the wealth of primary documentation of the colonial opium trade. Spence's brief but valuable view of opium, "Opium Smoking in Ch'ing China," (1975), establishes the need to keep this aspect of European imperialism in mind when studying the region's history.

to settle down. Their aim was initially to dominate, or at least to milk, the opium trade between India and China with Singapore as the choke hold. For a variety of reasons this proved impossible. To survive, they became commission agents, buying and selling Western goods for Eastern on behalf of larger merchant firms in India and the West.

After a very few years they discovered that the opium trade to China was too big and volatile for them even to profit from, let alone dominate. This became quite clear after the economic crises of 1835–39, when drastic fluctuations in the price of opium and in the international economy forced them to accept the instability of their situation and to restrict their range of activities. The founding of Hong Kong as a free port further challenged Singapore's position as a global entrepôt, as did the French intrusion into Indochina and Dutch "liberal" policies in the Indies and the opening of a number of free ports there. The problem with free trade was that no one had a monopoly on it.

While these events deprived Singapore of its unique status, they quickened economic activity in Southeast Asia as a whole. When Singapore's agency houses found it necessary to seek a local economic base, there was a good deal more business to do. They strengthened their connections with the local Chinese merchants and through them developed links to the sources of Southeast Asian produce, which they might trade in either China or Europe. They also attempted primary agricultural production on their own. In the 1830s, they tried to grow spices (mostly nutmegs) in Singapore, but this was a failure. At the same time, they began to push local products like gambier and gutta percha into European markets. Rather than insulating themselves from the vagaries of the capitalist world order, however, the British merchants simply intensified and extended the impact of those forces into the local Asian economies. As the range of the entrepôt shrunk, the intensity of its influence increased around Singapore's immediate hinterland and then began to spread out again with renewed vigor into the Malay Peninsula, Sumatra, Borneo, and Siam.

In this shrinking circle, opium continued to play an increasingly important role. As drug dealers, the British merchants initially employed opium as one of their major forms of capital. Generally speaking, hard currency and specie were in short supply in Southeast Asia; much trade had therefore to be carried out in kind. The availability of a commodity like opium, which had an acknowledged and reasonably predictable resale value, gave British traders a decided advantage in local markets. Opium thus lubricated their penetration of the kongsi economy, and instead of selling drugs to China, they settled simply for selling drugs to local Chinese. Opium was the trap in which the kongsi economies were captured by colonial capitalism. Having trapped the local economies, British merchants were able, perhaps even forced, to leave the details of the opium trade to others, but they relied on its presence.

The remarks of W. G. Gulland, a pillar of the European mercantile community and a member of the Legislative Council in 1883, are illustrative of the importance of opium and of British ambivalence toward it:

> For the opium trade, pure and simple, in itself, I care nothing; it is wholly in the hands of Jews and Armenians, and I know little about its ins and outs: but there is no doubt that Opium enters largely into, and forms an important part of, the Native trade of this city, as of almost all other eastern settlements. All those prahus and junks which we see lying off Tanjong Ru are insignificant in themselves, but they are all small parts of one great trade. They come here to sell their produce and buy return cargoes: some buy one thing, some another; but they must all have Opium to a greater or lesser extent, and unless they get what they want without let or hindrance, I fear they will go another year to some of the neighbouring ports.[3]

We cannot understand the economic life of nineteenth-century Singapore without understanding the role of opium; for the health of the local economy was largely dependent upon its price. Because opium was a major exchange commodity for local Straits produce, its price affected the values of all other commodities. No issue of a Singapore newspaper was complete without a quotation of the local opium price, and quotations of prices in Calcutta, Hong Kong, and the Chinese Treaty Ports were regularly available. Its rises and falls marked periods of crisis and prosperity in the colonial entrepôt.

Beyond this, and of even greater permanent importance, the distribution of opium to the increasing population of local Chinese constituted the first and the most enduring link between the colonial administration and the population. As a result, the mechanism for retail distribution of opium, the opium farm, became the political and economic focus of the Singapore Chinese community. The farm provided the crucial link between the British economic and administrative order and the Chinese brotherhoods. Thus, from the beginning to the end of the nineteenth century, the opium farm was the Chinese power

3. *Legco*, 28 February 1883, p. 8.

center of the colony. Its history is an important guide to the dynamics of the history of the Singapore Chinese.

The Opium Trade in Asia

The trade in opium to China was begun by the Portuguese and the Dutch as early as the seventeenth century, but it did not attain major proportions until after the British had taken Bengal (see map 2) in 1757. There were by then significant areas of poppy cultivation in the "upper provinces" of Bihar and Benares (Varanasi). The cultivation, which had previously been monopolized by the nawab, was appropriated by the servants of the Company who were posted to Patna and Ghazipur. There followed several decades of sporadic expansion through "private trade" by the Company's opium agents before the Company itself assumed control of the opium monopoly and began to rationalize the system of licenses, advances, and deliveries by which the cultivation was organized. During the 1780s a firm market was developed in China.

By the 1790s, the Company's management of the opium trade had attained what was more or less its final form. The Company limited itself to monopolization of drug production in India and then sold the opium at regular auctions in Calcutta to "country traders." The country traders carried the opium to the Nanyang and on to China, where they sold their cargoes to smugglers off the China coast and changed their silver at the Company's offices in Canton for bills of exchange on Europe, India, or America. The Company used the silver to cover its tea purchases in China and defray its massive debt in Britain. By the beginning of the Napoleonic Wars, it was perhaps the most lucrative element of the Company's commerce in Asia. Although expansion continued into the 1880s and minor adjustments were continually made, the system was essentially fixed.[4]

The Company's opium agents made cash advances to Indian peasants who grew poppies and harvested the opium. Ultimately, the raw opium was delivered to one of the two Company factories in Patna or Ghazipur, where it was cleaned, weighed, dried, and packaged. At the factories the opium was shaped into balls weighing about 3.5 pounds

---

4. Marshall, *East Indian Fortunes* (1976), pp. 118–19. "Country traders" were private traders based in India. They were mostly British, often in partnership with Indian firms. They were initially restricted to trade in the "country" of India and Southeast Asia and China, and were forbidden from infringing on the EIC's monopolies.

and packed into specially manufactured mango-wood chests. Each chest contained forty balls, twenty on each of two layers packed into pigeonhole sections.

The opium in each chest weighed about 140 pounds and was roughly equivalent to a *pikul* of 133.3 pounds (100 *catties*). This was called "provision" opium, and was meant to supply the overseas trade. Opium leaving the Patna factory was styled "Patna opium" and that from Ghazipur was known in the trade as "Benares opium." These two varieties were the staples of the Company's trade. Each had its own distinctive "taste" and appealed to a different group of consumers. Benares opium tended to be a little cheaper than Patna, but this was not always the case. The factories also produced "excise opium," packaged in a somewhat different manner for consumption inside India. All the provision opium was shipped to Calcutta, where it was sold at auction. By the nineteenth century, the auctions were dominated by agents and speculators and were held at monthly intervals.[5]

Prices at these auctions tended to vary considerably depending upon the perceived quality and quantity of the crop, the anticipated price it would bring in China, and finally, the speculative mood of the traders themselves. In the first half of the nineteenth century, January auction prices were often determined by the previous year's sales, whereas by March, a clipper ship would have returned from Canton with news of the sales of that year's crop and auction bids would be adjusted accordingly. As international communications improved, the lag time shortened. Once the drug was sold, the Company was theoretically finished with it. It was the property of the traders who carried it to China.

There had been pressures from the British traders since the 1770s for the establishment of a British base in the Indonesian archipelago. Settlements at Pinang, Benkulu, and even the ill-fated one at Balambangan were all attempts to answer this need. None of them ever really filled the purpose. The port that best met the needs of the trade was the Malay-Bugis entrepôt at Riau near the modern town of Tanjung Pinang on Bintan Island. Before 1784, Riau drew together the Chinese junk trade from Siam, Fujian, and Guangdong and the Bugis trade from the Java Sea and the Straits of Melaka. Despite the lack of security for British traders, Riau served as an important staging area for the vessels plying between Calcutta and Canton, because it was a collecting point for the tin, pepper, spices, and other goods of the

5. Watt. Reports of these auctions were a regular feature of all Singapore newspapers of the period. They included the figures (in rupees) for the high and low and average bids as well as the total quantity sold.

archipelago which had a market either in China or the West. If authorities on the China coast were strictly enforcing the antiopium laws that season, the Europeans could sell opium directly to Chinese traders at Riau in exchange for ceramics, tea, silk, and other Chinese products.

The colonies of Chinese laborers in Southeast Asia provided another small but reliable and growing market for the English traders' opium. Before 1800 the major opium consumers in Southeast Asia seem to have been local chiefs, and not the Chinese, though it is difficult to be certain. As the population of Chinese laborers increased, they became the region's major opium consumers. Southeast Asian sales were insignificant, however, compared with sales in China.

Although the new trading configuration at Riau was highly successful, it was short-lived and collapsed after 1784 when the Dutch sacked the port.[6] The next twenty-five years were chaotic ones in the Straits of Melaka as a result of the Napoleonic Wars and the British conquest of Java and other Dutch possessions in the region. Although the economy of the Malay world declined, the British trade to China continued and prospered. There was no crisis in the opium trade. Napoleon had eliminated the Dutch as a power in the archipelago, and there was thus no real threat to British trade, especially so long as Britain held Melaka.

With the coming of peace in Europe, the English agreed to return the Dutch territories they had seized in Southeast Asia. Melaka was handed over in 1818, and the Dutch reoccupied Riau in the same year. This appeared to leave British trade in the archipelago in a vulnerable position, with no safe harbor between Pinang and Canton. In what he perceived as a crisis atmosphere, Thomas Stamford Raffles decided to take matters into his own hands and founded a port at the eastern end of the Melaka Straits to serve the China trade. He arrived at Singapore Island in January 1819. The new settlement, founded as a free port, seemed the answer to the country traders' prayers. William Jardine, who arrived at Singapore five months later, wrote to his agents in Calcutta of the prospects of the new settlement. He had formed the "highest opinion of Singapore as a place of trade" but noted that little trade could take place, as there were as yet no merchants there and little capital. He felt, however, that the freedom from customs duties and port charges would soon draw considerable trade:

> I am of opinion that a person settling here for a few months with a few thousand dollars as a circulating medium (which they greatly want) might carry on business to great advantage. I dare say that Opium might be now retailed at $1,300 per Chest but there is no one individual who

6. I have discussed these events in some detail in Trocki, 1979, pp. 21–34.

Table 1. Trade of Bengal to the East Indies and China, 1814–1818 (rupees)

Goods	1814–15	1815–16	1816–17	1817–18
Opium	1,935,017	2,384,719	1,798,229	1,700,855
Cloth goods	2,082,843	1,945,477	2,292,578	2,579,194
Other	2,201,255	2,507,995	2,514,192	1,753,298
Total	6,219,126	6,838,191	6,663,949	6,033,347
Adj. total*	5,035,164	4,377,200	3,841,782	5,115,823
% Opium	38%	54%	47%	33%

Source: Parliamentary Papers, Report Relative to the Trade with the East Indies and China from the Select Committee of the House of Lords . . . , 7 May 1821 (House of Commons, 1821), pp. 314–19.
*The larger "Total" is all goods shipped from Bengal. The "Adjusted total" is exports only to Southeast Asia and China, not including the Maldives, Mauritius, New South Wales, South Africa, and Mozambique. The percentage of opium is figured on the basis of the smaller total since little opium was going to these other places.

could afford to buy so large a quantity as a Chest, the Sale of which must be the work of many days. . . . Mr. Bernard, son-in-law of the Major [Farquhar], who is Master Attendant is an inexperienced youth and knows not to take advantage of his opportunities—I offered to sell him Opium for Government Bills on Bengal but could not prevail on him to venture on a purchase.[7]

Jardine went on to note that he had just sold five chests of opium at Melaka for $1,100 each.

What one finds interesting about this letter, aside from his attempt to offer Bernard an "opportunity," is the fact that Jardine mentioned opium in no less than four different contexts in a letter that was not two pages long—handwritten. This is only a minor indication of the importance of the opium trade and of its centrality to almost all British commerce in the East at that time. As the figures in table 1 show, during the four years before the foundation of Singapore, opium constituted anywhere from one-third to more than one-half of the total value of produce shipped from Bengal to the East. It was the single most valuable commodity of the India-China trade. The rhythms of the opium trade more or less governed the economic development of nineteenth-century Singapore. Thus the rises and falls of the opium price in Canton or Calcutta offer a window on the health of the economy of the British colony.

On the whole, the Singapore market had little impact on the price of opium. The forces that generally determined the opium price were outside of Southeast Asia; events in India, China, or both were usually

7. Wm. Jardine to Larruleta & Co., 24 May 1819, Jardine Collection, Oxford, pp. 74–75. I am grateful to Ruth McVey for providing me with a copy of this letter.

crucial. In most cases, the supply level in India and the demand situation in China were the most important variables; for these were the two major poles of the trade. China normally absorbed 75–80 percent of India's annual opium output. Singapore's trade was but an eddy in this great river of opium flowing through the archipelago on its way east.

As the center for the trade in Southeast Asia, however, Singapore became the transmitter of global economic forces. And at a certain point, Asian economic forces became so thoroughly intermeshed with Western ones that they began operating together. As the elements of the global capitalist economy became bound together during the nineteenth century, the shocks from a boom or a crash, a war or a change of government in Calcutta, Canton, Paris, London, or New York could be transmitted to Singapore. Whatever its origins, an event's impact often arrived in Southeast Asia through the medium of opium. It is thus appropriate to treat opium as the primary instrument of capitalist penetration in the region.

About 20 percent of India's annual production of opium was landed at Singapore. Although some of that was transhipped to China, much of it came to be consumed in Singapore itself or else redistributed to Singapore's network of markets in Southeast Asia. This network included the states of the Malay Peninsula, Borneo, and Sumatra, Java, the Philippines, and the other islands in the eastern part of the archipelago. Most of this trade was carried on by Malaysian or Chinese traders and thus called the "native trade."

At the beginning of the century most of the European merchants who established houses in Singapore had their eyes not on the native trade but on the long-distance China opium trade. Since Singapore was really the only British port between the western part of Southeast Asia and Canton, they expected it would play a significant role in the long-distance trade to China. As the century progressed, however, the opium trade and Singapore's place in it took a different course. Singapore lost much of its role in the China trade in opium, forcing its European merchants to work the local markets in order to survive.[8]

The Crashes of 1837 and 1839

The Asian trade at the beginning of the nineteenth century was still operating according to principles and conditions of the past. Money

8. Wong Lin Ken, "Trade of Singapore" (1960), pp. 274–75; see also Allen and Donnithorn, *Western Enterprise in Indonesia and Malaya* (1957), pp. 38–39. Also Turnbull, *History of Singapore* (1977), p. 43.

was extremely scarce, for instance. Although prices in Singapore were always quoted in Spanish or Mexican dollars, very few of those dollars actually changed hands in Singapore. Most transactions were carried out in kind. European merchants who wished to obtain supplies of local produce were required to deal through Chinese intermediaries. They were generally expected to advance goods (e.g., Indian opium and such British manufactures as cotton cloth, iron tools, etc.) for three to six months before receiving consignments of Asian produce in return. Because they had no means of dealing directly with the producers or the suppliers of these goods, they had to rely on the chain of intermediaries. Under such conditions, trade was a highly speculative endeavor. There was no guarantee that a price agreed upon in January would still be profitable for both parties six months later. The market was opaque in the extreme, and as only an entrepôt, Singapore was simply a gathering place and not a final destination for most of the goods shipped there. For these reasons, many European trading houses were inclined to see the international opium trade as a far more secure and lucrative venture. This, however, was an illusion.

Opium played a crucial role in the Asian trade. Reports indicate that, in the absence of silver or other forms of hard cash, balls and chests of opium circulated as currency. It was, after all, the opium that drew both Southeast Asian and Chinese traders to Singapore in the first place. With trade underwritten by opium, there were serious problems when its price fluctuated. As figure 1 shows, the first part of the nineteenth century saw a series of rather extreme swings. The economic and thus the social and political history of Singapore was punctuated by these crises in the opium trade. The first of these came in 1835–37, when the opium market in Calcutta boomed and then collapsed. After a brief recovery, the market went into a drastic crash with the outbreak of the Opium War between Britain and China in 1839. Other crises were associated with the sharp price rises of 1844, 1857, 1860, and 1867. After 1870 the opium price was stabilized and thus ceased to act as an unpredictable factor. This stability came as a result of monopolies by the Sassoons and Jardines and the arrival of the telegraph in 1871. This predictability was, however, of marginal benefit to Singapore traders.

The 1837 crisis shows how tightly all of the various elements so far mentioned here had been interconnected. This was the first in the chain of events that ended with the Opium War in China and the Treaty of Nanking. In the decade after the founding of Singapore, the volume of opium produced in India and shipped eastward began to increase at an

Figure 1. Average annual opium price: Singapore, 1820–1901 (Spanish dollars per chest)

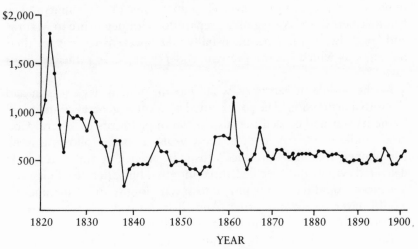

YEAR

Source: Compiled from various issues of SFP and ST.

unprecedented rate, and not all the increase occurred under the Company's monopoly. The rulers of independent Indian states were not slow to imitate a profitable enterprise. The state of Malwa in western India was particularly associated with this production, so much so that all non-Company opium produced in India and shipped through the port of Bombay came to be known simply as "Malwa opium" no matter where it came from.

As a result of skyrocketing Malwa production and the realization that the Chinese market seemed insatiable, the Company began to increase its own output of opium in the 1830s. Previously they had attempted to limit production to about four thousand chests in order to keep the price fairly high—around $1,000 per chest. The rapid increase in production, however, ultimately forced prices down. Between 1830 and 1835, prices fell sharply, reaching $538 per chest in the Singapore market by January 1835. In Calcutta, the price was even lower. The first sale of the year had brought record low prices of Rs 989 and Rs 980 (about $440 and $450—see fig. 1).

The trade reports in the *Singapore Chronicle* paint a picture of deepening depression between January and May of 1835. In those days, when trade was governed by the monsoons, January and February were usually slow months for business. Most of the Bugis traders, who had arrived from the south on the summer monsoon, had done their business and left. In the early part of January, the junks from

China had not yet arrived on the northeast monsoon. Likewise, the Indians were preparing to leave. The paper noted on 10 January: "The Kling dealers are making active preparations for departure to Madras and Pondicherry, these people usually take Specie as returns for their piece goods which for the present renders our Bazar rather scant of cash."[9]

By the middle of February, what was the annual slack season had slid into a depression. The paper noted a "want of general confidence" in the bazaar had caused the suspension of payments by several Chinese shopkeepers.[10] A letter in the *Chronicle* of the following week complained that the "produce" (usually pepper or tin) was rarely delivered within the specified three months, but often the European advancer would have to wait five to seven months and sometimes he would never receive the order. And, if it did come, it was often of inferior quality, or something else altogether.

Part of the problem was the limited market for European goods, which, outside of opium, was generally all that the British merchants had for capital. If they wanted to trade with China or the West, they needed Straits produce, and the only place they could get that was from the Chinese merchants who either bought it from Bugis or Malay traders or else from the kongsis. European merchants carried on trade at a tertiary level, making long advances of goods such as cotton cloth, ironware, or tools and offering substantial discounts to any Chinese or "native" traders who would take them. Resolutions by European dealers to end the system came to nothing because it was really the only way to move their merchandise.[11]

At the end of January, the *Chronicle* saw a glimmer of hope in a slight rise in opium prices, from $550 to $560 per chest: "We presume the Jews (who are the principal holders) will commence selling at above prices, on the usual credit of two months, payable in Cash, Gold Dust, Tin or Pepper."[12] The rise was a false start, however; by March, the price of opium had fallen to $530, and the paper was complaining of "hard times." The next week, commenting on the anxiety that had prevailed before the late arrival of an "Amoy junk," the paper noted that several Chinese firms had failed during the current depression and offered the thin gruel of nineteenth-century liberal consolation:

9. *SC*, 10 January 1835.
10. *SC*, 14 February 1835.
11. *SC*, 21 February 1835.
12. *SC*, 31 January 1835.

Still a good deal of agitation prevailing in consequence of the late failures. We are happy however to say that nearly all the "rotten fry" *have now died a natural death,* and we sincerely trust that the result will be a more wholesome state of things. We would *now* seriously recommend Piece Goods Houses not to push the Chinese dealers too hard for payments, which they will find much to their own interest. *"The rotten system"* must GRADUALLY *work its own cure.* The losses which several European establishments here have lately sustained have been to a very serious amount. [Italics and uppercase in the original.][13]

The writer, as it turned out, was indulging in wishful thinking. The depression continued into May, when the paper reported that the trade was "in the most depressed and miserable state." It reported the failure of a European trading firm, noting, *"Another* of the 'men of straw' has this week become bankrupt to the amount of Drs. 35,000."[14] This, apparently, was rock bottom and marked the end of the depression. There is evidence that trade during the second half of 1835 began to pick up, particularly in opium. By 1836, prices for Patna opium had climbed to over $700 per chest, and Benares opium was at $650 in the Singapore market.

These prices reflected a worldwide speculative boom that involved railroad shares in Britain, frontier land in the United States, and opium in Calcutta and Canton. Through opium, the boom was transmitted to Singapore. In March of 1837, the Calcutta market crashed,[15] and the Singapore price fell back to about $500 per chest. The Indian government bailed out the Calcutta and Canton speculators and absorbed a loss of nearly Rs 2.5 million. This was to ensure that the brokers in China and India would continue to have "capital to work the trade" in the future. But the Straits merchants in Pinang and Singapore, who had also joined the speculators and purchased opium at the first 1837 sales and stood to lose something like $20,000, had to swallow their losses.[16] Again, in 1839, when the price fell to $250 per chest after

13. *SC,* 14 March 1835.
14. *SC,* 2 May 1835.
15. John Prinsep, "Note on the Condition of the Opium Trade," Ft. William, 9 Aug. 1837, No. 5, India, Separate Revenue Proceedings, Range 208, vol. 19 (SRP). Prinsep, secretary to government in India, prepared a report on the opium market crisis in August of 1837. He attributed the boom of 1835–36 to the "money plethora of Europe" and the Calcutta opium market crash to the collapse of European markets in early 1837.
16. SRP, 18 October 1837, no. 6. The Singapore opium merchants who signed a letter seeking relief because of the drop in prices were W. D. Shaw, J. H. Whitehead, Joze d'Almeida, Alex L. Johnson, Thos. O. Crane, James Guthrie, A. Guthrie, P. Pool Tabor, Joaquin d'Almeida, E. J. Gliman, J. C. Drysdale, S. Stephens, I. d'Almeida, C. Currie, D.

Commissioner Lin Zexu confiscated the opium in Canton, the British government saved the opium traders of Canton and Calcutta and made sure they were compensated for their losses but was ready to glut the Singapore market with twenty thousand chests of "refugee" opium from the China coast. Straits merchants simply did not have the economic "stomach" to stay on the opium roller coaster, and Company officials were usually ready to sacrifice them to bail out the Calcutta and Canton merchants.

These spectacular price swings reflected the precarious footing upon which Singapore's economy rested. Any entrepôt's economy is always at the mercy of the general market fluctuations, and the overdependence upon opium made the position of Singapore even more unstable. The years after the Opium War did little to improve the general conditions of the trade; in fact they probably worsened. The Treaty of Nanking opened more ports but did not legalize the opium trade. It gave Hong Kong to the British Crown, thus providing a competitor for Singapore. With the opium trade still technically illegal, the market was favorably oriented toward dealers with well-armed ships and a well-organized system of delivery, like the Jardines, who now moved to monopolize the coast trade and keep out "men of small capital."[17]

The Singapore merchants were well aware of the need to seek sources of wealth and produce closer to their own hinterland. One move in this direction was the agricultural development of Singapore. During the first half of the nineteenth century a series of European schemes for nutmeg, clove, mace, coffee, pepper, and sugar cultivation all met with failure. There was simply no arena for Europeans in primary production in Asia. It was necessary to continue to work with and through the Chinese, who had access to the labor force and who

---

Fraser, M. F. Davidson, E. Boustead, W. R. George, J. Zechariah, Ian Purvis, and R. C. Healy. Cf. Buckley, *Anecdotal History of Old Times in Singapore* (1965), p. 301. Twelve of the above names appeared on a list of signers of a petition against levying duties at Singapore in January 1836.

17. Le Fevour, *Western Enterprise in Late Ch'ing China* (1968), p. 13; see also his discussion of William Jardine's monopolization of the trade, pp. 12–17. Jardine, originally a country trader and opium smuggler, founded his own firm in Hong Kong shortly after the island was annexed by Great Britain during the first Opium War. He later went into partnership with his onetime rival James Matheson, to form Jardine and Matheson. Their descendants were the "Taipans" of Hong Kong in the nineteenth century. The firm expanded its activities after the 1840s and continues to be a major force in the trade of Hong Kong, the China coast, and Southeast Asia in general to the present. Although it still has major holdings in Hong Kong, in the early 1980s it moved its headquarters to Bermuda in anticipation of the return of Hong Kong to China in 1997.

controlled the system through which investments were channeled and products were extracted.[18]

Chinese Agriculture in Singapore

As John Crawfurd had pointed out as early as 1825, the only crops that lent themselves to cultivation in Singapore were pepper and gambier.[19] Chinese planters who had migrated from Riau were successfully and profitably growing these crops on Singapore Island. While Europeans had been preoccupied with opium trading and failed agricultural schemes, substantial tracts of the interior had been settled by Chinese planters. Europeans took little interest in this cultivation largely because there was no market for gambier in Europe. The entire system was part of the Chinese kongsi economy and largely oriented toward the China market. Not until a tariff on gambier (which was used as a chemical for tanning leather) was lifted in England did British traders begin to take an interest in the crop and in the gambier market.[20] The first major shipments of Singapore gambier to Europe were sent off in 1836. Thus the very time the European merchants' position in the China-India opium trade was collapsing, gambier shipments drew them closer to the Chinese economy of Singapore. That economy had a dual basis that has received little attention in the written history of nineteenth-century Singapore. Pepper and gambier agriculture, although insignificant in its export value, was important because by midcentury it employed more than one-third of the entire Chinese population. And opium was a major item of consumption for most Singapore Chinese. If the estimates of numerous nineteenth-century commentators are even approximately correct, nearly two-thirds of all Singapore Chinese were regular users.

The gambier economy may have been the archetype of the "rotten

18. James C. Jackson, *Planters and Speculators* (1968); Turnbull, *Straits Settlements* (1975); Trocki, 1976, 1979.

19. John Crawfurd, a servant of the East India Company, was the Resident of Singapore from 1823 to 1827 and was largely responsible for putting the new colony's government on a sound footing. He traveled extensively in Southeast Asia during the first part of the nineteenth century on the Company's service and was its emissary to Siam and Vietnam. In 1825 he wrote the article "The Agriculture of Singapore," which was published in 1849. Crawfurd's major publications include *A Descriptive Dictionary of the Indian Islands* (1856), *The History of the Indian Archipelago* (1820), and *A Journal of an Embassy to Siam and Cochinchina* (1829).

20. Trocki, 1976, p. 140; and Trocki, 1979, chaps. 5 and 6.

Chinese laborer cutting dried gambier into cubes before packing it for shipping (National Archives, Singapore)

system" referred to earlier. Its organization and operation were initially results of kongsi enterprise. Pepper and gambier plantations were founded by a kangchu who mobilized labor and capital and pioneered a river valley. At its base gambier was in the early years a purely Teochew enterprise, fully dominated by the Ngee Heng. Coolies, planters, kangchus, and associated participants such as boatmen were all connected to the society, and the kangchu was probably a triad headman. This was the base of the economic pyramid.

Such planters were not self-sufficient, and the need for initial operating capital, or a "grubstake" led them to the merchants of the port. The suppliers of provisions were the Teochew pepper and gambier shopkeepers whose establishments lined Boat Quay. Their initial investments in the form of food, cloth, and tools supported the coolies and planters until the first crops came in. Normally, the first agreement was made between the shopkeeper and the kangchu, who may have been relatives and at least were linked by the triad brotherhood. Both held shares in the kongsi. Once planting began, the kangchu distributed the debts among the planters, who were responsible for repaying them in produce. The cost of advances was fixed at about four times the market value in Singapore. At the time the loans were made, the merchant received a guarantee of deliveries of produce at prices to be figured well below the Singapore market price. These margins were the merchants' profit.

On the next level in the pyramid of debt were the wealthier Hokkien commission merchants. They backed the Teochew merchants and probably made further adjustments to prices to secure their own profit margins. They also invested in the "pukat trade" and sent boats (pukats) through the Riau Archipelago and along the coasts of the Malay Peninsula and Sumatra to collect the produce of the region. It is not clear whether these merchants were directly linked to the Ngee Heng. The link between these Hokkiens and the Teochews seems always to have been a fragile one.

The peranakan or Baba merchants represented the top of the pyramid so far as the Chinese were concerned, but they were not the ultimate source of capital. Rather, they received orders for Straits produce from European merchants and accepted their advances of cloth, provisions, and other Western products. The peranakan merchants came from Melaka and Pinang families, and had a distinct advantage in possessing some knowledge of English. The Melaka families who had been established in the Straits for well over a century before 1800 had made good use of their opportunities to form personal relationships with British officials and merchants in the more than two decades (1797–1818) that the British occupied Melaka. These Anglo-Chinese relationships were crucial to the Singapore economy as they linked the Chinese to the European traders.

These connections were not static. Rather, they changed over the course of the century, passing through well-defined phases as the frontier area was pioneered and gradually became more settled. In the initial stages, as in Singapore before the 1840s, it is probable that the ownership of the plantations and the chukang remained in the hands of the local kongsi—the major planters and the one or two advancers. The line between labor and capital was rather vague. This, it seems, was the characteristic of the initial pepper and gambier society. It was a Teochew enterprise and was dominated by the Ngee Heng triad organization. As time passed, the ownership of the kongsi shares gravitated into the hands of the shopkeepers. Interests diverged: shopkeepers became creditors, and planters and everyone else in the chukang became employees and debtors.

Another change that took place was in the ethnic division of labor. Initially, many Teochews were culture-bound and reluctant to adopt British ways. Vaughan contrasts the Hokkiens with the Teochews, noting that the latter "yearn after China and many return as soon as they have saved money enough. They make it a point to send their children to China to be educated; not so the Hokiens, . . . [who] are satisfied with the education they can afford them in the Straits."[21]

There were, however, Teochews who gained respect and prosperity though connections with Europeans. Individuals such as Seah Eu Chin spoke good English and were able to make their own deals with Westerners. There was no monopoly on upward or downward linkages. The conventional wisdom among Europeans in Singapore during the nineteenth century had it that if a Chinese showed up at a British merchant's warehouse wearing a clean shirt, he could obtain an advance of all the goods he wanted and commence business on that basis. While this may have been an exaggeration, the frequent bankruptcies and financial crises that hit Singapore gave small-scale Chinese businesses a rather questionable reputation, which was the crux of the "rotten system" the Europeans found themselves stuck with; for the middlemen were necessary. Europeans could not deal directly with Asian producers, nor could coolies and planters sell their produce directly onto the European market.

The producers were always to some extent at the mercy of the town shopkeepers, but as time passed they became more vulnerable to the vicissitudes of the market economy in general. Drops in the price of their commodities could mean the sudden unemployment of many coolies and planters. Likewise, rises in the prices of the commodities they consumed, such as opium or rice, could have a similarly dislocating effect.

The world market also began to have an impact on the secret societies as this rearrangement of economic power occurred. As political and social power gravitated into the hands of the shopkeepers and the successful kangchus (who themselves often became shopkeepers), the status of the planters declined. The secret society may have become the vehicle through which the group of shopkeepers enforced their demands and their will on the planters and coolies. At some point, the leadership of the societies opted for economic power and found it to

21. Vaughan, p. 15.

their advantage to cast their lot with capital and became instruments of exploitation and coercion against labor.

Opium, the preparation, distribution, and consumption of which was the other integral part of the Chinese economy of Singapore, was not only part of the system of labor exploitation but actually made the system work to the profit of the shopkeepers, the secret societies, the revenue farmers, and the colonial government. Opium was the grand "common interest" of the Anglo-Chinese elite of Singapore. For the laborers, it was both the worst thing and the best thing available to them.

Opium was the worst because it was addictive, and habituated consumers were ready to sacrifice first their profits, then their labor, and finally their lives and futures to obtain it. In dulling their very real pain, opium made them insensitive to the long-term damage their exhausting labor was doing to their own bodies. They could literally work themselves to death without feeling much of the pain. Opium was the best because, in an environment so deprived, it was virtually the laborers' only source of pleasure. Not only did it substitute for women and banish loneliness, but it may have been more than a luxury when the workday was long and the toil strenuous.

Contemporary reports tell of laborers taking a break for a pipe of opium and then resuming their work "refreshed." Gambier planters not only had to clear jungle and brush for their plantations, but they also had to cut wood for the fires to boil the gambier. Mining coolies faced even more demanding exertions. Reports tell of men working throughout the day in bone-chilling streams, sluices, and pits up to their waists in water. In addition to the sheer physical and mental pain of their situations, these men also faced serious medical difficulties: ulcers festering in unhealed wounds, cholera, malaria, typhoid and many other fevers, and of course the primary killer of the tropics, dysentery. While not in any sense a cure, opium was a palliative that at least relieved the symptoms of these afflictions. It dulled muscular aches and pains, lowered fevers, stopped inflammations, stopped up bowels, and allowed the mind to forget, for a time, the grinding loneliness and desperation of their lives. In these circumstances, opium may well have been considered a necessity.

Economically speaking, opium was likewise an absolute necessity. Indeed, if one can make basic economic sense out of the statistics available for this period, it would seem that opium was required if the merchant capitalists of Singapore were to make an adequate profit. The capitalists who lent money to the planters and bought their produce also demanded a profit from the consumption of the coolies, particularly from their consumption of opium. This gave them a buffer against the vagaries of the market.

According to estimates made in 1838,[22] there were nearly 3,000 Chinese in Singapore who were involved in gambier cultivation, which accounted for nearly one-third of the Chinese population. In 1834, the total population stood at 26,329, and there were 10,767 Chinese.[23] In 1848, Seah Eu Chin estimated that something like 8,000 Chinese, nearly all Teochews, were working as gambier planters or coolies. The gambier economy thus accounted for the masses, particularly the Teochew masses. They, if anyone, made up the bulk of the pepper and gambier society.[24]

The large number of employees coupled with the low value of the crop created a highly unstable situation. If we are to accept the figures offered by one observer, gambier was not profitable:

> It is manifest that gambier would never pay, if grown by itself, at present prices. The gross value of the most extensive plantation [210 piculs] of gambier on the island at the market rate of $2 per picul is only $420 which would barely suffice to pay the mere wages of the ten men engaged on it, if taken even at $3.50 per month, although the proper average is perhaps $4 per month for each man. Even joined together, gambier and pepper are certainly not an enriching cultivation, and if it requires little outlay of capital, taken all in all it brings little in. Thus taking the price realized for 48,000 piculs gambier [Singapore's total production] at $2 per picul we have . . . $96,000 and for 15,000 piculs pepper at $5 . . . $75,000 for a value of the total annual produce of both . . . $171,000.

Labor costs for 3,000 coolies at $4 per month would amount to $144,000, which would leave $27,000 to be divided among the proprietors of 350 plantations. This would give an average profit of $77 each "without making any deduction for interest of capital laid out, materials used, carriage, and a variety of *et ceteras*." Yet the gambier planters assured the writer that a well-managed plantation would clear $400 per year.[25]

How could this be done? Or, in the economic terms, how were savings created to allow for the accumulation of capital for further investment? Usually, economic development has required savings at

22. Buckley, pp. 336–37.
23. *SC*, 24 January 1835.
24. Siah, "Chinese of Singapore" (1848).
25. Buckley, pp. 336–37.

the cost of laborers' wages. There were, however, particular problems related to Singapore's labor force. The same writer who described the gambier cultivation saw certain advantages in its use of labor: "It finds employment for numbers who, in a different state of affairs, were formerly found leaguing themselves together in bands for the purposes of midnight robbery and depredation, often causing the greatest alarm even in the immediate suburbs of town."[26] The labor force of Singapore was essentially a migratory group of adult male Chinese. Not only was it difficult to intimidate them, it was even more difficult to get them to work for nothing. Labor had to be offered a reasonable wage; otherwise it could easily pick up and move on. Virtually all of island Southeast Asia was, at this time, underpopulated, and labor was at a premium.

The "savings" problem was solved by opium. If two out of the four dollars that each coolie was paid monthly could be "recycled" through opium consumption, then the equation would be radically altered. There would be an additional "profit" of $77,000 added to the original profit of $27,000, which would bring the total to $104,000, which would put the average profit per plantation much nearer to $300. These figures do not include the cost of the opium and the general charges of the farm, but there was a great deal of profit in retailing opium. The mark-up between the market price of raw opium and the retail price of chandu was said to be 300%, and even *that* could be doubled by selling the residue a couple of times, as was regularly done. The above figures are not unreasonable.

The mechanism for profiting from opium consumption was the opium farm.[27] The opium farm was the monopoly for the retail sale of prepared opium, or chandu, to the population of Singapore.[28] This

26. Buckley, p. 337.
27. There is a small, but of late, rapidly growing literature on opium and other forms of tax farming in Southeast Asia during the nineteenth century. The pioneering pieces were Wong Lin Ken, 1964–65; the academic exercise by Lena Cheng U Wen, later published as "Opium in the Straits Settlements, 1867–1910" (1961); and Tong, "Opium in the Straits Settlements, 1867–1909" (1955). More recently there have been a series of analytic studies on revenue farming systems in the region, e.g., Butcher, "Demise of the Revenue Farm System" (1983); Rush; Hong, *Thailand in the Nineteenth Century* (1984); Brown, "Ministry of Finance" (1975); and Trocki, 1976, 1979, and "Rise of Singapore's Great Opium Syndicate" (1987).
28. Chandu, or opium refined for smoking, is a black-colored, molasseslike substance. It was obtained by dissolving raw opium in water, boiling it down, straining it, and reboiling it several times until most of the impurities were removed. The process was generally referred to as "boiling opium." Usually a three-pound ball of opium yielded a little more than two pounds of chandu. R. Little estimated a ball equaled 2,200 hoons. A user would take a *hoon* or two of chandu (1/100th of a *tahil*) on the end of a metal needle, heat it over a lamp until it began to boil, and then drop the fuming chandu into the bowl of his pipe and inhale the

concession was one of the most important elements of the Singapore economy. Very early in Singapore's history it became the main device whereby economic, political, and administrative control was extended over the Chinese population of Singapore. If the plantation owners and the advancers of capital were to recapture the coolies' wages and the other surplus value produced by the laborers, they needed a share in the farming system. If they were to reap the rewards of their investments, they needed to control both the production and the consumption of the labor force.

Here, the kangchu system of Johor offers an insight into the structure of the pepper and gambier agriculture of Singapore. The Johor *surat sungai* show that one of the principle rights of the kangchu was to sell opium to the coolies and planters in his kangkar. In Johor, the right was formally awarded to the kangchu by the Malay government. In fact, the kangchu held all farms (pork, pawnbroking, gambling, liquor, etc.). Although in Singapore, the British government did not award such rights to kangchus,[29] it seems sensible to assume that, in early nineteenth-century Singapore, the Singapore kangchus maintained the same rights within their areas in practice and probably worked with (or sometimes against) the government opium farmer. In any case, the role of the kangchu was crucial to the gambier cultivation, to the system of contracts between planters and shopkeepers, and to the revenue-farming syndicate. The kangchus also seem to have headed the local branch of the Ngee Heng Kongsi. Clearly, the kangchus made the system pay. The problem was, For whom did they make it pay?

Government by Opium

In *The Straits Settlements*, Mary Turnbull has remarked on the difficult financial situation of the British colonies, especially during the years of Indian governance before 1867. Since Singapore was a free

smoke. The process might be repeated several times, depending on the smoker's level of tolerance. In addition to the hoon, chandu was also retailed by the *chee* (10 hoons) and the tahil (one and one-third ounce). A very heavy smoker might use as much as a tahil per day. Chandu usually retailed for two to three cents per hoon until the 1880s, when the price began to rise. See R. Little, "On the Habitual Use of Opium in Singapore" (1848); the estimate of the ball's size is on p. 65.

29. A map put together by the local historians in Singapore working with the National Archives shows that in about 1851, there were about seven settlements on the north side of Singapore Island that bore the "kang" designation. National Archives, *Pictorial History of Nee Soon Community* (1987), p. 33.

port, there were no taxes on trade. As every issue of the *Singapore Free Press* proudly proclaimed just below the headline for the "Prices Current" page, "In this Port there are no Duties on Imports and Exports and Vessels of all Nations are free of all Charges." Because of the nature of gambier agriculture, which was beyond British control, there was no tax on land to speak of. All revenues were mainly from three sources: excise, licenses, and town property. The European merchants, who had the only effective "public" voice in the colony, absolutely refused to allow the imposition of any kind of tax on income or "commerce." This included port charges and even marine fees to pay for such aids to navigation as the Horsburgh Lighthouse or for the piracy suppression campaigns.[30]

The bulk of the revenues came from "excise" farms, the major one of which was opium. Some form of opium farm had existed since the foundation of the British settlement. Over Raffles's objections, Farquhar had organized the farm in as much as there was no other way of raising a revenue in a free port. The system was one that was well established in Southeast Asia and appears to have begun with the Dutch settlement at Batavia. Farms were well established at Pinang and all colonial settlements as well as in many independent states in Southeast Asia at the beginning of the nineteenth century, including Siam, Vietnam, and many of the Malay states. The practice of "farming out" the collection of taxes on certain items or services was not restricted to Asia but was characteristic of traditional economies everywhere, including the Ottoman Empire, the Indian subcontinent, and most premodern European states. It had its origins in biblical times, with the often-maligned publicans of Roman Palestine serving as the best known example. In the 1820s, it was the most ordinary way to raise a revenue given the circumstances.

Although there were other farms that made up the excise revenue of Singapore, the opium farm was by far the most valuable (see figs. 2 and 3). It generally accounted for about 50 percent of the total revenue. For a while there was a gambling farm, and during three or four years in the 1820s, it actually earned more than the opium farm. The Indian government, however, under pressure from Parliament, decided that it was immoral to collect a tax on gambling and so abolished the gam-

---

30. *SFP*, 5 March 1846; Turnbull, 1975, pp. 188, 194–95. In 1854, the government passed an act (Act XIII of 1854) to pay for the Horsburgh Lighthouse, which would have meant the collection of one anna (1/16th of a rupee, or about 3 cents) per ton on all vessels leaving Indian ports bound for the Straits or China. That is, it would only tax European vessels that actually passed the lighthouse. The merchants, however, vehemently objected and were able to exert pressures in London and Calcutta to have the tax repealed.

Figure 2. Opium farm value compared with total revenue, Singapore, 1820–1860 (Spanish dollars)

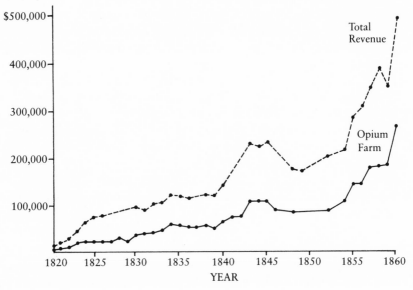

Figure 3. Opium farm value compared with total revenue, Singapore, 1860–1914 (millions of Spanish dollars)

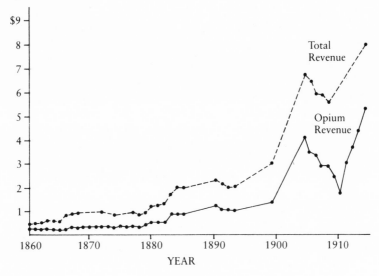

Chinese gamblers; scale for weighing opium on the left (National Archives, Singapore)

bling farms and attempted to outlaw the practice in 1828. The other major farm was the "spirit" or "arrack" farm, for the sale of liquor. It was rarely worth more than one-quarter of the value of the opium farm and was often worth less. Generally, it was held together with the opium farm, as a joint enterprise. Other farms included, at various times in the nineteenth century, siri (betel nut), *toddy* and *bhang*, pork, pawnbroking, and markets.[31] All of these latter farms combined rarely added up to more than one-tenth of the value of the opium farm. With the exception of toddy and bhang, all of the taxes were levied upon Chinese consumers and collected by Chinese farmers.

The farming system in Singapore evolved by trial and error. At first Farquhar had allowed the licensing of four opium shops, for which the government collected $395 per month. He made similar arrangements for spirits and gambling. Although he and Raffles quarreled about the

31. *Toddy* here refers to the fermented juice of the coconut palm obtained by tapping the flowers of the tree. The drink looks like diluted milk and is perhaps 5–10% alcohol. A pint of it will often suffice to intoxicate a person. *Bhang* is a form of cannabis that seems to have been smoked. The sources suggest that the leaf or flowers were used, rather than the resin, but they are not very definite. Both toddy and bhang were primarily consumed by Indians, and therefore the farmer was usually an Indian.

propriety of such taxes, this system remained in practice until Craw-furd took charge of the settlement in 1823.[32] At that time, the farms were not providing an adequate revenue. Crawfurd introduced the gambling farm and offered a justification for the farming system as it particularly related to "vices." For the first time, he put Singapore in a stable financial condition: "I feel thoroughly persuaded that the surest means of limiting and controlling this vice [gambling] is not to attempt to prohibit it altogether, but to place it under a strict system of license and as in the similar cases of the consumption of ardent spirits, opium and other intoxicating drugs, to make the practise of it as expensive as possible to those determined to indulge in it without driving them to the recourse of a clandestine place."[33] Writing in 1827, the resident councillor, John Prince, described the system Crawfurd had organized and recommended its continuation. He noted that the revenues had regularly increased since 1823 and attributed this partly to the in-creased population of Chinese, who were the major consumers of taxable items, and also to Crawfurd's "improved method of putting up the Farms in subdivided lots which may have the effect of preventing Combination among the bidders and of *exciting competition.*"[34]

By the 1840s the system of "letting" the farms had been more or less fixed, although the administrators continued to tinker with the pro-cedures. The farms were generally leased for periods of from one to three years. The method of letting them tended to vary: at certain times the farms were let by public auction, such as in 1847 when the resident councillor of Singapore, Thomas Church, wrote to his assistant, Capt. Adam Cuppage, "I beg to inform you that I have appointed Wednes-day, the 21st Instant for the sale of the Excise Farms and Markets for the Official Year, 1847/48, and request that you will do me the favour to cause the accompanying Notices to be affixed in the most conspic-uous parts of the Town for the information of the public, likewise order the Gong to be beat throughout the Town, including Campong Glam on the 9th, 16th, 20th and the morning of the sale."[35] At other times, the farms were let by sealed tenders or even by private sale. During the period before 1867, when the Straits Settlements were under the Indian government, the farms were let for the Indian official year (e.g., 1 April to 31 March).[36] After 1867, when the Straits Settle-

32. Song, p. 10.
33. Little, p. 75.
34. Prince to Anderson, 7 April 1827, *SSFR*, Singapore Diary.
35. *SSR*, CC 18, p. 202.
36. In some cases the term of farming licenses lagged a month behind the official financial year, and often contracts ran from 1 May to 30 April.

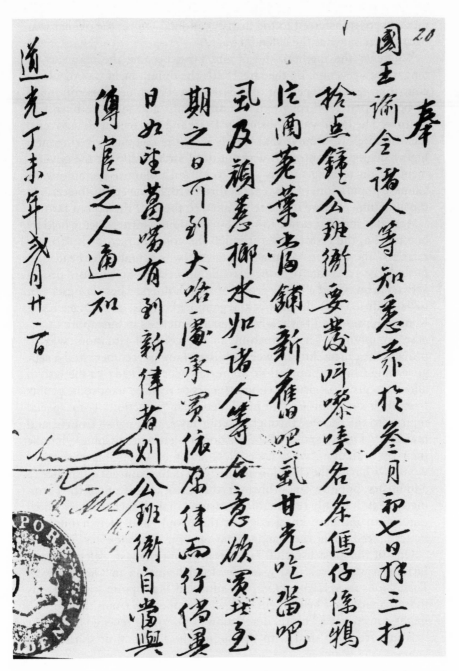

奉

國王諭令諸人等知悉兹於叁月初七日將三打

拾五錘公班衙要蒿叫嗉嘆名条碼仔係鴉

片酒菉葉當舖新舊吧氹甘克吃當吧

氹及頼豈獅水如諸人等合意欲買埠氹

期之日可到大咭厘承買依原律而行倘異

日如陸葛嗜有到新律者刈公班衙自當興

簿宦之人通知

道光丁未年弍月廿二日

Handbill written in Chinese advertising the auction of the Singapore opium farm, dated 30 April 1847, signed by Resident Councillor Thomas Church (*SRR*, BB 68, p. 20)

ments were transferred to the British Colonial Office, the official year became the same as the calendar year.

Whatever the method, the opium farm became the mainstay of Singapore's revenue. By the late 1820s the opium farm was regularly contributing 40–50 percent of the total local revenue. This continued to be the pattern throughout the nineteenth and into the twentieth century. The farm was abolished in 1910 and replaced with a government monopoly, a move that simply gave the colonial government a higher degree of control. It was not until after 1920 that the government began to take serious steps to curtail opium usage among its Chinese population. In the years before 1910, however, the interests of the government were intimately linked to those of the opium farmer.

Actually, it is inaccurate to speak of the opium farm as being held by one person, the farmer. Even though the colonial records invariably refer to "the farmer," in the singular, he was actually the head of a fairly large syndicate or kongsi, made up of a group of more-or-less active partners and a larger group of shareholders. These kongsis, not to be confused with the pepper and gambier kongsis, or the Ngee Heng Kongsi, represented fairly large financial interests in Singapore's Chinese community. Their function, in the colonial situation, was to provide the crucial link between a laissez-faire government and a self-governing Chinese population. Some defenders argued that the system allowed a group of private enterpreneurs to realize "handsome profits from their speculations" but precluded their "infliction of any special injuries to the people" through revenue laws, the English Courts, and lawyers.[37] Others spoke of the wisdom of letting the Chinese handle their own affairs: "what an endless series of smuggling and fraud would we have if the chandoo license were in the hands of our police to administer, but how smoothly everything works now under the Farming system. It is only reasonable to assume that all such matters which require an intimate knowledge of the people and their habits, are better placed under the management of some of themselves."[38]

One of the most forceful, but certainly not the last, defense of the farming system was that given by John Cameron in *Our Tropical Possessions in Malayan India*. He admitted that opium smoking was indeed a vice, and he thought that while some "over sensitive minds" might consider it a "moral dereliction" to derive a revenue from it, it was important to deal with the subject in a "practical spirit." The

37. *Administrative Reports of the Government of India* (IOR), V/10/4, pp. 9–10.
38. *ST*, 17 May 1862.

colony would need double or triple the number of police and would at the same time lose half its revenue if the practice were to be suppressed. He was quite frank about the pecuniary interest of the government and contradicted those who said that the purpose of the farm was to restrict consumption. On the contrary, he pointed out, "With the East India Company revenue was a matter of considerably greater solicitude than the moral condition of the large populations under their rule; and there can be very little question that the opium farm had its origin in the necessities of the local exchequer."[39] He went on to note, however, that since the farmer was forced to keep the price of opium fairly high, the opium was too expensive for the "laboring classes."

This assertion was not at all true; the opium farm relied heavily on the poor. Other commentators, such as R. Little, stated that gambier planters and their coolies were almost "inveterate" consumers of opium, as were others who generally engaged in heavy physical labor: "Now certain trades are greater consumers of opium than others. Amongst the principal are carpenters, box makers, blacksmiths, barbers, hunters, coolies, boatmen, and gambier planters including gardeners. These trades seem almost entirely to be devoted to the drug. I should say fully 85 percent are opium smokers." He went on to name the streets frequented by Chinese in various trades and pointed out that in Carpenter Street, Church Street, and South Bridge Road there were eighteen opium shops "principally frequented by Gambier people and gardeners, this being one of the principal entrances from the country to the Merchant's godowns."[40]

As early as 1829, the Resident, John Prince, laid heavy stress on the intimate relations between the colony's revenue and the prosperity of the gambier cultivation: "I am informed, however, that we may look forward to a decrease in the revenue for 1827/28 on account of the Gambier cultivation being nearly dropped as a losing Concern . . . and they [the Chinese] will probably quit the place for other situations more productive."[41] Thus, even at this relatively early date, when hardly any Europeans had even visited the gambier settlements, the opium farmers, as entrepreneurs, were collecting a significant portion of the colony's revenue from those planters.

The reliance of the British government on the farming system meant an alliance with a group of Chinese entrepreneurs. The revenue farm-

39. Cameron, 1965, pp. 216–17.
40. Little, pp. 20, 21; see also "Gambling and Opium Smoking in the Straits" (1856), pp. 66–83.
41. Resident's Diary, *SSR*, N 1, p. 312.

ers, particularly the opium farmers, were the major arm of the government so far as the Chinese population of Singapore was concerned. The system thus bore some resemblance to the old "kapitan China" system practiced in the Dutch territories and in Pinang, Melaka, and the Malay states. In Singapore, however, the alliance was always an informal one. There were no Chinese officers as such, although there were a few Chinese appointed as magistrates, justices of the peace, and members of the Legislative Council. Revenue farming was a business in that it was kept on a commercial and contractual basis and there were no official kapitans. Bidders competed for the farms, were expected to pay their rent on time, obey the laws, and give up the farms at the expiration of their contracts. Of course, things rarely worked out so perfectly, as Wong Lin Ken has shown in his study of the revenue farms of Pinang.[42] The study of the Singapore farms shows similar patterns of collusion, corruption, combination, and conflict.

The Dynamics of the Farm in Singapore History

The history of the farms reflects many of the patterns of social and economic conflict that divided Singapore's Chinese community during the nineteenth century. When the farms changed hands—that is, when one syndicate succeeded in outbidding another for control of the opium revenues—the takeover was usually marked by serious violence within Singapore's Chinese community, or perhaps more correctly, among the Chinese *communities*. Violence did not erupt at every auction, because even though auctions were annual (or biennial or sometimes triennial), that did not always mean a new syndicate took control. In fact, the emergence of a new syndicate was a relatively rare occurrence in Singapore. New revenue farming kongsis arose only about once every ten or fifteen years, and their appearance was always marked by major social upheaval.

One source of division among the Chinese was ethnicity. The two major speech groups, the Hokkien and the Teochew, had a history of animosity between them in China. As a result of this, it was often possible for contemporary observers to blame disputes, such as the 1854 riots, on "the ancient grudge brought from China." While there was something to this explanation, it was easy to ignore local sources of conflict within colonial society. The revenue farms had little to do

42. Wong Lin Ken, 1964–65.

with China. Nevertheless, speech groups generally attempted to monopolize the farms as they did certain trades and economic pursuits; thus, there was usually a Hokkien syndicate and a Teochew syndicate.

In the 1840s the division became apparent. Reports indicate that from the 1840s on, there were usually two viable syndicates bidding for the farms at any given time. Success required capital, organization, and knowledge of the market; for miscalculation could result in the loss of a great deal of money. These infrastructural needs simply precluded the existence of more than two syndicates. The existence of two did, however, assure that the price would rise from competition, something the government found desirable, and only one prize meant there would always be a loser.

Another disruptive element was the farmers' shaky tenure. Even though the potential farmer may have sought to become the agent of the government, losing the bid left him with no official or recognized position. The losing syndicate could readily become an enemy of the state and thus seek alliances with other opposing groups to make common cause with them. On occasion, disappointed farmers mobilized secret societies and other elements of the Chinese community to aid them in undercutting their rivals' monopoly. Since contenders for the farms were usually investors in pepper and gambier planting, their natural bases of support were their clients on the plantations. Thus one would expect the disappointed members of a Teochew syndicate to find allies among Teochew planters and kangchus. This, however, was not always the case.

If ethnic animosity is viewed as the cause of conflict, it is difficult to explain the fairly regular cooperation between members of the two speech groups. Likewise, since the fundamental issue here turns on the existence of *class* conflict, ethnic animosity is a causal factor that must be placed in perspective. One reason there was only occasional trouble between the Hokkien and Teochew syndicates is because there was usually only *one* effective farming syndicate, a combined Hokkien-Teochew syndicate.

A combined syndicate would obviously put all the revenue farmers in the camp of the colonial rulers and range them against the planters, or the coolies. Things were not quite so simple. The opium syndicate's interests were not always the same as the government's. The government was usually suspicious when there was only one syndicate, because that meant there was no viable competition, and therefore it was possible for the farmers to offer the government whatever they chose to bid, and this could frequently be quite low. Wong Lin Ken has shown that the establishment of a combination in Pinang in the 1820s made it possible for the farmers there actually to bid down the price of the farms. Between 1820 and 1824 the excise revenue of Pinang fell from $93,183 per month to $65,505.[43] While there were occasionally bad years in Singapore when the revenue fell, the sort of determined collusion seen in Pinang never manifested itself. Nevertheless, there were long periods of time, particularly between 1845 and 1859, and again from 1870 to 1879, when one syndicate maintained continuous control of the farms from contract to contract. During these periods, increases in the farm rentals were usually minimal.

The combination of both Hokkien and Teochew farmers at these times suggests that class interest (if we can conceive of the farmers as a group constituting a class) could prove a more powerful bond than ethnic solidarity. There is some reason for placing the opium farmers in the same faction at least at times when there was a combined kongsi. Support for this argument lies in the occurrence of serious social conflict when there was a combination between the farmers. It is, in fact, possible to show that conflict could result from either set of circumstances: a split over the farms or a combination of the farms.

Until the 1870s the key linkage was that between the opium farms and the gambier economy. The perennial conflict in Singapore's Chinese society turned on that relationship. Over the course of the nineteenth century, a series of shifts took place within the gambier economy. These changes were reflected in corresponding realignments in the farms and in the secret societies.

Although when Singapore was founded, gambier cultivation, as well as financing, seem to have been a Teochew preserve, at some point the Hokkiens began to move in. It is difficult to say exactly when this happened, but the period after 1835 seems a logical one, since that is when the British market opened up. At that time, people like Seah Eu Chin, who was already a fairly wealthy Teochew, entered the gambier-planting business on what seems to have been a much larger and more cash-oriented basis than the earlier plantations. He may have developed his own direct sources of finance among the European merchants. Hokkien merchants with access to European capital had formerly made advances to their clients among the Teochew merchants. This system began to break down after 1840. According to Seah Eu Chin's list, there were over one hundred Hokkien pepper and gambier dealers in 1848 but no Hokkien coolies or planters. By the 1850s, it

43. Wong Lin Ken, 1964–65, Table 3.

might have seemed to the Hokkiens that this was a good time to hire their own coolies and start financing plantations directly.

It seems logical to assume that the entry of the Hokkiens into the pepper and gambier business—in competition with the Teochew merchants—must have caused some friction and may have been the cause of some of the violence that came to characterize Chinese society in Singapore. The key question, then, is whether their involvement in the trade marked the intrusion of a real capitalist class into this "traditional" system—that is, did their intrusion signal a structural change in the systems, or did they simply come in as an outside ethnic group to crack the Teochew monopoly of the business? Another question is, What impact did the Hokkien intrusion have on the pepper and gambier kongsis of Singapore and their relationship with the Ngee Heng.

The intrusion could have been both structural and ethnic. Certainly the Hokkiens represented a challenge to a Teochew preserve, and on one level, the rivalry can be seen as simply commercial. On another level, though, did the Hokkien intrusion involve (wittingly or not) the substitution of "modern" institutions or systems of control for "traditional" ones? Did, for instance, the Hokkiens begin to rely on British police forces rather than the brotherhoods to provide security for their property? Actually, there is very little evidence that they did anything very different from the Teochews, at least at first. They seem to have organized their own secret society and simply gone after a piece of the business, as the events of the first major secret society riot, the so-called Chinese Funeral Riots of 1846, seem to indicate.

Whether this riot marked the initial entry of the Hokkiens into the gambier business is impossible to say. It is very possible that they were already involved. It does seem, however, that the Hokkiens attempted to extend their influence in 1846, beyond the position they had previously been content to hold. Moreover, a part of the class conflict argument depends on the alliance among Chinese merchants, the colonial state, and the European merchants: the so-called free trade society. Thus the role of the state itself is important here. The riots of 1846 bring together all the factors involved: pepper and gambier, secret societies, the advance of colonial control, the opium farms, and the commercial and other connections between the settlements of Singapore, Riau, and Johor.

4 Economic Struggle and
the Singapore Kongsis

The events that disrupted Singapore's Chinese society in the 1840s and 1850s are generally well known. There were three major civil disturbances, usually called "secret society riots": the 1846 Chinese Funeral Riots, the 1851 anti-Catholic riots, and the 1854 Hokkien-Teochew riots. That these occurred is not at issue; the problem lies in determining their significance. Most colonialist writers on secret societies and the Malaysian Chinese (e.g., Pickering, Wynne, Comber, Purcell, Blythe) have characterized these events as struggles for power within the Chinese population. Having gone that far, they fail to ask, "Power for what?" and proceed to treat the events as having been essentially illegitimate. Where this school has put forward causes, they have located them outside of the socioeconomic environment of Singapore.

Lee Poh Ping's suggestion that the conflict was an economic and class-based struggle between the free trade society and the pepper and gambier society does take into account economic divisions. His definition of the free trade society included the Melaka or Straits-born Chinese merchants, who were usually of the Hokkien speech group, in association with the British agency houses of Singapore town. The pepper and gambier society was represented by the kongsis and the smaller Teochew merchants of the town. While this analysis is, I believe, a more satisfactory one, Lee failed to demonstrate it. Nor were the "sides" in the struggles by any means so clear and consistent as he has presented them. But certain trends and patterns do stand out. The social and economic environment in which the disturbances took place reveal those trends and help determine what was at issue in each conflict.

There was a many-faceted economic conflict in progress. It was, at once, between laborers and capitalists; between Hokkiens and Teochews; between different revenue-farming syndicates; between different secret societies as well as between Europeans and Asians; and finally between adherents of conflicting views of the economic order. In the end, capitalist and colonialist forces were successful in dominating the Chinese economic order and in subordinating the labor force and the mercantile structure that supported the agriculture. The background of this economic conflict goes back to the crises of the mid-1830s associated with cycles of expansion and contraction in gambier and pepper planting. A series of "gang robberies" in the early 1830s and the numerous beggars in Singapore at the time have been seen as indicative of economic problems in the gambier agriculture.[1] These difficulties continued into 1835 and formed the background for the depression of that year.

The opening of a market for gambier in the West in 1836 thus was a welcome change and led to higher prices, which spurred an increase in planting. The low prices then maintaining for European manufactures (particularly cheap cloth and iron tools) as well as for opium and rice meant that the inputs of the system were cheap and plentiful. These conditions may have been what attracted investment from the Hokkien traders and drew the interest of Europeans. Another factor would have been the improvement in the relative security of the seas around Singapore Island, which was achieved by the quiet agreement made by Governor S. G. Bonham with Temenggong Ibrahim in 1837.[2] It became possible for the gambier *pukats* and *tongkangs* to travel between the Singapore River and places like Lim Chukang, Choa Chukang, Serangoon, and Kranji and other settlements on the north side of the island without fear of attack from Malay pirates.[3]

Prices for gambier and pepper hit highs in 1836 of $3 per pikul for gambier and $6.50 for pepper and then declined gradually until 1841,

1. Buckley, pp. 213, 224, and 235.
2. Trocki, 1979, pp. 69–74. Temenggong Ibrahim of Johor was the son of Temenggong Abdul Rahman (d. 1825), the Malay chief who had sold Singapore Island to Raffles. In the early 1830s Ibrahim had been suspected of involvement in the increased incidence of piracy around Singapore. In 1837, Bonham was successful in securing Ibrahim's assistance in suppressing piracy.
3. The pukat and tongkang were vessels used in the trade between Singapore and neighboring settlements in Riau, Sumatra, and the Malay Peninsula. These were Chinese junk-style boats about twenty to forty feet long and of about twenty-ton capacity. They were generally owned and operated by Chinese merchants in Singapore. According to Song, Seah Eu Chin got his start as a clerk on one of these vessels (p. 90). It is not clear whether these words were of Chinese origin. Such craft filled the docks along the Singapore River until the 1960s.

when gambier prices dropped below what appears to have been the optimum mentioned by the writer quoted earlier, of $2 per pikul. Pepper likewise dropped at about the same rate and by 1841 had fallen to just about $4 per pikul. Throughout these years, the cultivation appears to have been a paying proposition. It was aided, no doubt, by the relatively abundant supply of labor that regularly arrived in Singapore from China.

If there was friction between Hokkiens and Teochews during the 1836–41 period, or between the pepper and gambier planters and the Hokkien merchants, or between secret societies, or between whatever divisions existed in the population, there are no reports of violence. Trouble began—as is apparent in Charles Buckley's account, taken from the local newspapers, and in the government records—around 1841, when J. T. Thomson arrived to start surveying the island before levying taxes on agricultural land. At the same time, roads were being extended across the island so that, by 1846, roads (meaning perhaps bridle paths) stretched from Singapore Town to Kranji and to Serangoon.[4] Lee has suggested that the building of roads and the actions taken by the government to collect a quitrent represented the inroads of the free trade society and were thus the basic cause of conflict. Wong Lin Ken has challenged this view by pointing out that the land taxes were not effectively enforced until much later. Government records show that actual collections were first effected in 1856.[5]

The causes of violence given at the time by J. T. Thomson and others seem to have been the falling prices of gambier and the exhaustion of the supply of available land:

As the plantations multiplied and began to approximate each other's limits, disputes about boundaries commenced, and of later years have been the constantly recurring cause of strife and contention among the Chinese occupants; and, in particular, the right to reserve a certain extent of forest in the neighbourhood of each plantation, to supply their gambier-furnaces with fuel, has been the fertile source of disputes, and sometimes of bloodshed. When such quarrels occurred between parties of the same tribe, or belonging to the same brotherhood, they were generally settled by the intervention of friends on both sides, but, as the matter now stands, there is not a single week passes without applications being made by squatters for the assistance of the authorities to protect them from the alleged encroachments of some neighbours engaged in the same kind of cultivation as themselves.[6]

4. Lee, 1978, pp. 65–68.
5. Wong Lin Ken, 1980, pp. 160–62; SSR, AA 35, p. 68, 14 March 1856.
6. Buckley, p. 353.

After 1841, overproduction glutted the market and the price of both gambier and pepper continued to drop until 1848, when gambier hit a low of eighty cents per pikul. Between 1841 and 1843, however, the price of gambier did rise a little and just about made it back to two dollars in 1843, but then it went down again and continued to drop.

Thomson's remarks are useful in gauging the changing role of the Ngee Heng. He noted that previously the brotherhood had settled disputes between planters, and he remarked that by 1841 planters had begun to seek redress from the government to protect them from their neighbors. This situation suggests the arrival of persons who not only did not respect the authority of the Ngee Heng but who alternatively looked to the government for support. These newcomers were, it seems, planters who were backed by Hokkien merchants, or at least by merchants who had no previous connection to the agriculture and therefore no connection to the traditional system by which the brotherhood had run the agriculture.

The improved roads had created a situation in which shopkeepers were able more easily to reach the planters to collect debts and to enforce their contracts. Falling prices of gambier in the marketplace would have meant that the shopkeepers' own creditors would have been calling for repayment. The shopkeepers in turn seem to have applied increasing pressures on their debtors in the countryside. By August 1843 the shopkeepers were experiencing difficulty in collecting. The *Singapore Free Press* reported that the gambier merchants who "formerly used to call at the plantations periodically to collect interest and installments from the proprietors" had stopped doing so. According to the papers, they were afraid of "tigers."[7] While there may indeed have been tigers, it is equally possible that the disappearance of an unwelcome visitor to a plantation could have been easily blamed on a tiger. If, however, shopkeepers could not collect outstanding debts, they were hardly likely to allow new ones to be contracted unless they had some reason to expect repayment. Whether because of tigers or the Tiger Generals of the secret society, a "bad investment climate" was created.

Investors probably stopped backing new plantations around the mid-1840s, but the ones already cleared and planted were producing more than the market could bear and the oversupply drove prices down even further. As Low Siew Chek's research shows, production continued to rise until 1844, when gambier exports reached about 175,000 pikuls. They dropped sharply and fell to about 90,000 in

7. *SFP*, 3 August 1843.

1846, and by 1848 had risen to 180,000 pikuls again. The planters were competing for an inelastic market by increasing production.[8]

The significant drop in production in 1845–46 marked a period of deep crisis in the agricultural system. It seems sensible to view any outbreaks of violence among planters as related to the fall in prices, the overproduction, and the appearance of a new group of planters and capitalists attempting to operate outside the old kongsi arrangement. These conditions provide the context as well as the most probable cause for the Chinese Funeral Riots of 1846.[9]

Chinese Funeral Riots

All the statistics for the years 1845 and 1846 suggest economic collapse and catastrophe. These include the low gambier prices and the substantial decline in production, which must have been accomplished by simply abandoning many of the plantations. This meant, then, many impoverished and unemployed Chinese coolies in the town. Reports from the time suggest that the economic difficulty was not confined to Singapore alone. There was also high unemployment in the nearby Dutch settlements, particularly in Riau, whose gambier plantations shared in the conditions of the Singapore economy—indeed, were the same economy. Because Singapore was a free port, people could move in and out as easily as goods. There were accusations that the Dutch were simply rounding up destitute Chinese in Riau and Sumatra and hiring Malay traders to take them to Singapore. In March and April of 1846 there were reports that even Dutch warships were dumping the excess population of their prisons in Singapore.[10]

In 1845 reports of severe poverty were being published in the newspapers. Of the thirty-six thousand Chinese then resident in Singapore, nearly one-third were said to have no visible means of support. Police reports stated that nearly six thousand were starving and that one hundred persons a year were dying from hunger: "Poverty is stalking

8. Low Siew Chek, "Gambier and Pepper Planting in Singapore 1819–1860" (1955), App. 1. Buckley, pp. 336–37, 348, 353.
9. If the following discussion seems tendentious, it may be because no commentators other than myself and Mak Lau Fong (Trocki, 1979, pp. 99–117; Mak, 1981, pp. 41–49) have really considered the economic causes of this first serious secret society conflict in Singapore. Even Lee (1978), whose entire argument depends on the demonstration of socioeconomic conflict and class struggle, has chosen to neglect this incident altogether in his analysis.
10. ST, 6 October 1845; SSR, CC 16, no. 332; SSR, V 11, pp. 178–79, 187–88.

through our streets and in the purlieus of the Town, where the haunts of vice, indigence and disease are unobserved by the European part of the community. Many are daily dying for lack of labor and food. . . . During the current year sixty instances of death from starvation have been brought to the notice of the Police. Others take place and pass unreported, whilst a vast number die from disease occasioned by absolute destitution of which no record is taken."[11] The grand jury held hearings on Chinese poverty in October and reported that the death toll had risen to seventy. The problem, as the jurors saw it, was that too many Chinese were being landed at Singapore.

The market reports for the period painted a dismal picture of the economy. In December 1845 the gambier price was reported to have fallen to $1.40 per pikul because of the lack of tonnage to Europe. The Bugis trade for the 1845 season (May to August) had been light, and not much in the way of European goods had been purchased. During the 1846 junk season (December 1845 to March), not much business was done.[12] In February the *Straits Times* market report spoke of continued depression:

> Transactions have not been of much importance during the week, and no renewed activity will be imparted to our Market before the Junk Traders begin to lay in their return cargoes—Dealers, generally low of stocks, refrain from laying in more than is absolutely necessary for immediate use. The accounts from China by Junk Traders are considered unfavorable, and that market is represented as being overstocked with British Goods—with this knowledge our shopkeepers feel no inducement to enter into speculative investments.[13]

The economic hardship of the period was certainly one reason for the funeral riot, but other factors and events should be taken into consideration. For instance, while there was indeed overcrowding in Singapore, people were apparently already leaving for Johor. The first settlers had left Singapore and were setting up pepper and gambier plantations on the Sekudai River in October of 1844.[14] In December 1845 the same newspaper that in October had complained of too many paupers now expressed concern that the cultivators of "this valuable article of commerce" (gambier) were leaving because of fights over timber rights. The editor suggested that the government should

11. *ST*, 16 September 1845.
12. *ST*, 11 November 1845; *ST*, 10 December 1845.
13. *ST*, 18 February 1846.
14. Trocki, 1979, pp. 85–109.

do something to maintain the gambier cultivation in Singapore. The problem was more complicated than simple overcrowding, low prices, and unemployment.[15] If the only problems were the surpluses of labor and produce, then there would not be much sense in the planters going to Johor, nor should there have been cause for concern among contemporary observers that this "excess" population was leaving.

The crisis of the gambier cultivation appears also to have been related to the Hokkien takeover of, or at least participation in, what had been an occupational monopoly of the Teochews. If we accept Mak's explanation of secret society conflict—which for him began in 1842 in Singapore—this factor seems to be an important element in the Chinese Funeral riot of 1846.[16] On the surface, the two sides appear to have been the Tien-di hui (Ngee Heng or Ghee Hin) and the Quan Tek hui (also known as Quan Yat Huey, Quan Quay Hoey, etc.). The latter group has also been identified with the Kien Teck hui, branches of which were found in Riau, Singapore, and Pinang at about this time.[17] According to Comber, Wynne, and Newbold, it was associated with the Hokkien and Straits Chinese merchants. It was much smaller than the Ngee Heng/Tien-di hui, which was generally seen as a Cantonese, essentially Teochew, group. There had been a number of incidents, many of them connected to disputes over gambier land, before the riot. The appearance of a Hokkien secret society dominated by wealthy taukehs at a time of economic crisis is an important element in the background of this riot.

Another question worth raising here, but one that has no clear answer, regards the role of British merchants and authorities. Lee has suggested that an alliance between the Straits Chinese merchants and the British formed the core of the free trade society. Circumstances, both in 1846 and at other junctures, suggest that British authorities were covertly involved in supporting certain factions in these struggles. There is, however, no direct evidence at this point, but the relationship between the Singapore police and the Quan Tek appears likely. Whatever the British role at this point, Dutch authorities in Riau had taken sides in the conflict.

15. *ST*, 27 December 1845.
16. Mak, 1981, pp. 41–49.
17. Blythe, 1969 (pp. 58–59), quotes a report on secret societies compiled by S. G. Bohnam in 1830, which notes the existence of three societies in Singapore: the "Thean-ti Hoey" (Tien-di hui), the Quan-ti Hoey, probably the Quan Tek hui, and another called the "Shoo So-kong Hoey." The Quan-ti Hoey "was believed to be nearly extinct, for Bonham had been told that its members had joined the T'in Tei Wui." Blythe suggests that the 1846 appearance of the Quan Tek hui was a revival.

A major impetus for the disturbance seems to have been connected to events at Riau shortly before the Singapore riot. On 12 February 1846 the *Singapore Free Press* reported that the Dutch Resident of Riau had decided to crack down on the Tien-di hui: "Acting on the information of a newly appointed 'Capitan China' [he] has apprehended about a hundred persons which has caused such a panic that already about 1,500 Chinese have left Rhio and come to Singapore, some of whom have gone into the jungle while others remain in town."[18] This account, given by Buckley, connects Singapore's troubles to events in Riau. The local ruler, the Yang di-Pertuan Muda, had allied himself with the Quan Tek hui and had, in fact, lent them some of his own cannons to protect themselves from the Tien-di hui. The appointment of the new kapitan China and the round-up of Tien-di hui members in Riau during February 1846 had spread panic and instability into Singapore. Obviously, the Quan Tek hui and its kapitan had challenged the Tien-di hui's previous domination of the pepper and gambier agriculture. It appears that the Hokkien merchants of Riau, with the probable support of their Singapore partners, had set up their own plantations on Galang Island, just south of Bintan, in order to escape the influence of the Teochew-dominated Ngee Heng.

There were thus two "expansion" areas being settled at this time. In Galang, the planters seem to have been associated with the Quan Tek, while those who left Singapore for Johor were associated with the Ngee Heng. In both Singapore and Bintan, it is unclear which if any faction controlled the plantations; probably control was divided in both areas. Later events certainly give this impression.

The riot in Singapore must have been set off either by inept police work or collusion by the magistrate, Thomas Dunman, in the midst of this highly charged situation. The head of the Tien-di hui in Singapore, a person known as Ho Yam Ko or Ho Ah Yam ("Ko" simply means "elder brother," which was a common title for a secret society leader), had died. The members of the society had applied to the police for a permit for the procession, but there had been a disagreement over the route. Apparently the triad leaders wanted to lead the procession from the temple on Rochore Road through the middle of Kampong Glam and then on to the Chinese burial ground near the military cantonment on the western side of the town. The police refused them permission to take this route and designated another one that would follow Rochore

18. *SFP*, 12 February 1846.

Road and then skirt the most populous part of Kampong Glam. The police also put a limit on the number of people to be allowed to march in the procession.

The regulations no doubt frustrated the Ngee Heng members, but they were certainly suspicious of the government's sincerity and sympathies when on 3 March, the day of the procession, they saw one Ho Cheo Teck (or Chew Tock) walking beside Dunman as his "interpreter." Chew Tock was the head of the Quan Tek hui. There were, according to Comber's account of the disturbance, some two thousand to three thousand members of the Quan Tek hui (which Comber identifies with the Ghi Hock or Ghee Hock) drawn up at the intersection leading to Kampong Glam. Obviously, the ideal setting for a fight. The funeral procession was headed by the leader of the Ngee Heng, one Chew Swee, who had with him some six thousand members—far in excess of the agreed number. When the procession attempted to turn into Kampong Glam, the police drew up a line to stop them. Dunman called Chew Swee to ask why he had broken the rule.[19]

According to Assistant Resident Captain Cuppage, "There was a great deal of noise and confusion during which one man who had the appearance of a stranger from the Country, called out 'Pak' and several other members joined. He was immediately seized by Mr. Dunman and myself," who turned the coolie over to some police peons, and then the riot started. The governor, Maj.-Gen. William Butterworth, later reported that both heads of the societies were beaten up and that the chief culprits were "a party of coolies from the Jungle who appeared to be unknown to both parties."[20]

Many observers have simply accepted Blythe's explanation in his *The Impact of Chinese Secret Societies in Malaya,* which points to "ideological" differences. He noted that a funeral was an important event for the Chinese, where they could display the wealth, power, and prestige of the deceased. He pointed out that funeral processions were frequent occasions for secret society fights: "A procession provided a setting for the display of power and arrogance by the society, and the opportunity was frequently sought when members were thus massed together, bearing the emblems and insignia of their brotherhood, to insult members or officials of rival societies as a result of which a quarrel would flare up."[21]

Contemporary reports suggest, however, that this disturbance was

19. Comber, pp. 65–73.
20. *SSR,* BB 63, no. 218; *SSR,* R 13, no. 66, p. 446.
21. Blythe, 1969, pp. 67–68.

connected to other events. Observers noted that the participation of persons from Riau was prominent. On 14 March 1846, Tan Tock Seng, the prominent Straits Chinese merchant, wrote a letter to Resident Councillor Church complaining of another riot he had witnessed. He asked for action from the government and pointed out that some of the people had come from Riau.[22] In his report, Church asked for additional military support, as he felt the disturbances would continue:

> It appears a bitter and hostile feeling exists between the members of the two Secret Societies, Tan Tay Huey and Quan Yah Huey and both parties are prepared to proceed to open violence; I have been confidentially informed by the Resident of Rhio that at Bintang there had been most sanguine contests between the members of the rival Hueys, accompanied by the burning of Villages and considerable loss of life, a goodly number of the adverse party have crossed over to Singapore and are industriously engaged in exciting and fomenting disturbances with a view to revenge.[23]

The disputes at both Singapore and Riau were fought between members of the two rival societies, which clearly had branches in both places. The refugees from Riau no doubt added to the ferocity of the battle against the Quan Tek hui in Singapore. After the 3 March riot, other disturbances took place as well. In addition to the disturbance reported by Tan Tock Seng on 14 March, there was a gunfight on 19 March between the members of the two societies in Kampong Glam. On 30 March a gang of Ngee Heng members attacked and robbed the house of Thomas Hewetson, a magistrate's clerk. Although Comber reports a truce between the two societies toward the end of March, it is clear from later events that ill-feeling ran very deep.[24]

The following year a party of Ngee Heng members attacked Galang, led by a refugee from Riau who had settled in Singapore and become fairly wealthy. He was named Neo Liang Guan (or Neo Yang Kwan), and he owned a number of plantations around Seletar. In 1847 he apparently organized the daring raid against the pepper and gambier plantations, or bangsals, which had been opened on Galang Island:

> Their plans were laid with the greatest skill, and the effect was most complete. They took the inhabitants of the different *bangsals* or *kam-*

22. *SSR*, BB 63, no. 227; *SSR*, R 13, p. 447.
23. *SSR*, CC 16, no. 315.
24. Comber, pp. 71–73; Buckley, pp. 445–46; *SFP*, 19 March 1846.

pongs most completely by surprise, affording time neither for defense nor escape. The inhabitants were given to the sword, while everything in the different *kampongs* was destroyed, the houses and their furniture being burnt, and all trees, pepper vines and gambier plants cut up and laid waste. Twenty-eight bangsals or plantations were thus treated in the course of one night, upwards of one hundred persons having been killed; their bodies having been found, in nearly every case, deprived of the heads, and shockingly mangled and disfigured.

While there is no indication of what subsequently became of Neo Liang Quan, his bangsals on the Seletar River seem to have been the pioneering settlement that later became Chan Chukang and Nam To Kang; still later, the area was renamed Nee Soon Village.[25]

The two secret societies were fighting for control of the pepper and gambier agriculture, both in Singapore and Riau. In both places, the Quan Tek appears to have gained some measure of official support. In Riau, the Quan Tek hui's leader was appointed kapitan. Even in Singapore, the leader of the Quan Tek hui, Chew Tock, had gotten closer to the government than the Ngee Heng leaders. It is difficult, however, to see the face of deep-seated rival forces in these two societies alone.

Part of the difficulty of writing the history of secret societies in Singapore is the apparent ad hoc character of many of them. With the exception of the Ngee Heng/Ghee Hin umbrella society, many societies only appeared at times of crisis and then disappeared. On the occasion of a fresh crisis, an opposing society would be reborn, sometimes under a new name, and sometimes old names reappeared. But, it is often difficult to trace threads of continuous history for many of them. Even when names seem to have a certain continuity, one is often left with the impression that the names alone were reborn and that the societies themselves became dormant once their reason for being had been eliminated. After the 1846 period, the Quan Tek hui seems to have disappeared and was not heard of again. It is possible that the Ghee Hock, which arose in 1854 and was periodically active until 1879, did indeed represent some of the groups formerly associated with the Quan Tek, but there is no way of proving this.[26]

25. Pitt, "From Plantations to New Town" (1987), pp. 195–96. See also reports in Buckley, pp. 463–64; and *SSR*, U 13, pp. 56–57.
26. The Ghee Hock is a bit of a mystery. Comber's account (pp. 69–72), in which the Quan Tek hui is consistently referred to as the Ghee Hock, is questionable. There is no evidence from any other records that the Ghee Hock existed before 1854. The rise of this society appears entirely associated with the 1854 Hokkien-Teochew riots. Virtually no other

It is clear, however, that speech group affiliation was an important element in the conflict: the Quan Tek was associated with the Hokkiens, and the Ngee Heng was a Teochew society. But, there was an economic difference as well. The Teochew Ngee Heng was a part of the old-line kongsi brotherhood, although it is difficult to measure the limits of its egalitarian spirit. Probably it was by then under the domination of planters, kangchus, and shopkeepers, who used the society to intimidate coolies and to preserve a monopoly over the agriculture. Its strength was in the rural areas, whereas the Hokkiens seem to have had greater influence in the towns, both of Singapore and Tanjung Pinang at Riau.

Taken altogether, the events of 1846 and 1847 suggest a Hokkien attempt to dominate what might be termed the "commanding heights" of the economy. From there they confronted the Tien-di hui, which dominated at the grass roots or "mass" level. Membership estimates from this period suggest that the Ngee Heng was far larger than the Quan Tek.[27] Seah's list of Chinese occupations in his article published in 1848 shows about one hundred Hokkien pepper and gambier dealers and two hundred Teochew pepper and gambier dealers. The list also shows that there were no Hokkien pepper and gambier *planters* at this time. All planters were either Teochew or "Macao," meaning Cantonese.[28] The Hokkiens lacked traditional and cultural links to the laboring population, making it necessary for them to form alliances with the governments of Singapore and Riau and to use their wealth and access to authority to check the growing power of the Cantonese society, which had always dominated the pepper and gambier agriculture.

The movement of the society's headquarters to Johor in March 1846 suggests something of a retreat by the Ngee Heng, but the raid on Galang indicates that the old society had not left the field and that the outcome was still in doubt. In fact, two or three years later, the Quan Tek had, it seems, disappeared, but the Ngee Heng persisted. These events also tell something about earlier conditions that confirm a number of suggestions raised by Vaughan and Mak.

Both Vaughan and Mak maintain that until the 1840s, there was

---

researcher including Wilfred Blythe (1969, pp. 79–80) has associated it with the Hokkien speech group. Blythe, on the contrary, suggests that it was a Teochew society. Certainly its leader, Chua Moh Choon, was identified as a Teochew by Song (pp. 175, 187, 202).

27. Newspaper reports from the period estimate the Ngee Heng, or Tien-di hui, had a membership of ten thousand to twenty thousand, while the Quan Tek membership was put at only about one thousand. Quoted in Comber, p. 61.

28. Siah, 1848, p. 290.

only one secret society in Singapore, the Ngee Heng or Tien-di hui, and that during these years it split into rival factions that continued to fight throughout the century.[29] As causes, Vaughan has pointed to what Mak calls "traditional" differences, meaning clan, speech group, place of origin, and surname. Mak, in contrast, has stressed the economic factors, seeing conflict arise out of challenges to an occupational monopoly maintained by an established kongsi. Mak, however, has not really examined a particular occupation. The picture that I have presented here, so far, shows that occupational specialization was a far more complicated business that has hitherto been realized. Probably there were many kongsis, each focused on a particular skill, or craft, area, block, street, or kangkar. It is just that the sheer weight of numbers of people involved in the pepper and gambier business; their domination of the entire countryside and of a major sector of the town; their offshore connections to Riau and later Johor—all these factors—made this business the pivotal economic monopoly. It was not a monopoly of a single occupation, nor of a single speech group, but of an entire economy, which was held by a rather unstable coalition. This coalition consisted of large and small merchants, both Hokkien and Teochew; of planters, kangchus, boatmen, secret society soldiers, and coolie brokers; and finally, of a mass of coolies. By 1845 the coalition was destroyed.

The Rise of the Lau-Cheang Syndicate

The development of European interest and the entry of what Lee calls "free trade forces" into the traditional pepper and gambier system after 1836 seems to have been the crucial factor in destabilizing the established division of the spoils within the monopoly. The riots of 1846 indicate the final split within this old monopoly. To say, however, that one society or speech group or economic faction was victorious and one was defeated would be premature at this point simply because it is not exactly clear what was at issue. Understanding the conflict over control of the agriculture is impossible without considering the Singapore revenue farms; for the changes and the conflict in the secret societies and in the pepper and gambier agriculture that characterized the years 1845–47 were mirrored in the revenue farms, particularly the opium farm.

29. Vaughan, pp. 99–100; Mak, "Forgotten and Rejected Community" (1978), pp. 35a, 35–40.

Revenue farm conflicts occurred not only in Singapore but also in Riau and Johor. The appointment of the new Quan Tek kapitan in Riau must have signaled a change in control of the revenue farms in the Dutch settlement. There was also a great deal of concern over the fate of Johor's revenue farms, which now became a major issue for the Singapore government. Before 1844, when there were no settlers in Johor, there were no revenue farms there. But, with the establishment of pepper and gambier plantations there, Temenggong Ibrahim was immediately approached by a Chinese identified in the government reports as "Ang Ah."[30] The only word of him was that he was attacked in Singapore by employees of the Singapore opium farm. The Singapore farmer was concerned that not only would the Johor farmer deprive him of customers but Johor would become a base for smuggling opium into Singapore. Ang Ah, or more likely Sim Ah Nga, was a Teochew and probably a member of the Ngee Heng, whose action suggests a retaliatory move by the kongsi to undercut the established revenue-farming syndicate. This was the first occurrence of what would later become a perennial ploy in Singapore/Johor revenue farm conflicts. The pepper and gambier settlements on the north side of the island facing the Straits of Johor were impossible to patrol effectively. The government grasped the difficulty immediately and took steps to get both the Johor and Singapore farms under one management.

Governor Butterworth wrote to India in 1846 asking for permission to merge the two farms. He pointed out the proximity of Johor and explained the ease with which smuggling could be carried out and the detrimental effect it would have on Singapore's revenue. His plan was to offer the temenggong three hundred dollars per month for the opium farm and fifty dollars for the spirit farm. These sums would be paid by the Singapore farmer and simply added on to the cost of the Singapore farm. At the same time, Johor would then be under the same revenue laws as Singapore, and the temenggong and his followers would help to enforce the law in Johor.[31] Events connected with the Singapore farms show this to have been a welcome arrangement. The previous few years had been unsettling for both the farmer and the government. While there is very little information about the farms before 1845, the pattern of events seems to mirror that in the pepper and gambier agriculture and the secret societies: a monopolistic coalition had collapsed around 1845–46.

30. Buckley, p. 430. I believe this person was in fact one Sim Ah Nga, who was later named as a partner of Tan Seng Poh (see herein, chap. 5, n. 50).
31. *SSR*, R 13, no. 138, 11 September 1846.

Table 2. Singapore opium farm annual rent as a percentage of total revenue, 1820–1882 (Spanish dollars)

Year	Rent	Total revenue	Percentage
1820–21	7,345	15,925	46.1
1821–22	9,420	21,870	43.1
1822–23	14,200	31,490	45.1
1823–24	22,830	46,536	49.1
1824–25	24,000	66,999	35.8
1825–26	24,384	75,734	32.2
1826–27	24,600	77,312	31.8
1827–28	24,720	—	—
1828–29	32,640	—	—
1829–30	24,720	—	—
1830–31	39,240	96,331	40.7
1831–32	40,680	88,167	46.1
1832–33	41,280	103,260	40.0
1833–34	48,000	104,543	45.9
1834–35	60,720	122,600	49.5
1835–36	57,600	119,265	48.3
1836–37	54,840	114,219	48.0
1837–38	54,840	—	—
1838–39	58,230	121,645	47.9
1839–40	48,600	118,223	41.1
1840–41	65,000	142,900	45.5
1841–42	75,000	135,000	55.6
1842–43	76,164	—	—
1843–44	107,885	232,449	46.4
1844–45	107,885	223,182	48.3
1845–46	107,896	232,273	46.5
1846–47	90,000	—	—
1847–48	82,500	—	—
1848–49	84,360	175,550	48.1
1849–50	87,567	172,375	50.8
1850–51	87,567	—	—
1851–52	82,669	—	—
1852–53	88,058	204,110	43.1
1853–54	98,000	192,000	51.0
1854–55	109,090	216,352	50.4
1855–56	147,818	288,156	51.3
1856–57	147,900	308,436	48.0
1857–58	181,230	350,362	51.7
1858–59	185,509	388,033	47.8
1859–60	186,548	352,117	53.0
1860–61	266,751	492,853	54.1
1861–62	266,115	527,015	50.5
1862–63	266,791	569,177	46.9
1863–64	286,549	674,875	42.5
1864–65	270,767	610,887	44.3
1865–66	269,556	670,931	40.2
1866–67	300,000	878,057	34.5
1867	360,600	963,051	37.3
1868	355,550	989,370	35.9
1869	360,600	855,174	42.2
1870	360,600	875,690	41.1
1871	360,600	913,953	39.4

Year	Rent	Total revenue	Percentage
1872	390,650	1,023,759	38.1
1873	360,600	989,183	36.5
1874	346,500	891,818	38.9
1875	398,000	967,235	41.1
1876	383,000	1,062,733	36.0
1877	413,300	1,003,059	41.2
1878	372,900	904,500	41.2
1879	440,700	1,002,881	43.9
1880	600,000	1,277,413	47.0
1881	600,000	1,316,545	45.6
1882	600,000	1,375,585	43.6

Sources: Compiled from various references in *SSR, SFP, ST,* Little, Buckley, and Newbold, 1836.

British records are oddly skewed. They say little about the identity of the farmers themselves. The only hard data available are those from the yearly budgets. The government records give no information on the organization of these early farms in Singapore. Song Ong Siang reports that Tay Han Long, the father of Tay Ho Swee, was reported to have been the first opium farmer in Singapore. There is also a report that Choa Chong Long was an opium farmer and that Tan Che Sang was a gambling farmer.[32] The identity of the first Chinese kapitan of Singapore has been established as one Tan Kousing.[33] Outside of this, little else can be said. The impression one gets is that the farmer was most likely a Melaka Chinese, or someone who had gained the confidence of persons in the colonial government and mercantile community. He was most likely a member of a coalition of Straits Chinese merchants who apparently monopolized this connection to the European sector of the economy during the early years of Singapore.

Dr. Little's listing of amounts paid for the opium farm between 1822 and 1848 (table 2) shows a clear pattern.[34] The initial dozen years or so were a sort of settling-in period. Crawfurd, in particular, tinkered with the system in order to maximize the government's profit. He tried breaking the farm into five regional distributorships; he tried a gambling farm and a few other experiments. By the early 1830s, the system, whatever it was, seems to have stabilized.

32. Song, p. 39. Lee, 1978, pp. 25–26. Lee does not give an exact reference for Choa Chong Long's and Tan Che Sang's roles as revenue farmers.
33. I am grateful to David K. Y. Chng, director of the References Services Division of the National Library, Singapore, for bringing this document to my attention. A copy of the letter bearing Tan Kousing's signature is reproduced in *History of the Chinese Clan Association of Singapore*, National Archives, Singapore, p. 32.
34. Little, p. 62.

Between 1833 and 1840, the opium farm revenue hovered between $40,000 and $55,000 per year. Although it had gone up to $60,000 in 1834, it had fallen back to $48,000 by 1840. These consistently low prices at a time when population was clearly rising and when the economy was relatively prosperous meant only one thing, that one syndicate had the farms and was in a position to keep down the rent, although they did not actually reduce it, as had happened in Pinang in the 1820s.[35] In 1840, however, the government received a substantial increase. One syndicate, perhaps the same one (but spurred by competition), took the farm for $65,000. The following year, 1841–42, the contract seems to have been made for two years at about $75,000 per year. Then, in 1843, a new farmer, and probably a new syndicate, emerged.

Dr. R. Little, the government surgeon, has provided some of the first "inside" information on the Singapore farms. He reports that Kiong Kong Tuan, a Hokkien from Pinang who had married a daughter of Choa Chong Long,[36] had taken the farms at a "considerable advance." For the period 1843–46, three years, Kiong had bid $8,990 per month. That was just over one-third more than the highest rent in the previous contract and more than double the rent of 1840. The 1846–47 farm contract, however, indicates that something went wrong. There was a decline—to $7,500 per month.

Even without Dr. Little's report, it is possible to tell what had happened here on the basis of numbers alone. The period between 1833 and 1843 suggests domination by one farmer or one syndicate. The sharp rise associated with Kiong Kong Tuan's takeover indicates that he was a newcomer and had bid a high rent in a fight to take the farms away from the old syndicate. The somewhat lower rent of 1846–47 is, itself, enough to tell us that he lost money and may have even lost the farms. Normally, what happened—and it most certainly happened in 1843–46—was a great deal of smuggling, engineered by the former holders of the farm, who, having lost the privilege, set out to destroy their opponent. This scenario was to repeat itself several times during the nineteenth century. In the end, the two opponents eventually made a deal, formed an umbrella syndicate that included all the major "players," and then held the farms for a substantial period until they in turn were pushed out by a newcomer.

In this case, we have no idea of the identity of the farmer before

35. Wong Lin Ken, 1964–65, pp. 77–78.
36. Song, p. 39.

Figure 4. Opium-farming syndicates, 1843–1860

1843–1846	Opium & spirit farms of Singapore Farmer: Kiong Kong Tuan	Opium & spirit farm of Johor (1846 only) Farmer: Sim Ah Nga

1846–1847	Opium & spirit farms of Singapore and Johor Farmers: Kiong Kong Tuan, Tay Eng Long & Cheang Sam Teo

1847–1860	Opium & spirit farms of Singapore and Johor Farmers: Lau Joon Tek & Cheang Sam Teo, the "Lau-Cheang Syndicate"

Sources: Compiled from *SSD* and *SSR*.

1843. In 1845, however, even before his contract had expired, Kiong Kong Tuan had apparently taken a partner, Tay Eng Long, and given him control of the opium farm (fig. 4). Whether or not Tay Eng Long had been affiliated with the previous farms is impossible to say. He may also have helped to bail out Kiong Kong Tuan.

Little thought that Kiong's losses resulted from his attempt to raise the retail price of opium. He must have done so in order to pay the government the rent it demanded; his competition was able to undersell him. Little reported, "When Mr Kong Tuan had the farm the retail price of opium was very high and smuggling was so great that he was a loser by the speculation. By the Farmer who succeeded him, the price was lowered, so that he realized a handsome monthly sum of profit; and now smuggling . . . [is less] than 3 to 5 chests a month." Kiong Kong Tuan did not immediately give up revenue farming altogether, but Little and Song suggest that he had learned his lesson and decided to stay with spirit farming. He was again spirit farmer in 1846–47, but there is no data on the next few years. Song reports, however, that Kiong died in 1854.[37] The years 1847 to about 1850 were important: those who formed the Lau-Cheang syndicate took over the farms.

An important fact that would help in determining the alignment of the opium farm holders with the pepper and gambier agriculture would be the speech group of the farmers. Seah's list shows seventy "Revenue peons and chandu and arrack preparers," all Hokkien. Choa Chong Long and Kiong Kong Tuan were both Straits-born

37. Little, p. 75; Song, p. 39.

Chinese, the first from Melaka and the second from Pinang. Lee has classified these Chinese as belonging to the free trade society. Tay Han Long and his son Tay Ho Swee may have been Hokkiens; Song mentions both of them in his book but without indicating their speech group. Tay Han Long was a partner in the opium farm of Cheang Sam Teo, according to Song, and Tay Ho Swee was a partner of Cheang Hong Lim (Sam Teo's son).[38] Since it is known that the Cheangs were a Hokkien family, it is probable that the Tays were also Hokkien. Tay Eng Long, who is mentioned in the *Straits Settlements Directory*, but not in Song, was probably Tan Han Long's relative. The overall impression is that at least until 1849, or thereabout, the principals in the opium farm were always Hokkiens.

The events surrounding the farms between 1846 and 1849 are worth some attention. There is some documentation for the sale of the 1846 farms. The 1846–47 farm contract saw a drop in the rent of the opium farm, from $8,900 to $7,500 per month. Total revenue, the drop in which was even more substantial because not only opium, but almost all the excise revenue, was affected, fell by Rs 5,000 (or about $2,300) per month, or nearly 14 percent. Resident Councillor Church noted the cause for the decline was the serious loss suffered by the previous farmers (who would have been Kiong Kong Tuan and/or Tay Eng Long) and that a major reason for their loss was the serious drop in demand for opium because of the poor economic situation: "The almost unprecedented low price of Pepper and Gambier, the principle products of the Island, the Cultivators are exclusively Chinese. They contribute more to the Revenue than any other class of inhabitants."[39] He also mentioned a problem related to the inflation of the copper currency. Normally Chinese opium smokers purchased their opium for copper duits or tokens, but the farmer had to buy his opium and pay his rent in silver. The duits had originally been minted as one cent of a silver Spanish dollar, but the exchange between copper and silver had been fluctuating. In 1846 duits were selling at about 650 to 700 to the dollar. Rutherford Alcock, the British consul in Shanghai, reports that by 1848 in China they were about 1,400 to the dollar. But Buckley reports that in Singapore they had swung the other way and were selling for 82 to 85 to the dollar in 1848.[40] These numbers indicate speculation and may not reflect the true state of the day-to-day economy, but they must have destabilized retail purchasing patterns.

38. Siah, 1848, p. 290; Song, pp. 39, 119, 168–70.
39. *SSR*, CC 16, no. 570.
40. Buckley, p. 471; *Returns of the Trade of the Various Ports of China*, 1849, p. 75.

The other major reason Church gave for the decline in the value of the farms was the "inadequacies" of the revenue laws. Apparently a number of loopholes had been discovered. Moreover, the Chinese had discovered European lawyers, who could exploit the weaknesses of the law. From this time until 1851, Straits government officials continually petitioned their superiors in India for a revised revenue code. In 1850 the revenue officers had apprehended three Chinese in the act of boiling raw opium to make chandu. The law stated that only the *possession* of chandu was illegal. The defense lawyer thus argued that since the drug had not yet become chandu, the men were guilty of no offense. They were acquitted. The resident councillor indicated that this case had set a "very bad precedent": "If a person can with impunity boil Opium to a certain stage so that it is not *exactly* (although 5 minutes would make it so) prepared for smoking, the privilege of the Farmer is nominal, and unless a remedy is applied, the Revenue will materially suffer, and boilers of Opium be found in every street of the Town and Districts in the Country."[41]

While both Tay Eng Long and Kiong Kong Tuan were listed as the opium and spirit farmers for 1846–47, it seems likely that their enthusiasm for the venture was weakening. One set of their problems was related to the pepper and gambier agriculture. The farms were dominated by Straits-born or Hokkien Chinese, and they were running into difficulty in dealing with the Teochews, who dominated the agriculture. This struggle cannot be separated from the conflicts between the two speech groups which were breaking out at the same time. While it is entirely possible that there had formerly been Teochew shareholders in the syndicate that backed the farms, the riots of 1846 and 1847 certainly must have made it more difficult to maintain the Hokkien-run opium monopoly among the Teochew kangchus, planters, and coolies.

The leadership of the revenue-farming syndicate changed almost unaccountably over the next two years, the 1846–47 and 1847–48 contract years. In May 1846 the list of farmers was much the same as the previous year (table 3). Tay Eng Long was still the opium farmer; Kiong Kong Tuan, the spirit farmer. The person listed as "Ko Sway" in the 1846 directory, who held the pawnbroking farm and the Kampong Glam market, seems to have remained; in the 1846 listing he was identified as "Kho Swee Boon." The other farmers were changed. The toddy and bhang farmer was Mootoo Tammy instead of Sippo Pillay.

41. *SSR*, AA 22, no. 66.

Table 3. Singapore revenue farmers, 1845 and 1846

Farm	1845*	1846**
Opium farmer	Tay Eng Long	Tay Eng Long
Spirit farmer	Kiong Kong Tuan	Kiong Kong Tuan
Pawnbroker	Khoo Swee Boon	Khoo Swee Boon
Kampong Glam market	Khoo Swee Boon	Khoo Swee Boon
Toddy and bhang	Sippo Pillay	Mootoo Tammy
Siri farmer	Ko Jan	Cheang Sam Teo
Chinatown market	Kiong Kong Tuan	Cheang Sam Teo

*The SSD for 1846 gives the names for the farms from 1 May 1845 to 30 April 1846.
**The SSR, CC 16, no. 476, gives the names of the farmers from 1 May 1846 to 30 April 1847.

These changes, on the surface, seem minimal, but one is important: "Ko Jan," who had formerly held the siri farm, was replaced by one "Chea Teoh," who had also taken the Chinatown market, formerly held by Kiong Kong Tuan.[42] Despite the irregular spelling, "Chea Teoh" was in fact Cheang Sam Teo. By 1847 he had emerged as the dominant figure in the farming syndicate.

In May 1847, after the sale of the farms in that year, the resident councillor spoke of Cheang Sam Teo as if he had been the opium farmer for the entire previous year: "Relative to the arrangement made with the Temonggong by the Renter of the Opium Farm, and to add that this exclusive privilege for retailing the Drug *continues in the same hands as in the year 1846/47,* it has not been considered necessary to attempt to disturb the existing agreement entered into between His Highness the Temonggong and *Chung Teoh the Opium Farmer,* a copy of which accompanied my dispatch of 25 August 1846 . . . [italics added]."[43] This indicates that by some means or other, Cheang Sam Teo took charge of the Singapore and Johor opium farms at some time between May and August 1846 and was responsible for making the deal with the temenggong for the Johor farms.

It is difficult to place Cheang Sam Teo within the factions involved in the pepper and gambier conflict. Surface indications suggest he was affiliated with the Hokkien side. He was China born but had once been in partnership with the Hokkien Tay Han Long. And later, Tay Ho Swee (son of Han Long) and his brother-in-law Teo Kit were also partners in the Cheang opium-farming syndicate.[44] This was thus a

42. SSR, CC 16, no. 476.
43. SSR, AA 18, no. 62.
44. Song, pp. 168–70.

Hokkien syndicate; yet Kiong and his father-in-law, Choa Chong Long, also Hokkien-Babas, were not closely allied to the Cheang syndicate. There were two Hokkien factions arising from the two subgroups: H'ai Ch'ang and Ch'ang Tai. The lines dividing cliques and factions were more complex than scholars have earlier suggested.

Cheang Sam Teo's relationship with Johor shows how murky the picture really was. Relationships are very difficult for an outsider to fathom. Johor's pepper and gambier agriculture was founded by Teochew "refugees" setting up an alternative base for the Ngee Heng Kongsi. While it may have been entirely possible for Cheang Sam Teo to make a deal with the temenggong to take the revenue farms, it might have been difficult to maintain a monopoly among Teochew kangchus and planters closely allied to the Ngee Heng. If the Singapore Teochews were powerful enough to boycott the Hokkien-held farms of Kiong Kong Tuan, it is difficult to see why the Johor Teochews would agree to do business with Cheang, unless he was willing to offer them something in return. It would have made sense in the long run for Cheang to bring them into his syndicate. This may be what happened.

While there is no copy of the official list of farmers for the 1847–48 or the 1848–49 periods, a stray piece of correspondence from early 1849 indicates that a new partner had emerged at the top level of the syndicate, one Lau Joon Tek. In March 1849 the resident councillor of Singapore reported that he had received a request from the "opium farmers, Cheo Two and Lau June Teck." The appearance of Lau Joon Tek in the opium farms is significant because he may have been the first Teochew in a position of prominence in the farms.[45] It is possible that he, or some other Teochew, may have been a shareholder or silent partner before this time, but there is no evidence one way or the other. His appearance at this point, however, seems to mark a sort of truce between the major commercial factions in Singapore. That is, it appears that a coalition of the major people in the secret societies and the pepper and gambier business (taukehs) had decided to divide the territory among themselves and stop the fighting.

Without direct evidence, this conclusion is only speculation, but circumstances do suggest it. First of all, the Lau Joon Tek/Cheang Sam Teo partnership became a long and prosperous one that held the farms

45. *SSR*, BB 67, no. 188. The identification of Lau Joon Tek as a Teochew is tentative. I am told by one informant that the pronounciation Lau Joon Tek would make him a Teochew, but others say that the Hokkien pronunciation of those characters is not very different. David Chng Khin Yong of the National Library of Singapore favors the Teochew reading of the name. Mak Lau Fong has stated that it could be Hokkien. Personal communication, March 1985. My own sense of this is that he was Teochew.

from 1847 or 1848 until 1860. This apparent combination of a Hokkien and Teochew farming syndicate eliminated all opposition; in fact, during the 1850s, the farms were simply being sold to this kongsi by private sale without even a public auction or a request for tenders.[46] Second, during the initial years of the combination, there was a cessation of major secret society disturbances.

The lack of a major confrontation between the secret societies is significant in 1848 because reports show that the economic situation was every bit as bad as that of 1846. The price of gambier was at an all-time low of eighty cents per pikul. Many plantations had been abandoned, both in Singapore and Riau. Wages, which depended on the price of gambier, had fallen. An article on remittances to China remarked, "In the session which had just ended, the remittances were very small in amount, owing, in the case of the merchants and traders, to the unprofitable state of trade for some time past, and, in the case of the agricultural coolies, to the inadequate price which gambier had for many months commanded, and which has seriously affected their wages the amount of which is dependent upon the price of the product." Likewise the year-end article in the *Singapore Free Press* quoted in Buckley described a worldwide depression and a falling off in local productions, both of gambier and gutta percha. It also noted a decrease in the Chinese junk trade and the Bugis trade and went on to sum up: "These and other causes have produced a great exhaustion of means on the part of many of the smaller native traders—Kling and Chinese—amongst whom several failures took place. The very low price to which gambier fell, produced much distress among the planters, who found it almost impossible to obtain the means of existence."[47] The only bright spot was the low price of rice, which was all imported. It is equally possible that fewer immigrants arrived, as there were fewer junks. This may have eased tensions, but the misery index was every bit as high; yet, the secret societies were strangely quiescent.

In fact, the only reported disturbance of any note during 1848 was clearly so luckless and so unsuccessful that the lack of organizational support is obvious. The description, given in Buckley, of the blundering, "plundering" expedition carried out by about one hundred Chinese from Singapore stands in sharp contrast to the well-organized and ruthlessly executed attack on Galang led by Neo Liang Quan in the previous year.[48] Economic pressures failed to bring about a confronta-

46. *SSR*, AA 35, no. 56 with enclosure.
47. Siah, "Annual Remittances to China" (1848), p. 36; Buckley, pp. 497–98.
48. Buckley, pp. 463–64, 470.

tion between the societies in this year. Another interesting fact is the complete disappearance of the Quan Tek hui. The obvious conclusion to be drawn here is that the societies had resolved their differences. Or, perhaps more correctly, the leadership, of whatever factions there were, had made peace.

The essence of that peace is reflected in the new leadership of the revenue farms. The newly formed partnership of Cheang Sam Teo and Lau Joon Tek suggests the outline of the arrangement. The two partners apparently represented, in some fashion, both Hokkien and Teochew interests, at least at the elite level. It may even be that the two were also the leaders, or at least representatives, of the secret societies, or of factions of the secret society. Lau Joon Tek's death in 1859 or 1860 did coincide with reports of the death of a major secret society leader (see chap. 5).

What did this mean for the confrontation between the pepper and gambier kongsi and free trade interests? Some tentative conclusions suggest themselves. The disturbances between 1842 and 1846 all seem to have been initiated by the ascendant Hokkien/free trade group, which had links to Straits Chinese families from Pinang. They formed their own secret society, the Quan Tek hui, and took over the farms in Singapore; one of their members became the kapitan in Riau and perhaps took over a number of plantations, displacing many of the earlier Teochew settlers. They also opened up their own plantations on Galang. They may have taken over a number of plantations in Singapore as well. In both places they probably acted with the support, perhaps even the collusion, of colonial authorities.

The pepper and gambier society, as Teochews and as the Tien-di hui/Ngee Heng, regrouped and retaliated in late 1846. Some moved to Johor and established a base there, probably with the temenggong's blessing. The raid on Galang was a clear statement that these were serious people who could not be easily pushed around. The attempt to organize a separate revenue farm in Johor headed by the mysterious "Ang Ah" was perhaps yet another move in the power struggle. If we accept the implicit connection between the opium farm and the secret societies, then the position of the Ngee Heng in Johor was a strategic coup. As a result, a truce was made and the Teochew leaders were accepted—for the first time it appears—as equals in the upper levels of the Singapore socioeconomic structure.

The only other Teochew leader to have gained recognition at this level was Seah Eu Chin, and his role is problematic. He was clearly a major figure in the expansion of pepper and gambier agriculture in

Singapore in the years between 1836 and 1848. Lee has placed him in the camp of the Melaka Chinese, or with the free trade society.[49] There may be good reason for this. His command of English, his acceptance by Europeans, and his overall closeness to the colonial power structure suggests a clear class orientation. He was fairly close to the Melaka Chinese and had little reason to rely on the more traditional structures of the pepper and gambier kongsi. That he entered the pepper and gambier business at a late stage—only in 1836, when it had become an item of demand among European traders—is further evidence of the free trade orientation. His Teochew background would have made him the perfect vehicle to help the Straits Chinese merchants gain access to the pepper and gambier business. It is also probable that he held shares in the revenue farms before 1846 and would have continued to partici-pate. By the 1840s Seah Eu Chin's role in the overall economy was that of an investor, a capitalist. As time passed, more and more of the pepper and gambier merchants, both Hokkien and Teochew, began to fall into debt with him.[50] It was this debt structure that cemented the free trade society.

The weakness in Seah's position was his lack of "military" support, the function of secret societies. If we suppose the Quan Tek hui was the tool of Seah and a group of Hokkiens and Babas, some things are explained. Presumably the failure of the Quan Tek to subdue the Ngee Heng had been a setback. Then the death of Ngee Heng leader Ho Ah Yam probably provided an opportunity for intervention, or at least an alliance. There is evidence of a power struggle within the Ngee Heng after 1846: its leaders, or people acting in leadership positions, ap-peared and disappeared rapidly. Chew Swee, who had led the Tien-di hui in the funeral procession, gained a temporary notoriety and then was heard of no more. Tan Tek Hye wrote the letter to the newspaper announcing the Ngee Heng's move to Johor, styling himself "Keeper of the Quinquangular Seal."[51] Tan Kye Soon became the kapitan of the new settlement of the pepper and gambier society as the kangchu of Tebrau in Johor.[52] Neo Liang Guan led the attack on Galang. Tan Ah Tow was mentioned in 1850 as a Ngee Heng leader as well.[53] Possibly Lau Joon Tek also held a high position in the society.

Lau's appearance at this time, as well as his rise to prominence

49. Lee, 1978, pp. 22–23.
50. Song, pp. 19–20.
51. *SFP*, 19 March 1846.
52. Trocki, 1979, pp. 101–6.
53. Comber, p. 73.

during the 1850s, is mysterious. There is little information on him. Song, who mentions virtually everyone else of importance at the time, is silent; but Song did tend to focus on Hokkiens and mention only the most prominent Teochews. Managing the farms took money, and Lau was the "monied man." Where did he get the money? And how did he get so rich without getting famous? He may have been helped by a loan from a wealthy benefactor. If he was a leader of the Ngee Heng, he would have had substantial access to funds from the members, although because times were hard, a leader who did not immediately ask for a major levy to buy the farms (as Comber suggests) could have elicited more popular support than a rival.[54] Of course, a person could become independently wealthy as the revenue farmer, if he played his cards correctly, and Lau did very well in the long run. But he may have begun to lose his constituency among the rank-and-file, or at least among the cadre of the society. Control of the leadership did not necessarily ensure continued control of the entire membership.

The Riots of 1851 and 1854

Observers pointed out significant differences between the riots of 1846 and the two major outbursts in the early 1850s: the anti-Christian disturbances of 1851 and the great Five Catties of Rice/Hokkien-Teochew Riot of 1854. Both disturbances seem to have been largely ethnic and lacking clear involvement of the major secret societies. At least, secret society involvement determined the lines of opposition less than other factors.

Most students of these riots have laid the blame on outside elements: ancient grudges brought from China; contemporary divisions within Chinese society (this was the period of the Taiping Rebellion); and the obvious ethnic divisions. Comber and Blythe have pointed out that in 1851 the Christians represented an alternative brotherhood, with its own values and ideology, which was beyond the control of the established societies. Buckley has noted that the Catholics were said to be drawing recruits away from the secret societies and that their presence in the interior meant the triads could no longer operate away from alien eyes.[55]

Lee has seen class conflict in these riots—a reaction to the inroads of

54. Comber, p. 76.
55. Comber, pp. 77–93; Blythe, 1969, pp. 69–71; Lee, 1978, pp. 67–75; Buckley, p. 543.

the free trade society. He argues that the British "allowed" Catholics to open settlements, a practice resented by the Teochews, many of whom were laborers on the Christians' plantations, and thus their secret society led the attack against the Christians. Lee also claims, incorrectly, as Wong Lin Ken has shown, that the price of gambier was very low in 1851, when actually it was quite high. According to Low Siew Chek's figures, it was nearly three dollars per pikul in 1851.[56]

There are other problems with Lee's explanation besides his failure to demonstrate the low-price motivation. While it may be said that the British "allowed" the Christian Chinese to settle in the interior, the same held true for everyone else. There were still no quitrents being collected, and there is no evidence that the government was any more favorably disposed to the Christian Chinese than they were toward the "heathen" Chinese, as they usually called them. The fact that the Chinese Christians were Roman Catholics and were connected with French priests of the Missions étrangères de Paris did nothing at all to gain them favor among British Protestants, many of whom were Scottish Presbyterians and also members of the Masonic Lodge, Zetland of the East. So far as the government was concerned, the Christians were just as much to blame for the trouble as were the non-Christians. Vaughan pointed out that "the Hong Kahs, as the Chinese Christians are called, became a powerful body. Just as in joining a secret society the converts regarded themselves as a community of brothers, and were as ready to fight as the worst of the heathen around them." This same attitude was reflected by Governor Butterworth and the resident councillor, Thomas Church.[57] Thus, one should be cautious about assuming that the Christian Chinese necessarily represented the free trade forces.

The suggestion that the Ngee Heng considered the Roman Catholics an alternative brotherhood seems a compelling motivation. There were occasions during which rumors spread through the Chinese community regarding alleged human sacrifice, kidnapping, and cannibalism on the part of the Christians.[58] It is also true that the Christian planters were reported to be "well-to-do" or "prosperous."[59] It would

56. Lee, 1978, pp. 66–69; Wong Lin Ken, 1980, pp. 165–68.
57. Vaughan, pp. 33–34; SSR, R 19, no. 134; SSR, AA 22, no. 20. In his letter, Thomas Church reports on a mission he made to Kranji to quell a dispute between some Christians and "heathens" on 25 February 1851. The violence had been on both sides; the Christians had been attacked and then retaliated. One of the non-Christians had been shot, but it was not clear by whom. Church's whole tone, through this letter, can hardly be considered sympathetic in any way to the Christians.
58. Song, pp. 85–86.
59. Blythe, 1969, p. 71; McNair and Bayliss, Prisoners Their Own Warders (1899), p. 68; Lee, 1978, p. 69.

be useful to know what was meant by prosperous and whether that prosperity meant that the Christians did not use opium or that the Christian planters had taken control of their own opium supply. In either case, they would have earned the jealousy of the traditional order.

Despite the apparent coalition between Lau Joon Tek and Cheang Sam Teo, the monopoly was far from airtight; considerable smuggling being reported at this time. Especially during the latter half of 1850 and during the first couple of months of 1852, the opium farmer delivered numerous complaints and petitions to the resident councillor and the government. There was constant reference to smuggling being carried on in the rural districts.

In September the resident councillor wrote the governor complaining that "several Chinese who pass for persons of Character and respectability are deeply implicated" in the smuggling traffic. Since June 1850, when the three Chinese who were caught boiling opium had been acquitted, smuggling had increased. Certain Chinese merchants were simply buying chests of opium and then reselling it by the ball to whoever wanted it. The problem, as he saw it, was the "defective state of the Regulations." He pointed out that "Chinese and others desirous of becoming acquainted with the legal construction of certain Clauses of the Excise Laws have no difficulty in doing so."[60] On 17 February 1851, in the midst of the attacks on the Christian plantations at Bukit Timah and Kranji, the opium farmer sent a petition and Church warned, "The Farms will be resold in about 2 months, and if the opium Farmer in particular is not better protected than at present, a serious decline in the Revenue will necessarily follow."[61] In fact, he was right. In 1850–51 the farm rental had been $87,567 for the year, and in 1851–52 it fell to $82,669 (table 2). Despite the promulgation of a new revenue code in August 1851,[62] smuggling and difficulties over the opium farms persisted through the 1850s.

The Catholics were outside the secret society socioeconomic network. Therefore, if they or their coolies used opium, they must have gotten it illegally and thus have been infringing on somebody's privilege. Their punishment was particularly vicious. During five days starting on about 15 February 1851 the non-Christian Chinese, apparently led by secret society members, attacked the Christian plantations. About five hundred people were killed, and twenty-eight plantations were burned. The Christians fought back. A truce was negotiated

60. *SSR*, AA 22, no. 114.
61. *SSR*, AA 22, no. 13.
62. *SFP*, 21 August 1851.

with the help of Seah Eu Chin, and the "heathen" pepper and gambier merchants of the town compensated the Christians with a payment of fifteen hundred dollars, which was not felt to be adequate.[63] Disputes between Christian and non-Christian Chinese continued, and several petitions were filed regarding infringements on this or that planta- tion.[64] The fact that the pepper and gambier merchants were held financially responsible for the attacks on the Christians suggests causes related to the gambier economy. Likewise, the role of Seah here is intriguing; he must have been more than a disinterested broker. In 1856 he paid the government the fees for title deeds and took over direct ownership of a large number of plantations, many of them located around Bukit Timah, where the Christians had been settled. It is possible that Seah and his growing clique were outside the Ngee Heng power structure.

The Hokkien-Teochew riot of 1854, however, had much more ob- vious immediate causes. The year 1854 was a bad one for gambier in Singapore. There was a serious decline in production. Although some new plantations were being opened in Johor, there was still substantial unemployment. At about the same time, a much larger group of immigrants arrived from China. These were not the usual type of immigrants but were the defeated rebels of the Xiao Dao Hui, vari- ously translated as "Small Sword," "Small Dagger," or "Small Knife" society, who had been driven out of Shanghai and Xiamen. About twenty thousand arrived in Singapore's harbor between May and December of 1853 and were a major factor in destabilizing an already tense situation. Their fleet of twenty-two war junks carried nearly 250 cannons.[65]

The riot, Buckley said, grew out of the refusal of the Hokkiens to contribute to a subscription to aid the rebels. This, he says, led to the general riots between Hokkiens and Teochews. Blythe has added the suggestion that the rebels seeking a contribution were Teochews. He believes that one result of the riot was the emergence of a new Teochew secret society in Singapore, the Ghee Hock.[66] The rebels came, also, at a time when the price of rice had risen very high and when there was an apparent shortage in the town.[67] The reports state that the first out-

63. Blythe, 1969, pp. 69–71.
64. *SSR*, BB 92, nos. 188, 225.
65. *SSR*, BB 91, p. 177.
66. Buckley, p. 585; Blythe, 1969, pp. 76–80; see also Comber, p. 61; Song, pp. 202–3. Wynne (p. 94) explains it as a phase in the conflict between the Han and Hung leagues and also sees the Ghee Hock-Ngee Heng conflict as central to the riot.
67. *SSR*, BB 92, no. 195; *Straits Guardian*, 13 May 1854; Wong Lin Ken, 1980, p. 174.

break of violence occurred when a Hokkien argued with a Teochew over the price of a quantity of rice (some say five catties, some say less). The riot began on 5 May 1854 and continued for about twelve days, spreading from the town to the countryside after the second day. About five hundred people were killed and over three hundred houses were burned.[68]

There is no agreement among the various sources about the causes. Vaughan maintained that the dispute did not involve secret societies but was between speech groups.[69] Apparently the Teochews had gotten the other Cantonese, the Hakka, and the Hainanese to join them against the Hokkien. Blythe disagrees with Vaughan's explanation and points to the rise of the new Teochew society, the Ghee Hock, which may have drawn support from the Xiao Dao rebels. Whatever the case, one thing is clear: like the anti-Catholic riots, and those of 1846, much of the violence seems to have been centered around the pepper and gambier agriculture. Lee associates the riot with the appearance of Hokkien planters, who now came directly into competition with the Teochew planters. There were no Hokkien planters in 1848, but by 1854, this had changed. Their appearance—probably backed by Hokkien shopkeepers and perhaps now in control of the Singapore Ghee Hin society, which seems to have taken control of the revenue farms— suggests not only an infringement on what had been Teochew territory but an attempt to dominate it. It may have been at this time that the Hokkiens came to outnumber the Teochews in Singapore.[70] The rise to prominence at this time of Chua Moh Choon—as head of the Ghee Hock, as a Teochew pepper and gambier shopkeeper, and as a coolie broker—is significant. It may be that he was associated with either Lau or Cheang in policing the farms. When the next split developed over the revenue farms, the Ghee Hock emerged as one of the belligerent factions.

What should also be noted is the problems that continued from this time on in relation to the status of the joint farms with Johor. Apparently a directive had been issued by either the governor or an authority in India to discontinue the joint arrangement. The resident councillor explained the reason for the decline in the rent for 1853–54 and pointed out that when, "previous to the Sale of the Opium and Spirit

68. General accounts of the riot can be found in Wynne, p. 62; Song, pp. 87–90; Comber, pp. 86–93; and Buckley, pp. 585–91.

69. Vaughan, p. 99.

70. According to Seah (1848), the Teochews outnumbered the Hokkiens by more than two to one in the late 1840s. Within the next twenty years the Hokkiens came to outnumber the Teochews.

Farms, several Chinese made enquiries relative to Johore, I distinctly apprised them and also the Temenggong that consequent on recent orders received, the local Authorities did not intend to interfere, or exercise any influence whatever with reference to the Revenues of Johor." This uncertainty "discouraged" bidders at the auction for the Singapore farms. The purchasers, in order to protect themselves, apparently had to obtain the Johor farms on an individual basis. They found, however, they had to triple the rent they had been paying in Johor. The temenggong had, it seems, been content to receive $350 per month ever since 1846 up until 1853. In 1853–54 he was able to get an increase to $1,000 per month,[71] and this heralded the appearance of a disharmony of interests between Johor and Singapore. Johor, after 1855, appeared much more expressly the territorial preserve of the Teochew Ngee Heng. By 1858 and 1859, however, groups from the Singapore Ghee Hock were attempting to push their way in.[72] Ultimately, splits erupted within the farming syndicate and the secret societies over the issue of Johor, the new frontier of the pepper and gambier society.

It is important to understand that the pepper and gambier society in Singapore probably never existed as a pure "brotherhood" kongsi in the ideal form described by Wang Tai Peng in Borneo. Even Wang has suggested that by the beginning of the nineteenth century, the kongsis in Borneo and Bangka were succumbing to taukeh domination. Certainly this must have been a "natural" process. As the Chinese economic system came into contact with the outside commercial world, elements of exploitation and authoritarianism were sure to arise as the profit motive was promoted. This was the result of free trade.

When pepper and gambier agriculture came to Singapore, it already carried within it the seeds of this exploitative tendency. The taukeh element in the town already had control of the market and the outside connections necessary to service the cultivation system. But, the gap between town and countryside was large. Thus, in the early days of Singapore, the kongsi brotherhood dominated the Chinese settled in the interior, and its leadership seemed able to enforce its own law at will. The situation before 1846 was one in which the rural cadre together with allies in the town maintained a relatively equal balance of power. The taukehs needed the products and customers represented by the planters, and the planters needed the supply system and the market of the town.

71. *SSR*, AA 26, no. 76.
72. *JLB*1, nos. 27 and 28, 4 October 1859 and 15 November 1859.

The town also put the brotherhood of the interior in connection with the global market forces. As the cultivation expanded beyond the demand of its traditional China market and became linked to the European market, the price structures of gambier, pepper, opium, rice, and other important commodities became more volatile. As in any market situation, the buck always stops with the first producer and final consumer. For the planters and coolies in the jungle, the brotherhood was the only buffer between them and the market forces. This was the essential ground of the conflict. So long as the leaders of pepper and gambier society maintained a social and economic distance from the town, the brotherhood could police the system in the interests of rhetorical if not real "equality." That is: profits could be spread; underemployment could prevent unemployment; and most important, debts could be held over until better days. The primary consideration was the survival of the producing community. The moral economy of the pepper and gambier society was the moral economy of the peasant.[73]

The shopkeepers of the town could not do business on this basis, at least not in the long run. In the beginning, such an operating ethic might have been possible in some cases. If a taukeh ran up too many debts with European houses and the low price of gambier or other produce made timely repayment impossible, rather than squeezing his brothers and clansmen in the jungle, he could simply abscond and either take refuge with them or hop on a boat and leave his European creditors to absorb the loss. Europeans would still have to lend their goods to *someone*. Land values in Singapore were then meaningless, so there was nothing to repossess. Value was created by labor, and the brotherhood dominated the labor force. But, as time passed it must have become clear to Chinese merchants that the material rewards offered by cooperation with the European power structure could not be matched by the planters' society. First the shopkeepers and later the secret society leaders were drawn into the official authority structure of Singapore.

The key in the struggle was leverage. There were many forms of leverage: credit, communications, police power, a continuous supply of fresh immigrants, and other things available to the capitalists. Another major form of leverage was the opium farm. In the course of time, all of these came into the hands of the shopkeepers in their struggle to crack the power of the brotherhood. If, as in 1843, "tigers"

73. Scott.

became a problem and it became too dangerous for shopkeepers to visit the plantations, then it was possible to open new plantations more accessible to authority and perhaps less able to resist exploitation. But, the brotherhood could, by expanding to Johor, play the same game, and it could even destroy competition if it took a mind to.

The strength of the brotherhood, of the pepper and gambier society, was its control of labor and its isolation, or at least its distance from the centers of colonial power. So long as it possessed the coercive force to protect its mass base in the countryside, the taukehs of the free trade society had to meet the planters at least halfway and build alliances with them and arrive at compromises. In the long run, however, the leaders of the brotherhood could be bought. The opium farm provided the economic leverage that held the system together: there was no profit in pepper and gambier—for investors or planters—without opium. Gambier and pepper only paid for labor. Opium paid the interest and paid for the police. Shareholding in the farming syndicate provided the means whereby the major investors could collect their supplementary profit; and the management of opium shops provided the means of remuneration for the smaller merchants, kangchus, and important planters.

As market forces came into play, the balance of power could shift from one end of the spectrum to the other. Likewise, the dynamic nature of the agriculture itself, requiring the periodic opening up of fresh territory because of the gradual exhaustion of the soil and fire-wood resources, tended to prevent immediate stabilization of relations. In a frontier period, such as that which obtained in Singapore until the 1850s, the people in the jungle were very much on their own. And, as Lee has argued, once roads were built and the forces of the European state had, at least to some extent, expanded into the rural areas, the power balance shifted toward the center. The manipulation of price structures and land values and the ability to direct the flow of immigrants also gave power to the merchants. But since there was competition among the merchants, these changes also favored different groups of merchants at different times. The tendency to treat either the merchants or the brotherhood as monolithic forces is a major flaw in most discussions of conflict in Singapore Chinese society. It was perfectly possible for shifts in market forces to disrupt partnerships and arrangements. Moreover, people got old and died and were replaced by new generations. There was also simple greed. Merchants could decide to double-cross their "friends." Finally, there was the fickle nature of European authority.

Part of the chaos of the late 1840s was due to the deaths of people like Ho Ah Yam and the retirement of Kiong Kong Tuan. The death of Kiong, who had been in Singapore at least since 1826, signaled the passing of the first generation of Chinese merchants. Clearly, the rising generation of the late 1840s was represented by men like Cheang Sam Teo and Lau Joon Tek. The passing of the old leaders also meant the passing of their arrangements, and thus the systems tended to erode with time and had to be restored in each succeeding generation.

The reestablishment of these partnerships always took time and usually created conflict. The events of 1846–48 were to be repeated after a fashion again in the early 1860s and again in the 1880s. Such conflicts finally helped to bring down the farms altogether in 1910. The farming partnerships would split, and conflict would arise, and out of that would come a new partnership, usually one more in tune with current market forces and power balances. The establishment of a farming partnership such as the Lau-Cheang syndicate did not, however, end the conflict. It often set the stage for more obvious class conflict, or at least for a struggle between the exploited coolies and the allies of the merchants. But, even on these occasions, leadership often came from the taukeh class, and whatever leadership arose out of the brotherhood itself could often find a welcome in the circle of wealth and power at the center.

Yen Ching-hwang's study of the social history of the Singapore Chinese presents the argument that much of the conflict took place among mercantile factions organized in pang, or groups defined by speech and ethnic origins. Yen thus sees Singapore society as divided among Hokkien, Teochew, Hakka, Cantonese, and Hainan pangs. He points to important splits among both the Hokkien and Teochew pangs which bear upon the conflict discussed here. His stress on the power of linguistic differences and the ability of taukeh leadership to dominate these groups cannot be ignored and is correct insofar as it goes, but he fails to address the fact that the fruit of these struggles was control of specific economic resources, which in Singapore were the pepper and gambier agriculture and the opium revenue farms. The success of Seah Eu Chin in taking control of the Teochew pang and organizing the Ngee Ann Kongsi was directly related to his control of the agricultural system. As Yen points out, the strength of Cheang Sam Teo's position within the Hokkien pang rested on his control of his Ch'ang T'ai subgroup as well as of the revenue farms. While these explanations of mercantile factions are illuminating, Yen fails to ac-knowledge the alliance between the revenue farmers of the late 1840s and 1850s, represented by Lau Joon Tek and the Cheang Sam Teo.

This coalition of Teochew and some Hokkien ethnic and economic

interests gave force to their opposition to the interests represented by
Tan Tock Seng and his son Tan Kim Ching, and to some extent
explains a continuing opposition between the pepper and gambier
group, represented here by the Lau-Cheang syndicate, and the Straits
Chinese and Hokkien interests represented by Tan Tock Seng. Tan Kim
Ching was, moreover, the lightning rod for animosity as a result of his
attempt to corner the Singapore rice market and to force up the price
of foodstuffs in the colony. It appears that one result of the events of
the 1840s and 1850s was the exclusion of the H'ai Ch'ang faction of
the Hokkien pang (according to Yen) from the revenue farming syndicates of Singapore.[74] The other shortcoming of Yen's analysis is that he
too is restricted by the colonial and official boundaries of the colony.
As a result he does not take into account offshore links, especially
those with Riau and Johor in years between the 1840s and 1860s.

The problem was that there was only so much room at the center—
or at the top. There was usually a group of merchants who felt that
they deserved more, and there were always new "soldiers" arriving on
the boats from China, particularly when major upheavals occurred
there. At the same time, there were always plenty of dissatisfied coolies
to swell the ranks of a serious protest. An "arrangement" at the top
usually meant an agreement to perfect and protect the system whereby
those on the bottom were exploited. It also reduced employment
opportunities for the "police" forces. Thus a settlement, such as that
made in 1848 or so, left plenty of dissatisfaction. Groups like the
Catholics could arise, with an alternative system of brotherhood, and
either eschew opium or else produce their own chandu. (The latter
seems most likely.) Or, as in 1854, all the disaffected could, in hard
times, band together to attack what they perceived as the representatives of the system of exploitation.

74. Yen (pp. 181–91) maintains that the Hokkien pang was divided first between merchants from Chuanchou (Quanzhou) and Ch'angchou (Zhangzhou). This division led to the
split between the H'ai Ch'ang subgroup led by Tan Tock Seng and his son Tan Kim Ching,
and the Ch'ang T'ai subgroup led by Cheang Sam Teo and his son, Cheang Hong Lim. Yen
demonstrates these splits by pointing to the founding and support of various temples,
cemetary sponsorship, and other "charitable" organizations. Yen's analysis of the divisions
within the Teochew pang focus on the emergence of Seah Eu Chin's Ngee Ann Kun in 1830.
In 1848 it was renamed the Ngee Ann Kongsi, an alliance of Teochews around a temple and a
burial society. From the 1840s to the 1880s Seah and his sons dominated both the Ngee Ann
Kongsi and the Teochew community in Singapore. In the 1880s, however, other Teochew
groups dissatisfied with Seah leadership came to positions of power and ultimately organized
a powerful financial clique around the Sze Hai (Four Seas) Bank.

5 The Rise of the
Great Opium Syndicate

The 1860s were crucial for the kongsi brotherhoods of Singapore; for it was during this decade that the kongsis came almost completely under the control of a group of taukehs. Thereafter, they were dominated by monied interests rather than popular will. The taukehs that came into control of Singapore's Chinese community were the heads of the revenue-farming syndicates.

In 1860 the syndicate formed by Lao Joon Tek and Cheang Sam Teo in the late 1840s collapsed as its leaders died or retired. There followed a war of succession among hopeful replacements, during which the secret societies were fragmented and the taukehs organized surname groups to serve as their "muscle" in the streets. The Ngee Heng, which seemed to have reemerged after the Hokkien-Teochew riots of 1854 as the areawide umbrella kongsi (although unity was probably no more than a formality), had begun to fragment along ethnic (speech group) lines. The appearance of surname groups from within the secret society or societies, which occurred in 1861 and 1862, seems to have been an entirely new phenomenon and marked a serious erosion of kongsi solidarity while signaling the rise of the opium farmers as the predominant forces. In fact, during the 1860s, the societies regularly served as agents for the revenue farmers in the struggles for control of the local community.

The situation was complicated by the role now played by the new Malay ruler of Johor, Maharaja Abu Bakar. Like Tan Seng Poh and Cheang Hong Lim, he too had grown up in colonial Singapore. Like them, he too sought to use the power of the kongsis to enhance his own position within the sub-European power structure of the region. This

117

led to a confrontation that I have discussed elsewhere, known as the Tanjong Putri controversy.[1] I raise the issue again here to revise and to expand my earlier interpretation of the event. It must be placed within the context of the opium farm war going on concurrently in Singapore. Abu Bakar had joined in the struggle by allying himself with his own revenue farmer, Tan Hiok Nee.

The main event of the 1860s, however, was the struggle between Tan Seng Poh and Cheang Hong Lim for control of the Singapore opium and spirit farms. Tan headed a Teochew syndicate that was buttressed by the extensive pepper and gambier holdings of his brother-in-law, Seah Eu Chin. In the 1860s Seah retired and Tan took over as the manager of the Seah family business. Cheang inherited the opium farming interests of his father, Cheang Sam Teo, and thus came to head the Hokkien syndicate. Their conflict lasted the entire decade, or so it seems. Although there were periods of quiescence and apparent stand-offs, there was no real peace until 1870, when the two Singapore syndicates formed a partnership including Tan Hiok Nee of Johor. This was the "great syndicate" that combined the opium and spirit farms of Singapore, Johor, Riau, and Melaka under one company (fig. 5).

The result of the struggle was more than a mere truce between revenue farmers. Rather, it was an important transition in the development of Chinese society in Singapore and in the extension of the economic "reach" of Singapore. The contenders used the surrounding Dutch and Malay settlements as staging areas for their attacks on each other within Singapore. These activities brought those areas more completely within the sphere of Singapore's influence. The struggle in Singapore overwhelmed all other neighboring power centers both within and near Singapore and either integrated them, eliminated them, or seriously weakened them. This is particularly true of the triad brotherhoods, which by 1869 were sufficiently vulnerable to fall under the surveillance of the colonial police and accept registration.

A final point pertains to the economic impact of the opium farm coalition. The great syndicate's success was largely based on its strong position in the pepper and gambier agriculture. Tan Seng Poh together with Tan Hiok Nee stood at the top of pyramids of indebtedness that gave them control over the production and consumption of many coolies, planters, boatmen, shopkeepers, and others. I have elsewhere

1. Trocki, 1979, pp. 131–45. Abu Bakar, the son of Temenggong Ibrahim, dropped the title of Temonggong in 1868 and began calling himself "Maharaja," a title more generally recognized by Europeans.

Figure 5. Opium-farming syndicates, 1847–1879

1847–1860	Singapore and Johor opium & spirit farms Farmers: Lau Joon Tek & Cheang Sam Teo, the "Lau-Cheang Syndicate"		
1860–1861	Johor & Singapore opium farm Heng Bun Soon	Singapore (& Johor?) spirit farm Cheang Sam Teo	
1861–1863	Singapore opium farm Heng Bun Soon & Co.	Singapore spirit farm Cheang Sam Teo	Johor opium (& spirit)? farm Wee Bock Seng
1863–1865	Singapore opium farm Tan Seng Poh	Singapore spirit farm Cheang Hong Lim	Johor opium (& spirit) farm Tan Hiok Nee
1866–1868 (Transfer, 1867)	Singapore opium farm Tan Seng Poh	Singapore spirit farm Cheang Hong Lim	Johor opium (& spirit) farm Tan Seng Poh
1869	Melaka opium (& spirit) farm	Singapore opium & spirit farm	Johor farm Tan Seng Poh
	Cheang Hong Guan		
Jan–Nov 1870	Singapore, Johor, & Melaka opium & spirit farms Cheang Hong Lim (& Tan Hiok Nee?)		Riau opium (& spirit) farm Tan Seng Poh
Nov 1870–1879	The Great Syndicate: Singapore, Johor, Melaka, & Riau opium & spirit farms Farmers: Cheang Hong Lim, Tan Seng Poh, & Tan Hiok Nee		

Sources: SSD, SFP, SSR, Legco, ST, and Song Ong Siang, 1967.

suggested that the pepper and gambier business may have provided a living for nearly a hundred thousand people as of 1870, all of them living within a fifty-mile radius of Singapore.[2] This was the productive foundation of the syndicate's power.

2. Ibid., p. 155.

The Collapse of the Lau-Cheang Syndicate

To quote W. G. Gulland, a prominent Singapore merchant and a member of the Legislative Council in 1883, "For the better understanding of this matter in all its bearings we must go back to 1870–73, when Seng Poh and Hong Lim, after a desperate fight, made a long and lasting peace, and founded that great opium syndicate which has ever since played such an important part in the internal workings of this Colony."[3] Actually, it is important to go back even further than 1870, since that was simply the end of the "desperate fight," which appears to have begun some time around 1859 or 1860. Their struggle laid the foundations of the economy and society of modern Singapore and shows the fracture points and cleavage lines that divided the Chinese of that era, as well as some of the bases for the unity and conflict resolution that resulted in the great syndicate.

From the 1860s onward, a great deal more hard evidence is available regarding the composition of the farming syndicates and the affiliations of the major partners with other elements in colonial society. The Straits Settlements Records, the Colonial Office Records, and the Singapore newspapers contain considerable, if not always complete, information about the affairs of the Singapore revenue farms. The account I piece together here has not been told before and should add to our understanding of the nineteenth-century colonial world.

I have already alluded to the importance of revenue farms in the economy of the nineteenth century, not only in British Malaya, but throughout Southeast Asia. Every state in the region, colonial or independent, relied heavily on opium farms, all of which were operated by Chinese. This system put the major Chinese merchants into close partnership with the ruling order and provided a major link between European administrators and Asian society at large. It is probable that colonialism could not have gained control over the societies of this region without the active collaboration of these Chinese merchants. Although the societies of Java and Singapore stood in sharp contrast, James Rush's study of the Javanese opium farms shows the same dependence.

British logic in defending the farming system shows an awareness of this dependence:

I do not consider it desirable the Executive Officers of Government should manage the details appertaining to the Excise Revenue, the princi-

3. *Legco,* 1883, p. 7.

pal consumers and Vendors of Excisable Articles are the Chinese. Their propensity to smuggle is great, which can only be checked by their own Countrymen conversant with their habits and language and who have a direct interest in the discovery of offenders; although the experiment had been tried, there is not now a single Chinese [police] peon employed at this Station, they are not to be trusted, and they do not evince any particular disposition to become Peace Officers under the Executive. Should therefore, the direct management of the Excise Revenue with all its minutia be vested in the Resident Councillor, he would be driven to entertain Klings and Malays as Revenue Officers, the result may easily be imagined.[4]

Given the expectations people have of modern governments, this sort of statement might seem an admission of an ineffective system of rule. Not many governments today would confess to such a total inability to collect a tax from the largest body of its subjects. Modern sensibilities are not a good guide to the administrative methods of the nineteenth century. In fact, the opium farm, as it evolved in Singapore, tended to enhance the central authority in the long run. In a sense, the farms represented a continuation of the old kapitan system. The major difference was the regular, almost annual, renegotiation that essentially placed the institution of revenue farming on a more rational basis. This annual renegotiation theoretically gave the government the opportunity to seek the highest bidder and conduct the relationship on a businesslike basis. But there were, as we have seen, perennial problems.

Song Ong Siang quoted Gulland on the dilemma that the government faced when it tried to manage the revenue farms:

It was over the periodical letting of this monopoly that the Executive . . . in the eyes of critics, was always coming to grief. Neither wonder if they did, for it is no easy matter to go into any business transaction on his own ground with John Chinaman and come out of the deal on the right side. Moreover, it is not to the advantage of the Colony to wring the last penny out of the Farmer . . . and it is generally best . . . that the Farm should be in strong hands doing well for themselves by the business.[5]

If the government could get two or three syndicates bidding against one another, "then the letting is a comparatively easy matter." But that was a big "if," and as it turned out, syndicates found it profitable to merge. Thus the pre-1860s syndicate headed by Lau Joon Tek and

4. *SSR*, AA 22, no. 91.
5. Song, pp. 131–32.

Cheang Sam Teo proved, despite continual reports of smuggling and predictions of impending disaster, to be quite durable and apparently profitable. In 1863, Tan Seng Poh wrote to the government and noted that before the time when his syndicate bid for the farms, "the late Lao Joon Tek and his friends had the Opium and Spirit farms for a period of fifteen or sixteen years in their own hands and had made immensely large profits, indeed several of them made large fortunes therefrom to the great detriment of the Government Revenue."[6]

This was the problem. One syndicate could be greedy, but if two or three syndicates made letting the farms comparatively easy, they also made management difficult. This difficulty was compounded by the problem of Johor, and disagreements became more frequent after 1855. At the root of this problem was a fundamental population shift. Thousands of Chinese were deserting the exhausted soils of Singapore and moving across the Straits to open plantations in the virgin jungles of Johor. As the population grew, so too did the potential revenue for the Johor opium farmer. Likewise, it became even easier to smuggle opium between Johor and Singapore. Whatever the Johor farms were intrinsically worth, they also had a certain nuisance value.[7] So long as the Lau-Cheang syndicate held together, the Johor farms thus continued under the same management. Around 1860, however, difficulties arose.

The first of these difficulties was the death of Lau Joon Tek, a possibility hinted at in a letter from the resident councillor to the governor in 1860: "It is possible that the present Kongsee may not be able to renew the lease as a report has reached this from China of the death of Low Jun Teck the principal monied man of the Farms, this, if confirmed, may tend to derange their operations but I trust the rumours may prove unfounded."[8] His optimism was misplaced. No more was heard about Lau Joon Tek. In April 1860 the *Singapore Free Press* reported that one Heng Bun Soon had become the new opium farmer.[9] While the report in the *Free Press* suggested nothing amiss, within a few months there were hints that something had come unstuck.

Although the Johor and Singapore Farms were still joined and the spirit farms were, it appears, still part of the package, it seems that the

6. *SSR*, W 45, no. 127.
7. *SSR*, AA 18, no. 62.
8. *SSR*, AA 43, no. 42.
9. *SFP*, 19 April 1860. Actually the *SFP* gave his name as "Ong," but since other sources give his name as "Heng" and since he was apparently a Teochew, I use the Teochew pronunciation. There is very little known about him. Song (p. 118) notes only that he was a member of the Tan Tock Seng Hospital management committee in 1861.

relationship between Cheang Sam Teo (listed as the spirit farmer) and the new opium farmer was less than amicable. In February 1861, before the first year's lease had expired and before he assumed his option to take the opium farm for a second year, Bun Soon wrote to the government to ask for a remission in his rent because he had suffered losses because of what he called "the course of his immediate predecessor."[10] Apparently this was a reference to the previous farmer's having glutted the market with all of his unsold chandu at knocked-down prices a few days before turning over the farm—a common practice when the farms changed hands. It is hard to tell, however, to whom he was referring. Lau Joon Tek had died in China before March 1860. Bun Soon did not buy the farm until 14 April, and the monopoly did not actually change hands until 1 May 1860. One assumes the culprit here was whoever took charge of the opium farm in Joon Tek's absence. Later evidence points to his partner, Cheang Sam Teo, as the most likely candidate. The fact that he was still part of Bun Soon's kongsi and also the spirit farmer does not appear to have won his cooperation.

"Dumping" by the previous managers of the farm was, however, not Heng Bun Soon's only difficulty. He had taken the farms at a public auction and had bid considerably more than the previous rent. Between 1857 and 1860 the rent for the Singapore opium farm was about $15,500 per month, or about $185,000 per year (table 2). Bun Soon's bid represented a considerable advance. He offered $24,000 per month, or about $266,500 for the year. There is no indication that Bun Soon had received permission to raise the price of the chandu he sold, which was fixed by the government. Also, the price of raw opium had been rising since the Indian Mutiny in 1857, and during 1860 it had climbed to nearly $1,000 per chest, a level it had not reached since the early 1820s. (See fig. 1.)

The final difficulty was political as well as financial. Since 1846, when Tay Eng Long, Cheang Sam Teo, and Lau Joon Tek first put the Johor opium farm together with the Singapore farm, the price for the Johor farm had risen rather unevenly. Between 1847 and 1853, the temenggong had been content to accept $350 per month for his opium and spirit farms. When the Johor ruler began negotiations with another group of Chinese in 1853 (possibly with Heng Bun Soon) for the Johor farm, Joon Tek had been required to increase the Johor rent to $1,000 per month. In 1855, it went to $3,500 per month.[11]

10. *SSR*, W 37, no. 38 p. 27.
11. *SSR*, R 28, no. 109; *SSR*, S 23, no. 161; *SSR*, S 25, no. 72; *SSR*, U 32, p. 153; *SSR*, R 31, p. 1; *SSR*, AA 26, no. 76. Temenggong to Blundell, 17 April 1856, *JLB*1.

Turnbull, suggesting this increase was the result of the temenggong trying to "shake free" of the joint farms arrangement, has stated, "In April 1855, he made a bid to sell the Johor tax farms by public auction, but Blundell forbade this and persuaded Calcutta to insist on the joint disposal of the Singapore and Johor opium and spirit farms."[12] The fault did not lie entirely with the temenggong but rather with the governor and the Indian authorities, who themselves had forbidden the joint auction of the farms in 1854 (see chap. 4) but when the farmers objected, quickly backed down.

Between 1855 and 1860, during the tenure of Governor Edmund Blundell, the Straits authorities seemed eager to convince Indian authorities that it was to their interest to ensure the continuation of the joint farms arrangement.[13] At the same time, every effort was made to allow the temenggong to obtain increases for the Johor farms. In 1857 he was able to get his share converted to a percentage (22.2 percent) of the total for Singapore's opium and spirit farms.[14] And in 1860, he asked for one-third but only got 25%, or $8,000 per month. This may have been excessive, but the temenggong was then claiming a population of 30,000 (mostly Chinese), while Singapore's 1859 population was estimated at 74,000, and only 40,000 Chinese. Even the resident councillor was willing to concede a five-to-four ratio between the Chinese populations of Singapore and Johor.[15]

As the time approached for the 1860–61 contract to end, the difficulties began to come to a head. The temenggong died in December 1861 and was succeeded by his son, Abu Bakar, who had become deeply involved in the civil war in Pahang and was supporting Bendahara Ali and his son Tun Koris against the other son, Wan Ahmad. Abu Bakar was using the close connection the Johor princes enjoyed with the Straits government to enhance his influence in Pahang. As early as 1857 he had actually been arrested by the resident councillor of Singapore and charged with piracy for interfering with refugee boats from Pahang. It was charged that he was flying the British flag from his mast at the time.[16] Reports in the *Straits Times* were highly critical of the temenggong, not only because of his alleged attempt to take over Pahang, but also because of the manner in which he was said to involve Singapore's government in his ambitions.

12. Turnbull, 1975, p. 283.
13. *SSR*, R 28, no. 109.
14. *SSR*, U 32, pp. 152–55; *SSR*, AA 35, no. 56.
15. Temenggong to Blundell, 1 December 1860, JLB1; *SSR*, AA 43, nos. 43, 44; *SSR*, BB 113, no. 149.
16. *SSR*, V 25, no. 108.

The paper also claimed he was receiving too much for his farms. The *Straits Times* reported in April 1861, as negotiations were in progress for the 1861–62 farm auction, that the temenggong "was receiving from the Excise Farmers through the Local Treasury upwards of $5,000 per month more than the gross sale of excisable articles in Johor amounted to." It further charged that he had been using this money in his war against Wan Ahmad. The fact that he was paid straight out of the Singapore treasury was emphasized to the government's embarrassment.[17] A later report claimed that Abu Bakar had boasted to the Pahang chiefs that the Straits government had become the collector of his revenue and that they would back him up with force in any fight with Wan Ahmad.[18]

Thus in April 1861 the new Straits governor, Orfeur Cavenagh, found himself between the opium farmer complaining of his losses, the *Straits Times* raising embarrassing questions about the temenggong's activities, and the temenggong himself still demanding one-third of the joint farms. Cavenagh wrote to the Singapore resident councillor and told him to break off negotiations with the temenggong. The joint farms had come to an end. The Singapore farms would be offered to Heng Bun Soon for the same price as the year before, minus the 25 percent that had been going to Johor.[19] Or, instead of $32,100 for the joint farms, Heng Bun Soon was offered the Singapore opium farm for $24,000, which he took.

The report of the sale, which took place on 15 April 1861, contained another interesting item: the spirit farm was bought by Cheang Sam Teo, who had also held it the previous year. He paid the extraordinary price of $6,600 per month, an increase of $3,525 over the previous year.[20] It is clear that Sam Teo did not get the spirit farm without a fight. If nothing else, this sale signaled the end of whatever remained of the old syndicate, and the heavy bidding over the spirit farm was essentially a declaration of war between the two major Chinese mercantile factions in Singapore (fig. 5). With the opium farm in the hands of one and the spirit farm in the hands of the other, matters were not exactly even, but that soon changed.

The *Straits Times* warned the public to be wary of bidding for the Johor farms when the temenggong announced a separate sale at Tan-

17. *ST*, 13 April 1861.
18. *ST*, 4 May 1861. See also a consistent series of stories, letters, and editorials in the *Straits Times* supporting Sultan Ali and encouraging a "civil war" in Johor: *ST*, 9 February 1861, 2 March 1861, 16 March 1861, and 23 March 1861.
19. Resident Councillor to Governor, 2 April 1861, *SSR*, X 21; *SSR*, U 42, no. 125.
20. *ST*, 20 April 1861.

jung Putri: "We assume the responsibility of telling British subjects to be on their guard when bidding for these excise farms of Johor, as the numerous petitions against the tyrannical and arbitrary authority exercised by the Temenggong and his factotums—show that no faith can be placed in the promises of the present ruler of Johor."[21] The warning was ignored, however, and the Johor farms were sold for the same price as the previous year, $9,050 per month for both opium and spirit farms.[22] Although the head of the Johor farms was said to be one Wee Bock Seng, the key figure in the Johor syndicate was Cheang Sam Teo, who had set himself up to do battle with Heng Bun Soon's Teochew syndicate.

Cheang's position was a strong one. As spirit farmer of Singapore, he was permitted to maintain a factory and a staff of revenue officers, or *chintengs,* to police the farm. As it turned out, he had employed a staff of some eighty revenue peons when the spirit farmer usually had only about ten. The smuggling of opium from Johor began almost immediately. By 18 May, less than three weeks after the new fiscal year had begun, Heng Bun Soon petitioned the government to increase the punishment for smuggling. He claimed that his revenue had declined by two hundred dollars per day since the beginning of the month. He also offered to pay three hundred dollars per month to hire thirty extra policemen and five sampans to patrol the Johor Strait.[23]

The Singapore newspapers were suddenly full of items about people being apprehended with illicit chandu. The chintengs of the Singapore opium farm began taking stiff measures to stop smuggling, but the fine was only one hundred dollars, and naturally the heads of the farms and the chief figures behind the smuggling could not be caught. It was only coolies carrying ten or twenty tahils of chandu who were actually apprehended. So eager were the chintengs to get to the ringleaders that they were quite willing to overstep their authority and bend the law. In one instance, Heng Bun Soon's chintengs raided a house occupied by one Cheong Ah Seng and discovered some contraband chandu. Although Cheong admitted ownership of the chandu, the charges against him were dropped, and the opium farmer tried to prosecute the actual owner of the house, from whom Ah Seng was renting it: one Cheo Teng Swee. Those charges too were dismissed. As the Straits records suggest, "This somewhat extraordinary proceeding on the part of the

21. *ST,* 13 April 1861.
22. *ST,* 20 April 1861; i.e. $8,000 for the opium farm and $1,050 for the spirit farm.
23. *SSR,* X 21, no. 87; *SSR,* R 34, no. 79.

opium farmer may be accounted for by the fact that Cheo Teng Swee's being the stepson of Bock Seng the present opium farmer of Johor and a conviction against him would have been very desirable for the Singapore opium farmer."[24]

It was not long before the forces of the Johor farmer and the Singapore spirit farmer were openly fighting with those of the Singapore opium farmer. Around the beginning of June 1861 the revenue officers of the Johor farmer seized some chandu being smuggled into Johor by some men said to be working for the Singapore opium farmer.[25] A few days later in Singapore, the opium farmer went after Cheang Sam Teo himself and sent some chintengs together with the police to serve a search warrant on the spirit farm on Telok Ayer Street. The spirit farmer's chintengs refused to allow them to enter and a fight began. Ultimately, the police forced their way in and found $300 worth of chandu (possibly about sixteen pounds at $1.50 per tahil), but it was thought that even more had been hustled out the back door during the fight. The *Straits Times* called on the government to break its contract with Cheang Sam Teo: "The Spirit Farmer has now forfeited all claim to the fulfillment of his contract and the Government would simply discharge its duty, if it were to withdraw the spirit monopoly from a man who has thus abused his trust."[26]

This sounds like a sensible solution, but the government, or more correctly, Governor Cavenagh, did nothing. For someone hard-nosed in his dealings with Asian elites, Cavanagh's apparent tolerance toward Cheang seems out of character and suggests an agreement with the spirit farmer, perhaps even a certain favoritism for him by the authorities. The government should have been suspicious when Cheang had doubled the rent for the farm in 1861 and had greatly increased the number of chintengs, actions that could only be explained by an intent to smuggle, which was exactly what he did. Why was Cavanagh willing to look the other way when the Hokkiens bent the rules? The events connected with the secret societies also had a bearing on the answer.

At virtually the same time that the rift in the revenue farming syndicate was taking place, another conflict was unfolding in the streets of Singapore. At the end of March 1861, as negotiations were proceeding for the letting of the farms, a fresh outbreak of secret

24. *SSR*, X 21, no. 108.
25. *ST*, 4 June 1861.
26. *ST*, 8 June 1861.

society violence occurred. The term *secret* is used advisedly here, because some of the groups involved were not usually counted among the true triad societies; rather, they were surname or "clan" groups, which were called "*seh*" or "seah." A riot, or series of riots, began on 31 March, reportedly between the Seh Tan (or the Tan clan group) and the Ghee Hock.[27] Another fight was reported on 18 April; this time, Lee Ah Kwang, the head of the Ghee Hin, and Chua Moh Choon, the head of the Ghee Hock, were arrested.[28]

A rather interesting explanation of the society violence appeared in the *Straits Times* of 27 April. The writer claimed to have interviewed the headman of the Ghee Hock, who would have been Chua Moh Choon. His account of the riots was that "the Grand Triad Hoey" or the "Hoey of the Heaven and Earth and Man connection" (e.g., the Tien-di hui) no longer existed in the Straits Settlements. He said that the recent death of the late "Grand Master" had caused the various clans that made up the society to split apart and start fighting among themselves. He also said there was a struggle for power among the heads of the various clans. How the Ghee Hock fit into this struggle is left unclear.

Blythe is of the opinion that the Ghee Hock was made up of the Teochew "element among the Triad fighters from Amoy which was responsible for the riots of 1854 and for the formation of this new addition to the Triad complex of Singapore." He notes, however, that the first mention of the group is around this time, in a police report dated 1 May 1860. It was said to have had a membership of about eight hundred. Chua Moh Choon a Teochew pepper and gambier dealer and a coolie broker, was generally identified as the leader of the Ghee Hock throughout the 1860s and 1870s.[29] It was not, reputedly, a surname group; but then, no other commentators had previously described the Tien-di hui as composed of such components.

According to this account, the Tan clan had control of some of the most desirable prostitutes in Hong Kong Street. When a member of the Seh Lim asked for one of the women, he was refused, and this led to a fight between the Tans and the Lims. The Seh Chua joined on the side of the Lims. Later on, the quarrel was supposed to have been patched up. The Lims were to give the Tans a pair of candles, and the Tans would reciprocate with a "wayang koolit" for the Lims.[30] The Tans

27. *ST,* 6 April 1861.
28. *ST,* 18 April 1861.
29. *ST,* 27 April 1861; Blythe, 1969, p. 80; Song, pp. 175, 187, 202.
30. "Wayang koolit" (*wayang kulit*) in this case referred to a Chinese shadow puppet play. It was quite common for triad-affiliated groups to stage traditional Chinese plays to

also engaged some Chua musicians to "give musical attendance," but when the latter asked to be paid, they were refused and beaten, which led to further rioting. Yet another disturbance was reported on 18 May, when it was said that the Tans had staged a demonstration and had marched down Carpenter Street (the scene of many of these incidents), carrying a banner saying "The Tan Tribe is Supreme" (*Tan Seah Oaan*).[31] These were only three of the incidents that had occurred in April and May of 1861; there were many more. While there is no mention of the revenue farm dispute in these events, their timing places them in the same context, and the Seh Tan was later shown to be an important actor in the revenue farm organization.

In June the editor of the *Straits Times* complained that riots had become a daily occurrence over the past two months: "The street fights among the Chinese are positively becoming a chronic disease—a sort of permanent institution. Day after day, the peace of the Town is broken by fresh disturbances. Sticks, stones and bricks are freely used, heads are broken, and at last the police interfere and the riot is quelled only to break out afresh the next day."[32] The writer was particularly concerned that the governor had left town and taken most of the troops and three of the steamers up the east coast, where the temenggong had finally gotten him involved in the Pahang war.[33] As for causes, the *Times* editor felt that part of the problem was the government's attempts to suppress gambling, but mostly "it is the old grudge brought from their native country, and only requiring opportunity to break out into open hostility."[34]

There was no attempt by the editor, nor any commentator at that time or since, to link these feuds to the revenue farms. They did not find it worth noting the simultaneity of the breakup of the syndicate and the breakup of the "Grand Triad Hoey," as it was called. Likewise,

---

honor the various patrons of their societies (see Vaughan, pp. 48–49, 52–53, 58, 85–87). One assumes these were the typical Teochew or Cantonese "operas" based on Chinese epics such as "The Three Kingdoms" and "Water-Margin," which are still popular today among Southern Chinese. The Malay term *wayang kulit*, or simply *wayang*, was generally used in the nineteenth century to describe any kind of Asian dramatic performance and did not necessarily just refer to Malay, Thai, or Javanese folk operas based on the Indian epics, the Ramayana, and the Mahabharata. Chinese shadow puppet plays are no longer performed in Malaysia to my knowledge.

31. *ST*, 18 May 1861. This would have been particularly offensive to the Ghee Hock, since Carpenter Street was part of their turf and was even known to the Chinese as "Ghee Hock Street" (Mak, 1981, pp. 116–17).

32. *ST*, 1 June 1861.

33. *Administrative Reports of the Government of India*, 1861–62 (IOR), V/10/19, pp. 29–30. This reports on the governor's operations on the east coast.

34. *ST*, 1 June 1861.

the rise of rioting and of opium smuggling were treated separately. One suspects a sort of naïvete on the part of Europeans not making some connection. This obliviousness is particularly striking when, in the same issue of the *Straits Times* that carried the above report on the secret society riots, one finds small items such as the one about some Chinese living on Thomson Road who burned down their own house on 26 May in order that "an adjoining attap house occupied by an opium shopkeeper might be consumed. Their intentions were fulfilled. The opium shop was burnt down and all it contained destroyed. Our informant states that on the morning of the 27th [the next day] the Chinese all along the road seemed in very excited state. This is one of the latest developments of the clan feuds."[35] It might just as well have been the latest in the opium syndicate feuds—if there was indeed a difference.

On the basis of synchronicity alone, it may seem speculative to conclude that the revenue farm conflicts were related to the secret society or to clan conflicts. There is more explicit evidence that not only were they connected but events were now driven by the revenue farmers rather than by conditions within the societies.

Writing in 1879, Vaughan, pointed out that opium smuggling during the 1860s had been "rife . . . in consequence of Hokkien and Teo Chew gentlemen being interested in the Opium Farm. If the Farm was sold to one race only, the other would do their utmost to smuggle contraband chandu into the place and ruin their rivals."[36] Vaughan blamed the fighting and smuggling on the speech-group distinction, probably with some accuracy. The Singapore opium syndicate controlled by Heng Bun Soon was clearly a Teochew organization, and the group under Cheang Sam Teo was Hokkien. But this did not necessarily mean that all Hokkiens in Singapore had lined up behind the Hokkien syndicate, all Teochews with the other. The situation was not so simple; the social and economic divisions in the society were more complex. For one thing, the Hokkien farmers controlled the Johor farms, in an area essentially dominated by Teochews. By contrast, in Singapore, where the Hokkiens were becoming the majority, the farm was run by the Teochew syndicate.

Thus, while ethnicity might explain hostility between the two syndicates, it cannot explain the full scale of the instability and division behind the violence occurring at that time. The key element here was

35. Ibid.
36. Vaughan, p. 20.

the ability of one or two persons to forge a kind of unity among several elements. To run the farms, one needed money, knowledge, and organization. As of mid-1861, no one had all three. A change in generations was occurring. The old syndicate had fallen apart with the death of the "monied man" on the Teochew side of the equation, Lau Joon Tek. It is also significant that the "grand master" of the Tien-di hui had also recently died. By the end of 1863, Cheang Sam Teo had also apparently either retired or died. With their disappearance went the whole complex network of alliances, agreements, dependencies, and special relationships that had undergirded the former syndicate.

In some cases, the change was from father to son. Cheang Sam Teo was replaced by his son, Cheang Hong Lim. On the Teochew side, the succession was less clear. Lau Joon Tek seems to have left no offspring. Heng Bun Soon, who appeared as the head of the Teochew syndicate, did not last very long, and there is little information on his background. His successor, Tan Seng Poh, was clearly someone of the new generation. These changes in the farming syndicates were paralleled by similar generational and administrative shifts in the local governments. Abu Bakar had just succeeded his father as temenggong of Johor in January 1862, and Orfeur Cavenagh had just taken over as the new governor of the Straits Settlements in the previous year.[37]

The Temenggong and the Governor

Cavenagh, a military man whose entire background had been in India, was a stranger to the essentially commercial world of the Straits. He saw little reason to abide by the sort of compromises and arrangements that had heretofore been the essence of British rule in the region. He took a hard line with Johor, demanding the implementation of his interpretation of British treaty rights to the very letter.[38] He took an activist role in intervening in the affairs of local states when they concerned the welfare of "British subjects," a category that included

37. Buckley, p. 676.
38. The entire period between October 1859 and July 1861 was marked by numerous incidents leading to Cavenagh's request for a clarification of the treaties of 1855 and 1824 regarding the status of the temenggong as an independent chief and the territorial extent of the state of Johor. Finally, in July of 1861, after an incident between some Johor Malay officials and some Chinese fishermen, Cavenagh decided to claim the entire width of the Johor Strait as British territory. See the fairly voluminous correspondence in the SSR, esp. R 38, no. 2; R 40, no. 113; R 34, no. 94; R 34, no. 100; V 3, no. 333; R 34, nos. 105, 118; V 27, nos. 410, 414; V 33, no. 227; and V 24, no. 207. In addition, there is the correspondence in the JLB1 for this period.

not only Europeans domiciled in the Straits Settlements, and Chinese who had been born there or who had been naturalized, but virtually anyone (except Malays) who had been resident in the Straits Settlements for five years.

Cavenagh's chauvinism was matched by Abu Bakar's desire not only to carve an independent state out of the virgin territory of Johor but, if possible, to take control of other Malay states. The temenggongs had managed to rise in concert with the British and had a substantial influence in directing the implementation of European power in the Malay world. Abu Bakar was moving, in the early 1860s, toward establishing himself as the major force in neighboring Pahang and the Negri Sembilan.[39] At the same time, he had formed his own alliances within the Singapore Chinese community, through which he maintained a measure of control over the thousands of Chinese who were now moving into Johor. There too, a new generation had taken control. The founding Chinese kapitan, Tan Kye Soon, had been replaced around 1860 by his "adopted son," Tan Cheng Hung, as both kapitan and kangchu of Tebrau.[40]

The Chinese migration to Johor and the consequent proliferation of "incidents" increased the friction in the Johor-Singapore relationship. During the early 1860s the arrests of Chinese or clashes between authorities and Chinese in Johor brought the intervention of the Straits government. Many of these incidents were related to the expanding gambier cultivation in Johor and the multiplication of kangkar settlements there. The system by which the temenggong parceled out the rights to open up river valleys to kangchus, who then brought in labor and cleared the jungle for plantations, had become an officially regulated version of the informal, Chinese practice that characterized the agriculture in Riau and Singapore. The leaders of these settlements were also given the revenue-farming rights in their own territories. These were enumerated in the surat sungais, by which kangchus were appointed.[41] Among the Chinese, the entire system of arrangements was policed by the Ngee Heng society, which was recognized as the only legal society in the state.

The struggles that had characterized the gambier cultivation in

39. Trocki, 1979, pp. 118–23.
40. Trocki, 1979, p. 106.
41. See Trocki, 1979, pp. 160–85, where I discuss the kangchu system in Johor in some detail. The typical surat sungai (they were actually form letters) listed the river, or tributary, that was granted and named the kangchu and his kongsi and usually the number of shares each kongsi member held. The revenue concessions held by the kangchu were given as "opium, spirits, pork, gambling, pawnbroking, and others." I have published translations of these documents and a list of surat sungai issued in Johor between 1844 and 1890 in my article describing the system. Trocki, "The Johor Archives and the Kangchu System" (1975).

Singapore continued in Johor. It was not long before the Ghee Hock tried to move into the state and organize its own branches there.[42] The system of indebtedness and forced deliveries of produce that had typified the agriculture in Singapore was also followed in Johor. The merchants of Singapore had simply expanded their area of operation, and the exploitative nature of the system naturally led to outbreaks of violence just as it had in Singapore.[43] Now, however, British authorities treated these disturbances as international incidents rather than as simply "clan wars." So long as this outstanding political tension remained between Singapore and Johor, there could be no real peace within the farming system.

The violence and smuggling that had begun in 1861 continued for the next two years. When serious rioting broke out in August of 1862, a curfew was imposed and the headmen of the various societies were deputized.[44] This did not stop the smuggling and double dealing over opium. The government was either unable or unwilling to interfere. Perhaps this was the cost of "farming out" the revenue. The government had decided to let the Chinese handle it, and that was what they were doing. The results were not always acceptable. Sometime later, the number of revenue cases coming to court decreased, but that did not mean that the smuggling had ceased. The superintendent of police complained about the manner in which the Singapore opium farmer was using the law. He said that people would be arrested with contraband chandu and charged but that when the case came before the magistrate, the opium farmer (who was the plaintiff) would drop the charges with no explanation. He said that the opium farmer was simply forcing the defendants (or their employers more likely) to pay him off personally, rather than paying the fine (one hundred dollars for a first offense) to the government. The superintendent also faulted the way in which the courts determined whether a particular lot of chandu was contraband: they relied on the testimony of the tester employed by the opium farmer. The superintendent claimed to have tested the tester and found him wanting.[45]

By the beginning of 1863, as the time for reletting the farms was

42. *JLB*1, 4 October 1859.
43. Trocki, 1979, pp. 113–17.
44. *ST*, 30 August 1862; *ST*, 6 September 1862.
45. *SSR*, W 42, no. 203. In cases where the provenance of a quantity of confiscated chandu was in question, the court would call the opium tester to decide. The tester was the opium "chemist" employed by the farmer. He usually tasted the drug in question and then declared whether or not it was farm chandu or contraband. In this case, the police superintendant had brought a falacious case to trial and presented the tester with two lots of chandu, both of which had been surreptitiously taken from the same lot of farm chandu. The tester judged that one was the farm product and that the other was contraband.

drawing near, the various parties began to seek some sort of settlement. Heng Bun Soon had continued to take heavy losses, and as early as August of 1862 he had asked for a remission of his rent because of the excessive smuggling; but Governor Cavenagh had refused to grant it.[46] In January 1863, Temenggong Abu Bakar, still smarting from his defeat in Pahang, was eager to build good will with Cavenagh. He offered an olive branch: "Our Friend is well aware that for the last two years during which the Opium Farms of Singapore and Johor have been held by separate persons, there had been much trouble and annoyance both to Our Friend's Government and to our own from smuggling being carried on between the two territories, and that it has been impossible to repress it notwithstanding all the efforts used for that purpose."[47]

Abu Bakar suggested a resumption of the former system whereby the farms for Johor and Singapore were let together to the same farmer. The governor responded that he was agreeable to a trial of the old system but would not take any less for the joint farm than the current rent for the Singapore farm: twenty-four thousand dollars per month. He allowed that the temenggong could have whatever was bid in excess of that amount as the rent for the Johor farm.[48] That was not a very generous offer, nor was the tone of the governor's letter very gracious. Abu Bakar refused this offer, but negotiations continued, and although the temenggong finally agreed, the deal still collapsed.[49]

A settlement of the farm issue would have to include all the concerned parties. In addition to the two, or possibly three, mercantile factions in Singapore, there were also the interests of the various societies or brotherhoods and their goals of defending or enlarging their economic monopolies or privileges. At the same time, the settlement would have to gain the agreement not only of the Straits government but also of the Dutch authorities in Riau and the Malay government of Johor.

On 21 February 1863 a lengthy and irate letter was sent by three persons styling themselves "Agents and Attornies [sic] for Heng Bun Soon." They were Tan Seng Poh, Sim Ah Nga, and Choa Ah Long.[50]

46. SSR, V 36, no. 333.
47. SSR, W 45, p. 7.
48. SSR, V 36, no. 24, pp. 392–93.
49. SSR, W 45, no. 127.
50. The letter (Agents and Attornies of Heng Bun Soon to the Secretary of Government, 21 February 1863, SSR, W 45, no. 127) is signed "Tan Seng Poh, Sim Ang Ah and Choa Long" in English. There are also Chinese characters for two of the names, the characters given for "Ang Ah" are more appropriately rendered "Ah Nga." It is possible that this is the person mentioned as the original renter of the Johor farms in 1846; see Buckley, p. 430.

The key person here is Tan Seng Poh, the brother-in-law of Seah Eu Chin and the manager of the latter's substantial pepper and gambier interests. No reason was given why Heng Bun Soon did not write on his own behalf, but it seemed that he was nearly bankrupt and the three agents had taken over. They claimed that Bun Soon had (as of February 1863) lost $120,000 on the opium farm and that they expected the losses would amount to $160,000 by the time the contract had expired in April. Bun Soon was not bankrupt, they said, only because of his wealthy friends and supporters (themselves). At the time, the farms were so deeply in debt that any profit would simply go to pay the interest. They had thus decided to give up the farms at the end of the contract, but then they had heard that the temenggong would be amenable to a reunion of the joint Singapore-Johor opium and spirit farms. They said that they had hired the lawyer F. E. Pereira to negotiate with the Singapore and Johor governments on their behalf, in the hope of making an arrangement agreeable to all parties.

The letter laid out the terms of the arrangement that had supposedly been made: Heng Bun Soon and company would get the Singapore opium farm for the same price (this was already in their contract); they would also get the spirit farm for the same price. There would thus be no increase in rent for the Singapore government, and the farmers would have an option on the farm for yet another year at the same rates. The temenggong had agreed to take $7,500 per month for his farms, which was a decrease of $1,550 below the 1861–62 contract.

Clearly the sticking point had been that Cheang Sam Teo would lose the spirit farm. It was on this point that the British government had refused, claiming that it had the right to either give the farms to Cheang Sam Teo or else sell them at auction. In their letter, Tan Seng Poh and colleagues had replied:

> We are at a loss to conceive how the present Spirit Farmer can have a better claim on Government than Heng Bun Soon. The Spirit Farmer might say that he and his friends have held the farms for a great length of time, but His Honor knows and they cannot deny that they have always made profits by the farms and would not have ever increased the rent . . . [of the opium farm] but for the bidding of Heng Bun Soon besides for other reasons best known to His Honor . . . [meaning the smuggling] we most humbly and earnestly do submit that they deserve no consideration from Government whatever on the other hand the claim of Heng Bun Soon is a very strong one.[51]

51. *SSR*, W 45, no. 127.

The governor, however, refused to give in. There is no indication of why he took this course; perhaps he feared a lawsuit from Cheang Sam Teo because of a possible option clause in the 1862 contract. Or perhaps he feared a combination among the farmers would hurt the revenue in the long run. In the end, Tan Seng Poh accepted the best deal he could get and took the Singapore opium farm again as the agent of Heng Bun Soon. A Singapore paper sarcastically remarked that he did it "with a view to recouping his losses." In the end, little had changed in the lines of opposition between the two syndicates (fig. 5).

It has not been possible to document the arrangements made for the 1863–64 farms precisely. At the beginning of 1864 Tan Seng Poh was still presenting himself as the agent and attorney for Heng Bun Soon (Sim Ah Nga and Choa Ah Long seem to have disappeared), but the following year Seng Poh was listed as the head of the Singapore opium farm. It is also not clear whether Cheang Sam Teo kept the spirit farm in his name in 1863–64 or whether he had already been replaced by his eldest son, Hong Lim. By 1865, however, Cheang Hong Lim was listed as the Singapore spirit farmer.

This result—two opposing syndicates carrying on a kind of guerrilla warfare in the streets—is attributable to the governor's decision. Cavanagh clearly refused to bump Cheang Hong Lim and his syndicate out the of the farm. Whether or not it was his intention to maintain another syndicate and thus prevent a possible monopoly, that was certainly a result. So was the violence and smuggling. It is difficult to see what was gained, or even what Cavanagh thought he was gaining, from this course. It does not seem to have been the act of a responsible official. Unfortunately, we have no way of learning the rationales behind most of these revenue farm settlements. Even the contracts the government must have signed with the farmers have, for the most part, disappeared from the colonial records collections. And the colonial governors, who kept minute records of the most trivial undertakings, have left not one single record of their own negotiations with the revenue farmers.

The point I wish to make here is that there were hidden agendas and policies that have not made it into the historical record. But, the circumstancial evidence is clear. Cavanagh played favorites several times. Each time, the results were of questionable benefit to the common good. He should not have let the Cheangs bid double on the spirit farm in 1861. He should have accepted the peace offering of the temenggong. He should not have let the Cheangs keep the spirit farm in 1863 after they had been caught smuggling. And later on, one of his last acts was to give Tan Seng Poh a sweetheart contract that was very costly to his successor, Governor Ord. No one can say, at this historical distance, whether these decisions were the result of stupidity, corruption, or misguided cunning. One thing is certain: not all the conflict among the Singapore Chinese was the result of the grudge brought from China.

In Johor, the settlement made in April 1863 is likewise murky. It appears, however, not to have been a successful one, because in September 1863 documents from the Johor Archives indicate that the Johor revenue farms had been taken over by Tan Hiok Nee. The next year temenggong Abu Bakar announced the so-called Tanjong Putri regulations, which led to a long and bitter dispute between Johor and the Straits government and many of the Straits merchants as well.[52]

There continued to be reports of smuggling in the papers, but the incidence of arrests and secret society violence seems to have decreased. At least, they were not reported, either in the newspapers or in the government correspondence. The years 1863–64 were, however, bad ones for Singapore's economy. By the middle of 1864 the city was in a serious depression. Two major European firms had gone bankrupt, lots of Chinese firms had failed, and there were runs on the banks.

The Temenggong's issuance of the Tanjong Putri regulations in October 1864 may very possibly have been a part of the split over the farms, and possibly caused by Cavanagh's intransigence. They were certainly the Johor ruler's attempt to separate his economy from that of Singapore. The regulations required that all boats coming to and departing from Johor had to stop at Tanjong Putri (Johor Baru) and get a pass. The regulations naturally gave a great deal of power to Tan Hiok Nee.

Tan Hiok Nee, or Tan Yeok Nee, was an "outsider" so far as the economic power structure of Singapore was concerned up until this point. He was a Teochew who came to Singapore when he was young. He began a career as a cloth peddler and became friendly with the Malays of Teluk Belanga, the temenggong's kampong in Singapore. During the 1850s he began buying up rather extensive kangchu rights in Johor and became established as a pepper and gambier merchant in Singapore with a shop in Boat Quay. In this particular period he seems to have emerged as the chief ally of Abu Bakar in his struggle against

52. This dispute has been discussed in C. M. Turnbull's "Pepper and Gambier Trade in Johore" (1959) and also in my own *Prince of Pirates*, chap. 5, pp. 129–43.

Tan Hiok Nee, the major China of Johor and member of the Great Opium Syndicate, dressed in his "mandarin" robes (National Archives, Singapore)

not only the government of Singapore but also the combined forces of the Singapore revenue-farming syndicates and their secret society allies. Although there is no direct evidence, it is probable that he was a very high ranking member of the Johor Ngee Heng.[53]

By this time, there were perhaps fifty thousand Chinese settled in Johor, and even though they were scattered around, the fact that they all belonged to the same secret society and that most of them were Teochews gave Johor a higher degree of homogeneity than existed in Singapore. Also, the forces of the Malay government had been thrown together with those of the Chinese societies and kangchus. The kangchu system, as it came to be organized in Johor at this time, was the latest, and perhaps the last, transformation or reincarnation of the pepper and gambier society. It is important, however, to note that taukeh domination was clearly established. The old kapitan China of Johor, Tan Kye Soon,[54] who had been the kangchu of Tebrau from 1844 to 1859 and the Ngee Heng headman in the state, may have represented the old kongsi brotherhood. The ascendance of Tan Cheng Hung as kapitan and Tan Hiok Nee as major, however, marked a transition in the leadership and an alteration in the character of the pepper and gambier society. Here too, the dynamics of the marketplace were asserting themselves. Just because he was a capitalist did not mean, however, that Tan Hiok Nee would automatically make common cause with the Melaka Chinese or the established economic leadership of Singapore—at least not until he had been adequately compensated.[55]

The Chinese merchants of Singapore, with the backing of the Chamber of Commerce and the Straits government, protested against the Tanjong Putri regulations. The move was seen as an attempt by Johor to monopolize the pepper and gambier trade, and it would also have made it possible for the Johor people to control the flow of opium more effectively. The Straits government claimed the regulations were a violation of the 1824 Treaty and countered by reasserting the earlier claim to the whole of the Johor Strait as British waters. If that were the case, then Abu Bakar had no power whatsoever to force boats that had already entered "British waters" to stop at Tanjong Putri.

In the correspondence one can see, if nothing else, a continuation of

53. Trocki, 1979, pp. 125–27.
54. Trocki, 1979, pp. 102–5. I have incorrectly given his name as Tan *Kee* Soon in my earlier book. I am informed that the correct pronunciation of this character in Teochew is "Kye" or "Kai" and not "Kee."
55. Trocki, 1979, pp. 124–25.

the attitudes and stances that had led to the split in the farms. On the one hand, the temenggong was pushing for more autonomy and greater recognition; on the other, there was a countering resistance by the Chinese merchants backed by the ruling forces in Singapore to maintain some control over their investments in Johor. These amounted to nearly one million dollars by October 1864. Most of these investments, largely loans to planters, had been made between June 1863 and December 1864. During these eighteen months, 31 surat sungais had been issued. This expansion nearly doubled the area of settlement in Johor, and with the issuance of the regulations in late 1864, before the plantations had begun to produce, it appeared that Abu Bakar was trying to take the money and run.

The Tanjong Putri dispute and the lack of agreement over the farms continued through 1865 and into 1866. The combination of pressure from the British government and the Chamber of Commerce have been given as the reason for Abu Bakar's eventual reversal. By the end of January 1866, Abu Bakar had withdrawn his regulations and made his peace with Cavenagh. Ostensibly, the crisis was ended when Cavenagh had convinced Abu Bakar that it would be better to collect a land tax on the gambier plantations (which Cavenagh seemed to think were bamboo plantations) and got him a trip to England to meet Queen Victoria. Winstedt and Turnbull have accepted this explanation, but my own research in the Johor Archives gives no evidence of land laws.[56]

Toward the end of 1866, it likewise appears that some arrangement was made to bring Tan Seng Poh into the Johor opium and spirit farms. Subsequent events really point to a conflict between Seah Eu Chin and the Johor ruler. The Tanjong Putri regulations seem to have been aimed at the Seah Eu Chin interests, which Tan Seng Poh had come to represent. The agreement with Tan about the Johor farms, then, marked a significant compromise by belligerent parties. Another result of this period seems to have been the emergence or creation of a group that included almost all of the pepper and gambier shopkeepers in Singapore. This was the Kongkek, otherwise known as the Pepper and Gambier Society. Under the leadership of Seah Eu Chin, the group seems to have been able to act in concert to suspend all investment in Johor during 1865. I believe that it was this pressure, rather than Cavenagh's policies, that changed Abu Bakar's mind. The creation of the Kongkek and the simultaneous consolidation of Tan Seng Poh's

---

56. Trocki, 1979, pp. 129–43; Turnbull, 1959, pp. 176–80; Winstedt, "A History of Johor," p. 108.

control over the Johor and Singapore opium farms represented a significant realignment of mercantile forces in Singapore. It appears that this new configuration left little room (except in Johor) for the old kongsi brotherhoods represented by the Ngee Heng.

Organizing the Great Syndicate

Once the Singapore and Johor opium farms were joined, the Singapore spirit farmer, who was still Cheang Hong Lim, had less of an advantage. He no longer had a territorial base from which to smuggle. For a while, there were no reports of serious trouble, but there must have been latent problems all along. By the end of 1868, the arrangement came unstuck again. This time, it is difficult to say what went wrong.

Data on the farms is only available for periods when problems arose. When things went smoothly, no one saw fit to comment on the farms, let alone discuss the intricacies of who was getting what from whom and for how much. But each crisis provides another little pocket of information, which, while it offers some insight into the affairs of the revenue farm, provides no broad perspective or continuity. There was a serious break in administrative continuity in British Malaya in 1867, with the Transfer, whereby control of the Straits Settlements was taken from the defunct East India Company by the Colonial Office.

The Transfer took place at a time when there were a lot of new people around. Governor Cavenagh was replaced by Harry St. George Ord. Soon after his arrival in Singapore, Ord found himself faced with a problem in the revenue farms. Once again, Johor seemed to be at the heart of the issue. The Singapore/Johor opium farm had been separated again in some way during the switch in administrations. Ord blamed the division on his predecessor; he could not imagine how Cavenagh could ever have let the Johor farm get separated from the Singapore farm: "It appeared . . . that before the Transfer the Singapore and Malacca [Melaka] Farms were let at $429,000 a year. They were re-let in 1868 when they terminated. At that time they were let separately from those of Johor. He had never been able to understand how such a step could have been taken by the former government. It lost us a large sum of money, as well as the persons engaged in the business."[57] Since Tan Seng Poh held both farms in 1868, Ord seems to

57. *Legco*, 21 August 1873, p. 124.

have assumed that they had always been joined. Apparently the whole series of events between 1861 and 1866 had been quietly forgotten, or were never clearly understood by the new administration. But the Asians and permanent residents of Singapore remembered them. Certainly the farmers themselves, particularly Tan Seng Poh, were well aware of the history of the farming syndicates. European reports suggest that Tan pulled a very neat trick, either on Cavenagh or with his connivance.

Newspaper reports of 1869 and 1870 and some Legislative Council debates from 1873 have made it possible to reconstruct the following account. They indicate that Tan Seng Poh had kept control of the Singapore opium farm during the period between 1865 and 1868.[58] In 1867 or 1868, the Singapore fiscal year changed, but apparently the Johor contract had been written in such a way that the two farm contracts got out of synchronization (fig. 5).[59] This provided an opportunity for Tan Seng Poh; for when the contract for the Singapore farms ran out at the end of 1868, he still had a year to go on his contract for Johor. This placed him in a very strong position when it came time to bid for the Singapore farms for 1869. The *Straits Times* commented, "General Cavenagh—ordinarily so watchful—not very long before his departure acquiesced in the separate sale of the Johor farm. . . . The result of this blunder was very seriously to jeopardize the sale of the Singapore Farm, and it was for some time feared—so great was the dread of smuggling that no buyer would come into competition with the lessee of the Johor farm."[60]

Again, one must question the intentions of Cavenagh. One must assume, with the *Straits Times* writer, that Cavenagh should have known better than to let the Singapore farms get separated from Johor, particularly under those circumstances. In doing so, he left a virtual time bomb for his successor. Cavenagh had been playing hardball with Tan Seng Poh since 1863, and probably longer. It is difficult to accept the judgment that he had, in the final days of his administration, been duped by the Chinese revenue farmer. His decision, placed in the context of earlier decisions taken regarding Cheang Sam Teo, suggests a questionable pattern. The silence of the official record on these negotiations is likewise suspect. Circumstances suggest that Cavenagh

58. *SSR*, R 46, p. 130.
59. Temenggong to Secretary of Government, 25 January 1867, J*LB*1. Abu Bakar informed MacPherson that Tan Seng Poh had been given the Johor farms for two years and eight months beginning 1 May 1867, or until 31 December 1869.
60. *ST*, 29 May 1869.

deliberately looked the other way, and we may suppose that he did not leave Singapore the poorer as a result. He does not seem to have been the first colonial governor to do so, nor was he the last.

Ord faced the perennial problem: the choice between smuggling and monopoly. The government could encourage competition to ensure that it received a reasonable price for the farms, but this always meant that there was a loser, who then turned to smuggling. Yet if one syndicate was allowed to control all the farms (e.g., the spirit farm, the Johor farms, the Melaka farms, and, as we shall see, the Riau farms), then the farmers could increase their profits by offering the governments involved a smaller rent. In fact, between 1861 and 1867, Tan Seng Poh had managed to keep the rent of the Singapore farm down to minimal increases (table 2). He appeared to be positioned to keep the Singapore farms for yet another contract with no major increase in rent.

If, however, he hoped to slide by yet another year with no major increase in rent by holding the Johor farm, Tan Seng Poh must have been disappointed when another "kongsee, sufficiently wealthy and plucky, stepped in" and the rent rose from $300,000 per year to $360,000 per year.[61] The new contender was Cheang Sam Teo's other son, Cheang Hong Guan, the younger brother of Hong Lim. At the same time he got the Singapore opium farm, Hong Guan seems to have also taken charge of his brother's interest in the Singapore spirit farm. The government, having gotten its way in terms of a high rent, now had to sit back and watch Tan Seng Poh extract his own price for losing the contract.

The same issue of the *Straits Times* hinted heavily that Tan Seng Poh, the Johor farmer, was behind the smuggling, which had again begun. The writer noted that the imports of raw opium into Johor had doubled since the beginning of the year. In February and March of 1869 there were reports of a suit against Seng Poh by Hong Guan. The paper gave no details, beyond reporting that Seng Poh won the case on appeal to the Supreme Court.[62] There were numerous smuggling cases in the courts during the first three-quarters of 1869, and later reports indicate that the smuggling went both ways. Tan Seng Poh lost about thirty thousand dollars from the Singapore farmer (or his agents) smuggling into Johor. But he also inflicted an equal amount of damage to the other side.[63]

61. Ibid.
62. *ST*, 13 February 1869; *ST*, 16 March 1869.
63. *Legco*, 1873, p. 124.

Complaints were also raised about the "oppressiveness" of the revenue laws. The rise of smuggling had convinced the government to stiffen the penalties and to put rather extensive powers of search and seizure into the hands of the revenue farmer. It was possible for the revenue farmers to use the laws simply to harass people by leveling charges against them, having them thrown into jail, and then dropping the charges several days or weeks later without explanation.[64] In May of 1869 a person who had been arrested after being falsely turned in by an opium shopkeeper returned after his release and killed the informer.[65]

Tan Seng Poh had established a very effective organization. Smuggling from Johor resumed with a vengeance. He even had Europeans working for him as couriers of contraband chandu in cooperation with Chinese shopkeepers in Singapore.[66] Actually, the *Straits Times* pointed out, since the usual gross profit on chandu sales was about 300 percent, the Johor farmer could just sit back and sell chandu wholesale to whomever he wished: "There would be nothing wrong, nothing suspicious in his contenting himself with one hundred percent on extensive sales—it would be his interest and his fair right to work the extensive operations as frequently as possible, and yet this would leave any enterprising smuggler two hundred per cent profit to stimulate his action, and to apportion against his risks of capture, forfeiture and fine."[67] In an attempt to outflank Tan Seng Poh, Cheang Hong Guan bought the Melaka farms when they were put for sale in early 1869; this gave him a base from which to move contraband from Melaka up to the Johor kangchu settlements then being made on the Batu Pahat River.

By the end of 1869, Governor Ord decided to take a hand in matters. The Johor farms came up for sale in November, and even though Tan Seng Poh made a substantial increase in his bid (his 1869 rent was $9,000) by offering Abu Bakar $12,000 per month for the Johor farms, Ord put pressure on the maharaja to accept Cheang Hong Guan's offer of $11,000. The *Straits Times* expressed some satisfaction in announcing the result of the sale, noting that it would give Hong Guan "comparative immunity from the losses his income has sustained during the past two years through the extensive smug-

64. *ST,* 26 April 1869.
65. *ST,* 22 May 1869.
66. *ST,* 18 June 1869.
67. *ST,* 3 June 1869.

gling operations that have been carried on from Johor and the adjacent islands."[68]

Actually, their optimism was premature. Not only did the smuggling not end, but Hong Guan went bankrupt. By the time he finished out his contract for Singapore, his rent was about two months in arrears.[69] Nor is it entirely clear that all the damage was done by Tan Seng Poh and the smugglers of his Teochew clique. Apparently there had been bad blood between the two sons of Cheang Sam Teo. When Hong Guan went bankrupt in 1870, his brother Hong Lim took over the farms in his own name, and this caused a bitter feud between the two brothers. As a result, in 1872, Hong Guan was even willing to admit complicity in a crime in an attempt to convict his brother.[70]

The final nail in Hong Guan's coffin appears to have been Tan Seng Poh's acquisition of the Riau farm. Again, there is no data on exactly when this occurred, but the newspapers simply announced the formation of what was called the "great opium syndicate" in November 1870. It noted that the opium farmers of Singapore had succeeded in making an arrangement to end the smuggling: "This arrangement is, we learn, the amalgamation of the Singapore, Rhio, Malacca and Johor farms into one, and they have also we heard, admitted Mr Tan Seng Poh, former Singapore farmer and present holder of the Rhio farm into their partnership."[71]

It is difficult to tell, from the outside and from this historical remove, the degree and type of pressure necessary for Tan Seng Poh to effect this arrangement. Both sides, must have had to swallow considerable pride as well as substantial financial losses in order to strike a bargain. Although the newspapers showed no marked increase in the number of smuggling cases after 1869, there were some indications of struggle. There was a renewed outbreak of secret society fights between the Seh Tan and the Ghee Hock. Incidents were reported in August, October, and November.

The papers began to speculate that the triad disputes were settled when the headmen were sworn in as special constables. (This meant that they had to parade up and down the streets in the hot sun.) These

68. *ST*, 23 November 1869.
69. *STOJ*, 17 June 1870; *STOJ*, 1 February 1871.
70. *STOJ*, 28 March 1872; *STOJ*, 25 April 1872; Song, p. 168. Hong Guan sued Hong Lim, Wee Bock Seng, Low Tuan Lock, and Tan Beng Chie for a conspiracy to forge Cheang Sam Teo's will. He admitted that he himself was a participant. The suit failed and Hong Lim and the others were acquitted, but Hong Guan was jailed for forgery.
71. *STOJ*, 8 November 1870.

events coincided almost to the day with the formation of the syndicate. The relationship between the farmers and these particular secret societies was only made public almost thirteen years later, by another Singapore Chinese, when the syndicate had long since collapsed. Tan Kim Ching, who was called upon to give evidence against a smuggling conspiracy in 1883, described the Seh Tan as the largest and most powerful society in Singapore. He implicated them in the smuggling that had broken out in 1883 and linked them to Tan Seng Poh: "When Tan Seng Poh was engaged some years ago in smuggling against Hong Lim, the Opium Farmer, he had employed over 100 of the ablest and most discontented of the Seh Tans in carrying on his operations, and when he had forced Hong Lim to take him into partnership, he kept these men on as chintengs and they have so remained and are kept now by the Spirit Farmer."[72]

One result of the amalgamation of the farms was the elimination of the need for so many chintengs and other employees. As long as there were two separate farmers, each needed its own organizations and establishments. The formation of one syndicate meant that the farmers could cut overhead costs substantially. If Tan Kim Ching's testimony was accurate in identifying the Seh Tan as Tan Seng Poh's gang, the Ghee Hock may have been allied with Cheang Hong Lim. One wonders what happened to this organization when the two farmers decided to settle. One assumes that a lot of "soldiers" were put out of work. With the strongest of the groups controlling the opium, the rest had to fight for control of the "illegal" vices, gambling and prostitution. One of the final results of this dispute, then, appears to have been the demotion of many of the secret societies from what may once have been "legitimate" employment under the auspices of an opium farmer.

Reasoning backward from this premise, it seems fair to conclude that despite constant objections to their presence and activities, the societies had been necessary to the functioning of the colonial system—at least until about the 1870s. It was only after that time that most of them can be clearly classed as "criminal" organizations. Until then, as the series of events outlined here suggests, the societies were the major forces *for* whatever law and order obtained among the Chinese population of Singapore, particularly in the rural areas. If they could "obstruct" justice by preventing people from testifying against them, they could also exercise rigorous and close control over the

---

72. CO 273/119, Exco Minutes, 17 February 1883, p. 323.

population. As agents of the opium farmer, this power was legitimized under the authority given by the revenue laws. The farmers maintained, it was said, the most "minute systems of espionage" as well as possessing virtually unlimited powers of search and seizure. If what we today call a "controlled" substance was found in someone's possession, the burden of proof was on him to show that it was not contraband. This applied, by the way, to Europeans bringing home a bottle of brandy; they too needed a license from the spirit farmer.[73] The loss of this legitimate role in the colonial economy was disastrous for the secret societies. The desertion by their wealthy mercantile patrons left them deprived of an institutional link to the most profitable sectors of the economy.

This account points up a number of contradictions or at least paradoxes inherent in the colonial system. The first of these is that a system that championed free trade depended, finally, on a monopoly. A ruling power that took much pride in its laws and system of justice was dependent upon an "illegal" and virtually totalitarian system of social control to maintain its tax base. And the very economy of Singapore depended on the mechanism of the opium farm for capital accumulation to occur. The mainstay of Singapore's local economy during most of the nineteenth century was the pepper and gambier agriculture. The total value of pepper and gambier exported from Singapore and Johor only constituted a small percentage of the total trade, but these products were virtually the only local ones, and they were the basis upon which most of the local Chinese fortunes were made.

Tan Seng Poh's connection to the family of Seah Eu Chin placed him in an extremely good position regarding the farms. As investors, the gambier shopkeepers also decided which areas would be developed, where labor would be sent, and the entire pace of expansion. As Emily Sadka has pointed out regarding the relationship between tin mining and revenue farming in the Malay states, the investors were in a position to cut back investments and withdraw labor if they did not get the farm.[74] No wonder Abu Bakar and Tan Hiok Nee finally decided in 1866 to come to terms with the Singapore syndicate. Investment in Johor between 1864 and 1866 had virtually ceased.[75] In Singapore, the organization of the Kongkek held the monopoly. They controlled investment, they controlled the revenue farms, they controlled the

73. Letter from "C.Z.-N.," *ST*, 26 September 1863.
74. Sadka, *Protected Malay States* (1968), pp. 333–35.
75. Trocki, 1979, chap. 6.

labor force, and they also controlled most of the retail trade done with the pepper and gambier labor force, not only in Singapore, but also in Johor, Riau, and Melaka.

If we look further, to Song Ong Siang's *One Hundred Years History of the Chinese in Singapore,* it is easy to see that the relationship between the revenue farms and pepper and gambier was a rather consistent one. Many of those whom Song mentions as having pepper and gambier shops are also mentioned as being involved in the revenue farms. In fact, a glance at the names reveals that some of the most well known and respected Chinese of Singapore in this period were either directly or indirectly linked to the opium farms. In fact, these links extended over two and three generations. I have already mentioned the Cheangs and the Seahs and the Tans (the sons of both Seah Eu Chin and Tan Seng Poh were involved in the opium farms). Other members of this group were the Tays, including Tay Eng Long, Tay Han Long, and his son Tay Ho Swee, and the Lows, including Low Ah Jit and his sons Low How Kim and Low Cheang Yee.[76] Another important member of this group was Tan Hiok Nee, who, when he decided to retire from his position in Johor, returned to Singapore and built a large Chinese-style mansion on Tank Road and invested in Singapore real estate.[77]

These individuals and families, all of them Teochews (with the exceptions of the Cheangs), all in the same complex of businesses, all intermarried and financially interrelated, came to form an important clique within Singapore's Chinese community. The group demonstrated remarkable staying power. Despite the changes of time, the decline of pepper and gambier, of opium farming, and of individual families, the institutionalized power has remained a permanent feature of Singapore's social and economic landscape.

At the same time, although their origins and connections are less clear, the Cheang interests also had remarkable staying power. Song has noted that other prominent Singaporeans, in this case Hokkiens, were associated with this clique. Both the father and grandfather of Dr. Lim Boon Keng, the founder of the Straits Chinese British Association and the most prominent Singapore Chinese of his generation, had worked for Cheang Hong Lim in the opium farm,[78] and other notable families were connected to the powerful financial clique these Hokkien taukehs formed during these years.

76. Song, pp. 119–20, 131–33, 141–42, 151–52, 167–70, 191.
77. Song, p. 335. Tan Hiok Nee's house later on became the headquarters of the Salvation Army and has been renovated as a museum.
78. Song, p. 259.

6   The Collapse of
Singapore's Great Syndicate

Since the early years of the nineteenth century, the revenue farms had been organically tied to the local pepper and gambier economy and the Chinese social institutions associated with it. As the economy changed and pepper and gambier agriculture declined in the Singapore area, farmers came to rely less and less on these ties to the local social network, secret or otherwise. Neither patron-client networks nor brotherhood oaths were an adequate defense against the processes of commercialization of the economy and rationalization of the colonial political system. The farmers' links to the enforcement and distribution networks began to resemble those between employers and employees. Capital became more important than loyalty. Property rights came to displace kongsi control of cultivated lands. Shopkeepers in the town more often than not actually held title to the plantations in the interior of the island and in the Malay states now under colonial rule, rather than being forced to rely on debt relationships. Moreover, the roads were better, the communications more regular, the police more numerous, and the arm of government much longer and stronger.

Another aspect of this change was the demographic shift in Singapore. The period after 1860 had seen the growth of a large urban working class. People working in jobs in the harbor or in packing or preparation or in the basic food, water, and transportation services of the city, now came to outnumber the population of agricultural labor. The urban population was more diverse than formerly and perhaps more atomized and thus more amenable to formal economic and police controls than were the old kongsi villages of the pepper and gambier planters. The kongsi villages of Singapore themselves seem to

149

have become smaller and much more settled communities. Their population declined as gambier exhausted the soil and the firewood reserves gave out. It was not until the 1890s that new investors such as Tan Tye and Lim Nee Soon saw these communities as valuable prospects for crops such as pineapples and, finally, rubber.[1]

For Singapore's revenue-farming syndicates, which by the 1870s had grown fat by monopolizing the sale of opium to pepper and gambier planters and their coolies, these changes were good news and bad news. The good news was that their job was much easier. The bad news was that it was almost as easy for their competitors, and there were new competitors. The possibility that somebody with more ready cash than the Singapore farmers could enter the field and bid for the farms began to seem more real. In 1880, for the first time since Singapore was founded, a syndicate led by a non-Singaporean acquired the farms (fig. 6). The Pinang merchant Koh Seang Tat had come to Singapore with newly made wealth from the West Coast tin states and simply outbid the well-entrenched Singapore syndicate.

The appearance of Koh Seang Tat as a bidder for the Singapore farms was the first in a series of attempts by the colonial government to intervene more deeply than ever before in the policing of the farming monopoly. The members of the Singapore pepper and gambier syndicate retaliated by initiating a new round of smuggling. In 1883 a new governor, Sir Frederick Weld, who was willing to stretch the letter of the law, mounted an effective campaign to arrest the smugglers and claimed success in establishing governmental control over the revenue system. British control of the kongsis had also improved considerably with the growth of the Chinese Protectorate, which both registered societies and had begun to keep a record, however inadequate, of the vast numbers of Chinese laborers coming to Singapore.

The establishment of taukeh influence in the previous decade simply provided an avenue for the colonial administration to extend control over the Chinese population. The taukehs having served their purpose, the British were anxious to dispose of them. During the 1880s a major goal of the colonial establishment seemed to be to break the power their own revenue farmers had gained within the colonial power structure. Thus, after 1880, revenue farmers ceased to be magistrates and justices of the peace and instead became as replaceable and interchangeable as their own employees.

1. National Archives, *Pictorial History* (1987), pp. 23–31; see also Pitt, pp. 199–201.

Figure 6. Opium-farming syndicates, 1870–1885

Nov 1870–1879

The Great Syndicate: Singapore, Johor, Melaka, & Riau opium & spirit farms
Farmers: Cheang Hong Lim, Tan Seng Poh, & Tan Hiok Nee

1879–1882

The First Pinang Syndicate: Singapore, Johor, Riau, & (Melaka?) opium & spirit farms
Farmers: Koh Seang Tat, Koh Cheng Hooi, & Khoo Teong Poh
Partners: Tan Keng Swee, Tan Kim Fuan, Lim Kwee Eng, Ong Beng Tek, & Khoo Thean Poh

1883–1885

The Second Pinang Syndicate: Singapore opium farm
Farmer: Chiu Sin Yong
Singapore Syndicate: Singapore spirit farm
Farmer: Tan Keng Swee
Johor
Opium farmer: Lee Chin Tuan
Spirit farmer: Lee Cheng Wha
Riau opium & spirit farm
Farmer: Tan Moh Yong

Sources: Legco, 1883 and 1886.

Pepper and Gambier and the Great Syndicate

Pepper and gambier agriculture in and around Singapore reached its zenith in the two decades between 1870 and 1890. Kangchu settlements were opened on virtually every river of appropriate size in Johor.[2] At the same time, pepper and gambier plantations had been opened on most of the major islands of the Riau-Lingga Archipelago including Bintan, Batam, Galang, Lingga, Singkep, the Karimuns, and

---

2. See Trocki, 1979, pp. 161–85, where I discuss the links between the Johor plantations and the Singapore mercantile elite.

other small islands in the vicinity. The finance, staffing, and servicing of all of these settlements were focused in Singapore, where some seventy-five pepper and gambier firms, grouped together under the Pepper and Gambier Society (or Kongkek) dominated the trade in the articles.[3]

Despite continuing reports of its demise, pepper and gambier agriculture persisted in Singapore as well. It is true that it contracted and lost population as the land and firewood supplies were exhausted in the 1860s. At some point, however, this decline slowed down; the planting settlements in the interior of the island persisted and became much more stable communities than in the 1850s and 1860s. Not only was the gambier cultivation expanding in the areas beyond Singapore, but at the same time prices were generally rising. Between the late 1860s and the early 1880s, the price of gambier went from around $2 to over $7 per pikul. During the same years, the price of black pepper went from just over $6 to over $15 per pikul. By the late 1870s gambier exports were nearing the value of three million dollars annually.[4] They continued to climb to about four million dollars by 1890 and then leveled off for the next twenty years.[5]

The period between 1880 and 1885 was when the expansion of the gambier cultivation more or less peaked. Cultivation did continue to increase, but it increased in places like Sarawak, the Malay Peninsula, and the interior of Sumatra.[6] It is unclear whether the Singapore-based system of controls extended quite so far, but if it did, it may have been on a more decentralized basis than in Johor or Riau. Within Singapore the pepper and gambier cultivation had ceased to be the principal employer of labor, and this change greatly reduced the base of consumers for the Singapore revenue farmers. The system of financial controls and indebtedness that was dominated by the well-integrated machine put together by Tan Seng Poh seems to have been at its zenith in 1879, when he died.[7]

Tan Seng Poh's system of financial controls lay behind what Singapore merchant W. G. Gulland called the "great opium syndicate." The amalgamation of all the major farming syndicates including Singapore itself, Johor, Riau, and Melaka under the three-man partnership of Tan Sen Poh, Cheang Hong Lim, and Tan Hiok Nee drew its strength

3. "Chinese Hong List," SSD (1880), ix–xii.
4. Legco, 1880, pp. 116–23.
5. CO 273/327, G.D. No. 18519; G.D. No. 201, 30 April 1907, Statement F.
6. SSADR, 1904, pp. 542–52; SSADR, 1906, p. 310.
7. Song, p. 203. Tan Seng Poh died on 13 December 1879.

from the Kongkek and the Seh Tan. A surname group, the Seh Tan was Tan's police force, the chintengs of the revenue farm. The Kongkek merged all the pepper and gambier merchants into one large organiza-tion, with the dominant bloc the pepper and gambier holdings of Tan's brother-in-law, Seah Eu Chin. Tan Seng Poh thus held in his own hands the controlling elements of the local economy, which was a combina-tion of commercial capitalist enterprises constructed around "tradi-tional" forms of association and social control, the brotherhoods, or secret societies. It was a free enterprise monopoly. The system had created a considerable accumulation of labor and capital, and with the catalyst of opium, it had yielded great profits. Its construction had been largely the work of Tan Seng Poh. As Gulland said of him, "It is the duty of the head of the Farm to judge of the means and position of any probable opposition and to decide whether the new concern should be fought, squared, or to what extent taken into partnership. A very anxious time Seng Poh must often have had, but he was a very able man and appeared to manage matters highly to the advantage of himself and his friends, all of whom seemed to grow rich."[8] Tan Seng Poh's other business interests included the Alexandra Gunpowder Magazine, which he held together with Lee Cheang Tee and his nephew Seah Cheong Seah. Seng Poh was also a shipowner.[9] He gained recognition from the government, was appointed a justice of the peace in 1871, and was elected a municipal commissioner for three consecutive terms.[10]

Tan Hiok Nee, his counterpart in Johor, was perhaps even more highly ranked there. At some point in the early 1870s, he was made the major China of Johor by Maharaja Abu Bakar. He continued to hold his extensive kangchu concessions, mostly through intermediaries throughout eastern Johor, until the 1880s, when he seems to have sold them off and reinvested his money in house property in Singapore. During the 1870s, however, with Tan Seng Poh, he dominated the pepper and gambier business throughout the region.[11]

Cheang Hong Lim, the third partner in the triumvirate, was from the second generation of the family that had been a partner in almost all the Singapore farming syndicates since the 1840s. Hong Lim had his own firm, Chop Wan Seng. There is little information in Song on nature of his other business interests besides revenue farming, but

8. Quoted in Song, p. 132.
9. *SCD* (1863), p. 49.
10. Song, pp. 131–33.
11. Trocki, 1979, pp. 125–29, 134–35; Song, p. 335.

Yong Ching Fatt notes that he was a shipowner and an owner of house property in Singapore. Two of his most prominent partners were Wee Bock Seng, who had been involved in the Johor farm in 1861, and Low Thuan Lock. Hong Lim also gained a reputation as a philanthropist, founded a boys' school, built and maintained a public garden known as Hong Lim Green (now part of Hong Lim Park), and constructed a market, which also bore his name. Links to some form of triad organization are suggested by his links to the Geok Hong Tian Temple, which he also established, on Havelock Road.[12]

A measure of the acceptance and respectability enjoyed by the opium farmers is apparent in the newspaper report of the festival put on by the farmers in September 1869: "The Chinese Festival given by the Opium and Spirit Farmers here at their residence at Teluk Ayer, last Saturday evening, passed off very successfully. A large number of ladies and gentlemen were present, among whom were H.E. the Governor and Lady Ord, and several Government Officials. The illuminations were on a very superb scale, there being no less than thirteen lamp posts specially erected for the occasion."[13] Revenue farmers, secret society heads, wealthy merchants, and colonial officials had created a rather comfortable arrangement by midcentury. Just as it seemed to have become institutionalized, however, it was beginning to change, partly as a result of its own success and partly as a result of the new forces entering the region from Europe.

The Decline of the Secret Societies

The concentration of economic and political power represented by the great syndicate had a direct impact on the role of the Chinese secret societies in Singapore. These organizations, particularly the Ngee Heng, had formerly been dominant forces both in the pepper and gambier agriculture and in the revenue farming system. Where the agriculture persisted, the societies seem to have stabilized, as they did in Johor, where the society itself gained a monopoly. The nostalgic memories of Yap Pheng Geck of his boyhood home in the old kangkar of Sedili Kechil show the persistence of paternalistic and traditional patterns of society.[14] This bucolic atmosphere may have come to

12. *SSD* (1877), 101; Song, p. 169; Yong, "Chinese Leadership in Nineteenth Century Singapore" (1967).
13. *STOJ*, 10 September 1869.
14. Yap, *Scholar, Banker, Gentleman Soldier* (1982), pp. 2–16.

characterize the kangkars of rural Singapore as well. But these conditions in the rural areas were not matched by social peace within the rapidly changing urban society of Singapore.

On the contrary, the years after the establishment of the great syndicate were marked by repeated outbreaks of rioting, secret society disputes, and antigovernment protests. There were disturbances caused by fights between the Ghee Hin and the Ho Seng secret societies in March 1871; between Hokkiens and Teochews in October 1871; against the government in the so-called Veranda Riots in October 1872; between the Ghee Hock and the Ghee Hin in December 1872; and between the Ghee Hin and the Hai San in May 1874. The last major riot of the 1870s occurred in December 1876 and was directed against the government as a result of the new post office regulations.[15]

It is entirely possible that each incident simply erupted as a result of immediate and situational causes and had nothing to do with the ones that preceded or followed it. Because they occurred with such frequency, however, most observers sought general causes and patterns. In his report of November 1873, J. W. W. Birch, the first resident councillor of Selangor (in the 1870s), said there were two types of riots: those between "kongsis" and those directed at the government. He lumped the Hokkien-Teochew riots together with those between specifically named societies. He also pointed out that antigovernment riots, such as the Veranda Riots, could easily lead to "faction" fights among the various groups of Chinese.[16]

Other commentators at the time tended to blame the disturbances on the presence of *samsengs,* that is, toughs or secret society fighters. Much of the testimony given at the time indicated that these men were not perceived to be under the control of the leading members of any society. Comber has also noted a tendency in the 1873 report to blame the police, and he has questioned the tendency of the government to rely on both the guidance and testimony of such persons as Tan Seng Poh, the merchant Whampoa (Ho Ah Kay), Tan Swee Lim, and other so-called headmen. The reports do show that the government placed very heavy reliance on these persons.[17]

15. Basic sources for these disturbances are the CO 273/165, G.D. No. 59, 25 March 1871; G.D. No. 247, 24 October 1871; G.D. No. 263, 8 November 1871; G.D. No. 29, 2 May 1872; see also Song, pp. 166, 175, and CO 273/65, G.D. No. 14, 18 January 1873; G.D. No. 23, 30 January 1873; G.D. No. 39, 12 February 1873; G.D. No. 43, 13 January 1873; G.D. No. 84, 27 March 1873; and Lee, 1978, pp. 75–81.

16. "Memorandum by H.E. the Governor with Respect to the Suppression of Chinese Riots," pp. 154–55, CO 273/65, G.D. No. 14 January 1873.

17. Comber, pp. 140–53.

While it may indeed be true that the police were incompetent and, when given the opportunity, could act in an arrogant and high-handed manner, the other observations are also not without validity. In the first place, it does seem that during the administrations of Governor Ord and also Governor Archibald Anson (1867–80), the tendency was for the government to rely on the "headmen," generally meaning the revenue farmers and other prominent Chinese in Singapore such as Seah Eu Chin, Tan Kim Ching, Tan Beng Swee, Whampoa, and a few others. This reinforced the class stratification within Chinese society by essentially giving recognition to a merchant oligarchy through appointments to such positions as justice of the peace, magistrate, and municipal commissioner. Often these men included the very heads of the secret societies. Vaughan, writing in 1878, approved of this line of action, noting that since he came to the Straits in 1856, "no instances have occurred to the writer's knowledge of witnesses being sent out of the colony and the ends of justice being frustrated by the connivance of the Hoeys; and it is no unusual occurrence at the present time for the chiefs of the secret societies to give up offenders of their own societies to the police authorities." He went on to point out that the societies served a generally beneficial role in the administration of justice as carried out by the elders and headmen resolving their own differences: "Thousands of complaints, both civil and criminal are thus disposed of. Were all these complaints brought into our courts of law the staff of the Magistrates and Judges would have to be doubled or trebled."[18]

Vaughan's was not an isolated sentiment. In the *Straits Gaurdian* at about the same time, a lengthy article pointed out that the "Government has no direct means of communication with the lower class Chinese, and it is this work which the Secret Societies carry on."[19] What emerges here is an informal variety of indirect rule. So far as government was concerned, the heads of the societies had been co-opted into the service of the state. The colonial rulers had essentially foregone the government of the Chinese masses and left it in the hands of these leaders. This was the essence of the free trade policy.

Although the system was exceedingly cheap, it flew in the face of the professionalism of the new breed of colonial officers beginning to find positions in the Straits Settlements and pushing forward the expansion of the colonial state. The major opponent to Vaughan's laissez-faire view was William Pickering, the first "Protector" of the Chinese, who

18. Vaughan, pp. 110–11.
19. *Straits Guardian*, 17 February 1877.

was a proponent of a vigorous policy of registration and suppression of the secret societies. His views were highly acceptable to the new governor of the Straits Settlements, Sir Frederick Weld, who replaced Anson in 1880.[20] In the long run, this view tended to prevail, at least officially. Of course the laissez-faire policy was never the sort that was consciously formulated and promoted; rather, it just evolved and was defended after the fact in the terms given by Vaughan. The unstated corollary of that policy was the creation of a class of Chinese or native collaborators.

The other problem with the compromise policy of the earlier governors and administrators was that it carried its own set of contradictions and ultimately broke down of its own accord. As I explained in the last chapter, agreement among the societies' leaders and amalgamation of the farms meant reduced security costs but also unemployment for those groups not needed for farm security. With the Seh Tan providing the security, groups like the Ghee Hin were left to fight for control of the less lucrative and illegitimate vices of gambling and prostitution.

The only secret society that seemed to flourish during the 1870s was the Ghee Hock, led by Chua Moh Choon.[21] Not only did it probably have the largest membership in 1876, but Pickering claimed it was the best disciplined.[22] Blythe's remarks about Chua exemplify the ambivalent respect some Chinese leaders had won by this time:

> Pickering referred to his 'long career of intrigue' and declared that he was much feared by his countrymen, although in fact for some years before his death he had found that the best policy was to be on the side of the Government, and great use was made of him in keeping peace not only among members of his own society but also between other societies and

20. Weld's attitudes in Malaya have been characterized by Eunice Thio in *British Policy in the Malay Peninsula* (1969), pp. xv–xvi, 24, 108–9. He was a soldier of the British Empire who had begun his career in the Maori wars in New Zealand. He seems to have been something of a chauvinist and had little time for compromises with "natives." I have discussed his stormy relations with Abu Bakar of Johor, and a similar contempt for Asians characterized his relations with the Chinese. See also Lovat, *Life of Sir Frederick Weld* (1924).

21. Recently the gravesite of Chua Moh Choon has been discovered near Nee Soon Village by the Seletar River. Despite the fact that all nineteenth-century sources associate him with the Ghee Hock, the characters for Ngee Heng are carved on his tombstone: Chng, "On the Discovery of a Century-Old Grave" (1987). This suggests the Ghee Hock was some sort of offshoot of the original Ngee Heng. Blythe and some other writers have given convincing evidence to contradict Comber's contention that the Ghee Hock was a Hokkien society. The sources seem unanimous in showing it to have been a Teochew group.

22. Wynne quotes Pickering on p. 363.

clans. To the Chinese of Singapore, Chua Moh Choon was the embodi-
ment of power. His word was law because he had the means to enforce it.
Not only was he the unchallenged head of the largest and most unscrupu-
lous Hoey in the town but he was also in the confidence of the principal
officers of the Government, and was thus in a position to blacken the
name of anyone who failed to do his bidding."[23]

An important component of his power, in addition to the Ghee Hock,
which he personally controlled, was his role in the coolie-broking
business,[24] a particularly important one in a place like Singapore,
where the government took no hand in enforcing labor contracts. By
contrast, in Johor and the Netherlands Indies, if a coolie absconded, he
could be brought before a magistrate and returned to his plantation,
often with a penal sanction. In Singapore, the only agency to enforce
these contracts, upon which the pepper and gambier business depended, was the secret societies.[25] By the 1870s, Chua was one of the
major procurers of labor in the town.

The old Ngee Heng had fragmented and was now represented by the
ethnically based sections of the Ghee Hin.[26] The members of the secret
societies were moving in two directions. On the one hand, the more
affluent gained a degree of acceptance within the mercantile oligarchy
as many of the older leaders became shopkeepers. The societies under
their charge had gone from being brotherhoods of laborers to being
crimping agencies, the tools of the merchants. As such, they served the
forces of law and order. On the other hand, the societies dominated by
the financially unsuccessful were taking on the character of urban slum
gangs. This split in the brotherhoods was exacerbated by the continuing arrival of new "soldiers" from China.

The years 1871 and 1872 saw events in China quite similar to those
of 1853 and 1854. After the disruption of the Taiping Rebellion, the

23. Blythe, 1969, p. 211.
24. Song, pp. 175–76.
25. See Tan Seng Poh's remarks on the problem of absconding coolies in "Report of
Committee to Consider and Take Evidence upon the Condition of Chinese Labourers in the
Colony," *Legco* 3 November 1876: "As there is no written agreement, a man may run away,
and, if he is not stopped, may deny that he owes anything, and there may be a row. In Johor,
if a man runs away and is caught, he is taken before the Maharajah, who makes him go back.
It would be a very good thing if there was a law to punish runaway coolies. Among a
thousand men not nine make written agreements, they don't think it worth while. If there
was a law enforcing the agreements and punishing runaways, written agreements would be
universally adopted. At present you can only sue a man civilly, and of course it is not worth
while doing so, it is like running after the wind" (p. cclviii). See also p. 22.
26. Comber, p. 291. Comber gives a list showing that in 1878 the Ghee Hin was
composed of Hokkien, Teochew, and Hainanese branches.

northeastern part of Guangdong Province, especially the Teochew area around Shantou (Swatow) had fallen into a "chronic state of insurrection and class warfare." In 1872 Robert J. Forrest, the British consul at Shantou, reported that the whole district had formerly been divided into quasi-independent townships, each one under its own headman; feuds and clan fights prevailed throughout the country. The Chinese authorities had virtually no power over the inhabitants of these districts until 1869, when a British officer, a Commodore Jones, prevailed upon the "viceroy" of Guangdong to join him in sending a force against the villagers of Ou-ting-pei, a place with about ten thousand inhabitants and "the most powerful in all this turbulent district, and was chief of the so-called 'eighteen villages' which had leagued together against foreigners." The head of the Chinese force was a General Fang, who effectively "pacified" the district, mainly by beheading leaders and burning villages. The campaign led to a substantial emigration from the Shantou area. Forrest suggests that in the years since 1870 some one hundred thousand men had left the region, mainly for Saigon and the Straits Settlements.[27]

The influx of fighting men added to the instability of Chinese society in the Straits Settlements. While it is very difficult to get at the lower-class view of events, it appears that the sentiments of many of the lower-class Chinese in Singapore were directed against the very leaders upon whom the British government had come to rely. There is thus a clear suggestion of something approaching class warfare in the riots of the early 1870s.

There is little information on the first two riots in 1871 other than that the first was between two secret societies and the second between the Hokkiens and Teochews. The third, the so-called Veranda Riots, were the subject of a major government inquiry largely because the demonstrations were directed against the government.[28] The general tenor of the findings was that the riot grew out of a "misunderstanding" on the part of the police, who had issued an order to force hawkers of cooked food to remove their stalls from the five-foot ways or the covered sidewalks in front of the shop houses of the town. The removal of the food sellers was not the intention of the original ordinance, but somehow the police order never got cleared by the colonial secretary. The police who enforced the order were said to have demanded bribes and to have mistreated the hawkers and broken up

27. Forrest, "Political Summary" (1873).
28. "Report," *Legco*, 4 November 1872, pp. 1–4.

their stalls when they refused to pay. The hawkers went in a group and carried their protest to some of the influential Chinese merchants (e.g., Tan Swee Lim, Tan Seng Poh, Whampoa, etc.). This was the way the headman system was supposed to operate, but on this occasion, the hawkers got no satisfaction. Failing to get any sort of positive response, a riot began which was essentially blamed on the samsengs who "took advantage of the situation": "The persons principally engaged in the disturbances were without doubt 'samsengs' or fighting men, and the rowdies of the town, who took advantage of the dissatisfaction amongst the hawkers, a harmless and inoffensive kind of people, to create a riot for the purposes of looting and theft."[29]

The report also noted the recent arrival of the "hordes of rowdies and bad characters who have infested the district (Tay Chew) near Swatow." Mention was also made of the fact that some thirty-two hundred coolies had arrived on two steamers within a couple of days of each other and that these arrivals had crowded the town and left it under the control of the secret societies. The bulk of the eighty-page report essentially blamed poor police work and expounded what might be termed the "riff-raff" or "outside agitator" theory of riot causation. There are, however, several suggestions in the report that much of the protest was directed against the town's Chinese power structure.

Tan Seng Poh's carriage was attacked and Whampoa's windows were broken. The report also contains a translation of a placard put up by the demonstrators:

> There is a Hokkien Baba living in Kampong Malacca with an Englishman—(this man) with others farms the 12 monopolies, which consist of nearly all the kinds of business and labour carried on in Singapore such as medicine, barbers, tailors, etc.
> Now all these people by blood and sweat barely make enough to keep life together, and if these trades are to be farmed out, then surely evil and ruin will follow. . . . Now if this man is not killed it will not be acting in accordance with the will of Heaven.[30]

The general details of the placard show a good deal of misinformation. The "Hokkien Baba" may be a reference to Cheang Hong Lim, but there is no evidence that he lived with an Englishman, although he was no doubt seen by these newcomers as one who associated himself with the English. It is possible that the reference might have been to Tan

29. Ibid., p. 3.
30. Ibid., app. E.

Kim Ching, a shipowner, rice trader, an associate of the prominent Scottish merchant W. H. Read, and a man known to be associated with the Ghee Hin on the peninsula. The placard indicates that virtually everything was thought to be monopolized and that there were probably people going around, legally or illegally, collecting protection money. The perception among the lower-class Chinese was, accurate or not, that the entire system was centralized and farmed out to the highest bidder. A few years later, when the Chinese Post Office Riots occurred, it was assumed that the Chinese shopkeepers who handled the business of sending remittances to China were "farmers." Of course the government denied this, but the popular *perception* was clear, and probably the Teochew merchants who were engaged in the business did have a monopoly, official or not.[31]

My hypothesis is that the great opium syndicate merely represented a single aspect of what might be termed the *informal* power structure of the colony. The integration of the major farms and the resolution of differences by the major Singapore Chinese mercantile factions which took place in 1870 had given a focus to the various groups affiliated with them. The government's dependence on the farms and the recognition given to the farmers and to the other headmen was, to the average Chinese, a legitimation of the system by which these men exercised power. It was a tacit acceptance of the paramount role of *certain* secret societies or brotherhoods and of the exclusion of others. To the average Chinese, the move to chase the hawkers off the five-foot ways was simply one more attempt by the monopolists to tighten their control. The situation was only exacerbated by the arrival of so many aggressive newcomers where every bit of turf was already spoken for. The key element, however, both in the Veranda Riots and in the Post Office Riots, was a response to felt oppression. In fact, during the Post Office Riots, persons such as Tan Seng Poh and Low How Kim were actually named on the placards as the oppressors.[32]

The riots in the 1870s were quite distinct from those that convulsed the island in the 1850s. The latter arose out of economic competition between the pepper and gambier cultivators. The outbreaks of that period, and the long twilight struggle of the 1860s between the various groups as the great syndicate was being formed, must together have sorted out a great many of the issues that divided the Chinese in the

31. Lee, 1978, pp. 76–77.
32. Song, p. 191. Low How Kim was listed as the chief assistant of the opium farm in 1877. After 1880 he is said to have received help from Tan Hiok Nee and gone into the pepper and gambier business. See also *SSD* (1877), 102.

pepper and gambier agriculture. After 1870, there were no reports of violence in the countryside. Riots were confined to the city. The pepper and gambier agriculture seems to have been unaffected. Compared with the events of 1851 and 1854, the 1870s riots were mild. The quiet in the rural areas suggests that the system of domination developed under the opium syndicate was, if nothing else, effective.

The long-term problem for the government, however, was just that effectiveness. The system placed a great deal of power in the hands not only of the farmers but also of the Chinese groups supporting the system, probably including secret societies and other groups besides the Seh Tan. As of 1876, none of the Seh groups had been registered as "dangerous" societies. Vaughan, writing a few years later, indicated that groups like the Seh Tan should be placed in the "dangerous" category, but until the 1880s, only six societies were in that classification.[33] Moreover, people like Chua Moh Choon, the acknowledged head of the Ghee Hock, had acquired a degree of respectability by the 1870s.

If the dissatisfaction of the working-class Chinese helped to fuel the riots, the influence of the opium syndicate also bothered some British administrators, particularly Pickering. To him, the syndicate seemed an anomaly that placed too much power in the hands of private persons and relied too much on informal agencies for the operation of the government. During the 1870s he gradually brought several societies under surveillance, and by the 1880s he was in a position to help advance direct government control to another level.

The Conspiracy of 1883 and the Fall of the Syndicate

It is difficult to account for the collapse of the syndicate with a single cause; as in the past, several situations came to a head at the same time. There was another change of generations. By 1879 Tan Seng Poh and

33. "Report of Committee Appointed to Consider and Take Evidence upon the Condition of Chinese Labourers in the Colony," *Legco* 3 November 1876, p. ccxlv. This report listed nine dangerous societies, including two branches of the Ghee Hin, and gave total secret society membership in Singapore as 11,507. Pickering's list, dated January 1878, published in Comber (p. 291), listed ten societies. He had added the Hainanese branch of the Ghee Hin to the Hokkien and Teochew. His list gave a total membership of 12,371. Vaughan (p. 113) lists roughly the same societies but also the "Hin Beng Hong," which he claims was the Seh Tan society. The other two, "Yeat Tong Koon" and "Tong Ngu Hong," he also considered "tribal" societies like the Hin Beng Hong and "quite as dangerous as to the peace of the colony as the Ghee Hin."

Cheang Hong Lim had been involved in the farms for nearly twenty years. Seng Poh died in that year, and Chua Moh Choon, long an éminence grise in Singapore's secret society world, died less than six weeks later. It is unclear whether Seng Poh had even bid to keep the farms that year, nor is there any discussion in surviving sources of why the syndicate did not fight a little harder to hold onto the farms. It does appear, however, that the syndicate just sort of died of old age. Tan Hiok Nee seems to have disposed of his holdings in Johor at about the same time, or perhaps even a little earlier, and Cheang Hong Lim retired in 1879 as well.[34] Tan Seng Poh's business, it appears, had been taken over by his son, Tan Keng Swee, while Cheang Hong Lim had given his business over to the management of his young son-in-law, Lim Kwee Eng. Whether the old generation had turned over their affairs before or after they lost the farm is not entirely clear. The syndicate did, however, lose the farm at the end of 1879.

The new syndicate was not only composed of essentially new people but also of outsiders. A syndicate led by Koh Seang Tat, the most prominent member of the third generation of the Koh clan of Pinang, had come down to Singapore and outbid the local syndicate for control.[35] The fact that the challenger came from outside is again an indication of how complete was the power of the former kongsi. All of the competition inside Singapore had simply been absorbed or eliminated. There can be little doubt that the government was glad to see a new face in the auction. Opium revenues had ceased to rise with the population. The power of the Tan-Cheang-Tan syndicate had apparently become so pervasive that they had been able to hold the farms with only minimal increases for well over a decade. From 1867 to 1879, the yearly rent for the opium farm remained stuck between $350,000 and $400,000 (table 2).

These relatively low increases, less than $50,000 over a decade, indicate that the farmers and the other members of their syndicate must have been doing very well for themselves. Even the figures for the last three years are slightly deceptive. The contract for 1877–79 had been for three years or just over $400,000 per year, so the figures should be averaged. The bid of $600,000 per year by Koh Seang Tat was probably much closer to the appropriate value of the farm. After all, the population of Singapore had been increasing substantially

34. Song, pp. 202, 204, 335.
35. C. S. Wong, *Gallery of Chinese Kapitans* (1963), pp. 16–17.

during the decade, the price of gambier had been rising (table 4), and the price of opium itself had been completely stabilized.[36] All indications are that the consumption of opium had been increasing along with population and that the farmers and their shareholders enjoyed a very good thing indeed.

The Singapore syndicate was obviously not pleased when Koh took the farm away from them, but one method of fighting opposition is to join it. Koh Seang Tat had enough cash to outbid the Singapore syndicate, but being from Pinang, he probably lacked a local organization in Singapore. Koh was an experienced revenue farmer, having held the Pinang farms since 1873 and some farms on the peninsula for nearly a decade. He must have been aware of the difficulty he would face in Singapore if he had no locally based secret society or clan organization to back him. Aside from hoping the members of the old Tan-Cheang syndicate would accept a half loaf, he must have had other inducements. The encouragement of Archibald Anson must have seemed more than mere moral support; in fact it is likely that Anson had actively solicited Koh Seang Tat's bid. Like the former governors of the Settlements, Anson seems to have felt it his prerogative to manipulate the farms and to play favorites for an increase in revenue.[37] Another place Koh may have sought allies would have been among other Straits Chinese merchants in Singapore. Not a single Chinese merchant from an old Baba family had held the Singapore farms since Kiong Kong Tuan. In Singapore, the pepper and gambier clique was made up of relative newcomers. Their links to the kongsis gave them possession of a base among the masses as well as wealth. The combination had been sufficient to exclude the Hokkien Baba financiers who had formerly dominated the higher levels of the Chinese economy in the British settlements and held the Singapore farms before the 1840s.

Wynne, who divided the farming syndicates according to his idea of their secret society connections, has linked Tan Seng Poh and Cheang Hong Lim to the "Tokong" group and identified the "Triad" groups with the Straits Chinese merchant Tan Kim Ching. Some evidence suggests that they were the heads of opposing mercantile factions in

36. After a series of rather extreme fluctuations in the 1850s and 1860s, the Calcutta opium market had more or less stabilized at around five hundred dollars per chest, where it remained until the late 1890s, when inflation and other factors led to another increase (see fig. 1).
37. Khoo, 1972, p. 211. He notes that Koh had acquired the lease for the Trans-Krian farms in northern Perak "upon the establishment of British administration in Perak, through the recommendation of Lieutenant-Governor Archibald Anson."

Table 4. Singapore market prices for pepper and gambier, 1825–1909 (Spanish dollars per pikul)

Year	Pepper	Gambier	Year	Pepper	Gambier
1825	—	1.70	1868	—	—
1826	—	4.50	1869	6.70	3.10
1827	6.50	1.25	1870	7.35	3.02
1828	6.00	1.75	1871	9.15	2.85
1829	6.00	1.25	1872	10.70	3.47
1830	5.50	1.75	1873	11.50	4.42
1831	—	—	1874	15.35	5.10
1832	5.50	3.50	1875	13.30	5.35
1833	6.50	5.00	1876	8.75	5.50
1834	—	2.21	1877	8.20	4.20
1835	6.75	1.50	1878	7.55	4.55
1836	6.75	1.30	1879	7.30	4.25
1837	7.00	3.25	1880	10.50	4.40
1838	6.50	.85	1881	11.60	4.15
1839	6.00	2.12	1882	11.00	4.70
1840	—	2.50	1883	12.80	6.40
1841	—	2.50	1884	17.50	7.27
1842	—	1.75	1885	19.00	5.02
1843	—	1.75	1886	19.34	6.07
1844	—	1.50	1887	20.00	5.80
1845	5.00	1.50	1888	21.30	6.95
1846	6.50	1.35	1889	19.80	8.15
1847	3.60	1.25	1890	17.25	8.25
1848	3.35	.85	1891	11.17	5.80
1849	—	—	1892	9.70	5.95
1850	—	1.00	1893	11.12	6.45
1851	5.95	2.30	1894	10.00	6.60
1852	—	.70	1895	12.00	8.55
1853	—	3.95	1896	—	—
1854	7.25	3.30	1897	—	—
1855	6.40	2.05	1898	22.25	5.65
1856	7.80	2.50	1899	24.37	5.55
1857	—	—	1900	28.25	6.50
1858	—	—	1901	—	—
1859	7.00	2.90	1902	30.00	—
1860	6.60	2.50	1903	—	—
1861	—	—	1904	—	—
1862	—	3.35	1905	—	—
1863	—	4.13	1906	—	—
1864	5.70	4.08	1907	17.69	7.96
1865	—	4.44	1908	11.92	8.37
1866	—	—	1909	12.15	10.93

Sources: Low Siew Chek, 1955, *SSADR,* and various issues of *SFP* and *ST.*

Singapore during the 1870s.[38] Koh may have had at least promises of local secret society support from someone, but it is doubtful that it was Tan Kim Ching. Wynne has identified Kim Ching as a Ghee Hin leader, while Koh was clearly linked to the Tokong/Hai San camp in the Larut wars. This would have put the Koh and the Singapore syndicate in the same secret society camp, and it is clear that they were at odds here over a financial monopoly. While the division between Hai San and Ghee Hin cliques certainly characterized Pinang and the West Coast states and perhaps even Siam, it is not clear that the same divisions extended into Singapore. The inapplicability of Wynne's thesis here supports the idea that Koh probably expected most of his support from the colonial government.

Whatever the underlying alignments were here, Koh took two steps to cover himself. To ensure his profit, he raised the price of chandu by 8.5 percent. It had been six chees to the dollar (a chee was one-tenth of a tahil), and he raised the price to $1.80 per tahil (or from 16.6¢ per chee to 18¢ per chee). His next move was to ask the members of the old Singapore kongsi to join him. Gulland's account runs as follows:

> This Penang syndicate then went to the Singapore men and asked them to go into partnership with them, which they consented to do, probably with a view to damaging the Farm for the Penang men, rather than with any idea of making profit out of it for themselves . . . during the whole three years, smuggling was rife, particularly in third year, and there is every reason to believe that it was carried on at the instigation of the Singapore syndicate, with the intention of depreciating the Farm in the eyes of the Penang men.[39]

In fact, as early as August 1880, questions had been raised in the Legislative Council as to the solvency of the new farming syndicate. The governor was required to write to London reporting on the sta-

---

38. Wynne, p. 350. Wynne's division has certain flaws, one of which was that the secret societies controlled the revenue farms rather than vice versa; nevertheless, it may be correct in identifying the membership of the mercantile factions of the early 1880s. In the "Triad," or Ghee Hin, -dominated farms were the Melaka Chinese families of Tan Kim Ching, Lee Cheang Tee, Tan Beng Swee, and Tan Jiak Kim. They were linked to the Pinang triad group represented by Che Ah Him, Goh Siew Swee, and Chan Ah Yam. On the "Tokong" side, and probably linked to the Ghee Hock, was the Singapore clique I have already described: Tan Seng Poh, Cheang Hong Lim, Tan Hiok Nee, Tay Ho Swee, Teo Kit, and Lim Mah Peng, who were linked with the Pinang group of Khoo Thean Teck and Chang Keng Kui. Of course, if Wynne had carried his analysis through, he would have noticed that the conflict in Singapore in 1880 was between Koh Seang Tat of the Pinang–"Tokong"/Hai San group and the Singapore "Tokong" group.

39. *Legco*, 28 February 1883, p. 7.

bility of the farm and the "character and commercial standing" of "Mr. Tat." Governor Weld responded that he was impressed by Koh's ability to speak English "perfectly" and by the amount of capital (five hundred thousand dollars) that had been put up by the company plus the property deeds amounting to two hundred thousand dollars, which had been put up as security. He noted that the new company was "stronger because the old farmers had put their relatives and their capital into it."[40] Given Gulland's comments, the presence of Tan Keng Swee and Lim Kwee Eng was obviously more of a disadvantage than an asset.

While Koh's experience with the Singapore farm was hardly a success, his difficulties did not cause great concern. The real crisis came in early 1883. By late 1882, as Gulland noted, the Singapore men had achieved their purpose in joining the farm. Most of the partners in the 1880–82 farming syndicate of Koh Seang Tat refused to risk their money again, having finished in the red the first time. Koh himself had given up trying to do business in Singapore. Still, the few who remained of that syndicate formed a company and offered a bid of $63,400 per month (the monthly rent of the previous farm had been $50,000). The partners in the reorganized Singapore syndicate, offered $69,000 per month, which would have meant a yearly rent of $828,000. Gulland continued: "So far their little game was successful, but unfortunately for them another lot of publicans and sinners arrived on the scene from Penang and offered $85,000. I fancy the Executive Council was rather staggered by this figure."[41]

This would have meant an annual rent of $1,020,000. There was a meeting between the governor, the Executive Council, and the high bidder, Chiu Sin Yong. After further negotiation, it was later announced that the new rent would be $80,000 per month and that the retail price of chandu would be raised from $1.80 to $2.20 per tahil. Chiu's appearance was a great disappointment to the Singapore syndicate. When he came and asked them to join, Gulland tells us, they refused: "the Singapore gentlemen returned answer that the price (of chandu) was so exorbitant that they could have nothing to do with it, and they seem to have decided on a bolder line of action and determined to try to ruin the Penang men at the outset, and so force the Government to give the Farm to them, as the next highest tenderers."[42] The stage was thus set for a confrontation between the new generation

40. CO 273/104, G.D. No. 121, 20 August 1880.
41. *Legco*, 28 February 1883, p. 7.
42. Ibid.

of Singapore opium farmers—or would-be opium farmers—and the government. What followed in the first months of 1883 was a clear test of strength between the system that had dominated the Chinese of the colony for over a decade and the new and aggressively imperialistic governor, Frederick Weld.

The members of the old Singapore opium kongsi must have felt themselves to be in a strong position when Chiu Sin Yong gained the farming contract. Having been involved in the farms for over twenty years, the men of their organization knew the territory well. They were experienced at protecting themselves against smugglers and cheaters and knew most of the tricks. Not only that, they had used those tricks themselves to take control of the farms in the first place. Perhaps Tan Keng Swee and Lim Kwee Eng were new, but the men in the organization were probably experienced.

There is little information on Chiu Sin Yong, other than his Pinang origin. He was not known to be associated with Koh Seang Tat's syndicate. On the other hand, he was a partner of Khoo Thean Teck in the Pinang opium farm syndicate, a fact that would place him within the same general financial clique as Koh Seang Tat. Thean Teck was the head of the Toh Peh Kong or Tokong secret society clique and had held the Pinang farms before 1867. Wynne suggests that the Pinang riot of 1868 was caused by Khoo Thean Teck's anger at losing the farms in that year. He later held the Pinang and Kedah farms together with Chiu Sin Yong in 1890.[43] Chiu's willingness to bid for the Singapore farms may also indicate the support of one of the local mercantile or secret society cliques or even of Governor Weld or some other European official, although it is difficult to tell. The events of early 1883 suggest he had little sense of the local situation in Singapore. The fact that Tan Kim Ching later gave evidence against the Singapore syndicate should not be taken to suggest that Chiu was allied with him, for they seem to have been on opposite sides in the Ghee Hin/Hai San conflict.[44]

In many respects, the events of late 1882 and early 1883 were similar to those of the period after 1861. According to Gulland and a number of other observers—after the fact—the government had made one big mistake. They had allowed the spirit farm to be taken by a different syndicate. As it turned out, the spirit farmer was Tan Keng

---

43. Wynne, pp. 252–56, 326, 351; SSD (1910), 167; Song, pp. 427, 533.
44. It is thus difficult to explain Tan Kim Ching's willingness to testify, unless one assumes more pressing motivations on his part. Tan Kim Ching was probably under serious pressure from William Pickering to expose the inner workings of the Singapore syndicate.

Swee, who was backed by Cheang Hong Lim and Tan Hiok Nee.[45] To protect the spirit farm, all the chintengs of the old opium farm had been employed. This was the Seh Tan. Eighty chintengs were hired where it was said that only ten or eleven were necessary. This was exactly what Cheang Sam Teo had done in 1861, except he had not employed the Seh Tan.

It was also necessary to have an outside base from which to launch smuggling operations and to have an excuse to purchase large quantities of raw opium without raising suspicions. The headman of the Seh Tan, one Tan Moh Yong, also said to be a close relative of Tan Keng Swee, reportedly bought shares in the farms of Riau, which at this time included about fourteen islands in the northern part of the archipelago just across the Singapore Strait (e.g., Karimun, Bulan, Batam, Bintan, Sugi, Galang, Rempang, and most of the adjacent islands). In December 1882, just before the new farming syndicate took over, a great deal of opium was exported to these islands for storage, and even more was hidden in different parts of Singapore Island.[46]

A certain amount of dumping had been anticipated. A notice in the *Government Gazette* in December 1882 shows an attempt to forestall a blow at the farms from dumping. It stated that the privilege of the current farmers would cease on 31 December 1882 and that no "excisable article purchased from the present farmers can be used after the 3rd day of January."[47] This meant that the opium shopkeepers and private consumers were forbidden to stock up and would have to start buying opium from the new farming company at new high prices almost immediately.

The new farmer also appears to have taken steps to hit at the grass roots organization of the old farm by eliminating many of the old opium shops. The *Straits Times* reported that many of the old shops had been closed: "The Opium Farmer . . . has set his face against the small, dirty and miserable opium-smoking shops in town . . . the Farmer has established on his own account some forty or more very respectable-looking smoking houses. . . . These measures have . . . gained him some ill-will, but the general Chinese community will soon appreciate the boon of cleanliness and comfort while smoking their

45. CO 273/119, G.D. No. 81, 4 March 1883, p. 355. Weld claims to have learned from Maharaja Abu Bakar of the involvement of Cheang Hong Lim and Tan Hiok Nee in the conspiracy. See also *Legco*, 28 February 1883, pp. 8–10.

46. *Legco*, 28 February 1883, p. 7 and app. C, pp. 156–57; also CO 273/119, Exco Minutes, 17 February 1883, enclosed with G.D. No. 73, 26 February 1883.

47. *SSGG*, December 1882, Government Notice No. 511, p. 1294.

narcotic drug."[48] Undoubtedly, most of the new shops would be managed by people of his own choosing. Chiu Sin Yong also raised the cost of the opium shop license and at the same time raised the price for opium dross.[49] He also reduced the number of opium shops in the town.

The onset of smuggling was almost immediate. Gulland described the beginning of the new farm's contract: "Now, I take it that to pay $80,000 a month, the Farm must sell $3,700 worth of chandoo a day, but they took possession, on the 1st of January, to find that they could only sell to the extent of $800 worth a day, while the town was placarded with notices that chandoo could be bought at a certain place at the mouth of the river, at $9 per ten taels, the Farm price being $22 per ten taels." He said that for several weeks the police and the Chinese Protectorate (which for the first time now began to play a significant role in relation to the opium farm) ignored the farmer's complaints of smuggling. The British administrators were convinced that the farmer would seize upon the slightest excuse to ask for a reduction in the rent. In fact, when anticipating the time that smuggling would be suppressed, Gulland offered this advice to Governor Weld: "Now I should like to say a word as to the present Farmer. He will no doubt try to make capital out of what has taken place. He will probably come to your Excellency and say he has suffered great loss; will offer his books for inspection; but Chinese book-keeping does not amount to much; he probably has several sets of books." He went on to point out that it was necessary to maintain a strong front against the Chinese: "It would never do to allow the Chinese to think that, at the letting of these farms, they may play the game of brag with each other in offering large sums, and then, after getting possession of the farm, come to the Government, and obtain a reduction of rent."[50]

Up until this time, the government had "always taken it for granted that the farmer's interests were identical with its own."[51] Rule in the colony had become a joint affair in which the Europeans relied on the Chinese to take care of themselves and depended on the mercantile elite among the Chinese to manage affairs. But now the costs of

48. *ST*, 11 January 1883.
49. Opium "dross" was the ash or the residue left after opium was smoked the first time. This was generally recovered by the shopkeeper and resold at a cheaper rate. The residue from this second usage was also recovered and used yet again in many cases. Actually, it was from the dross that the shopkeeper made his profit, since the retailer was required to sell chandu at the same rate for which he had purchased it from the farmer.
50. *Legco*, 28 February 1883, p. 7.
51. Ibid., p. 8.

Table 5. Arrests for opium smuggling, 1880–1883

	Number of cases	Number of prisoners
January 1880	3	3
February 1880	8	12
January 1881	6	6
February 1881	7	8
January 1882	22	26
February 1882	36	47
January 1883	96	106
February 1–22, 1883	97	118

Source: Legco, 1883, "Report of Chinese Protectorate."

continuing that sort of system, costs that included accepting some sort of compromise with whomever won the battle for the farms, were no longer acceptable. Such costs had been tolerated in 1847 and 1848 and again from 1861 to 1870. Men such as Lau Joon Tek, Cheang Hong Lim, Tan Hiok Nee, and Tan Seng Poh had all, at one time or another, found it necessary to smuggle their way into the farming syndicate. The government may have awarded contracts to whomever they thought offered the best deal, but until 1883 the real power had always been decided in the streets.

Weld believed that had he not acted quickly, Chiu Sin Yong would have gone down faster than Koh Seng Tat. By the middle of January the papers were full of smuggling reports. Around the beginning of February, matters began to come to a head. In one day, two lots of smuggled chandu had been seized with a street value of thirty thousand dollars.[52] The head chinteng of the spirit farm had been caught with illicit opium. This was one Koeh Sun Chai, who had also been the head chinteng of the old opium farm. The government then offered a reward of ten thousand dollars for information on the smugglers, but as of 15 February there were no takers. The daily sales of farm chandu during the month of January had averaged only between nine hundred and one thousand dollars.[53] The attorney-general's report showed an enormous increase in arrests and revenue cases (table 5).[54]

There was very little sympathy for Chiu Sin Yong among the Chi-

52. *ST*, 6 February 1883.
53. *Legco*, app. C, 1883, pp. 156–57; see also *ST*, 15 February 1883.
54. CO 273/119b, Attorney-General's Report, 24 February 1883, enclosed with G.D. No. 73, 26 February 1883.

nese of Singapore. Consumers of opium, now forced to pay much higher prices for the drug, undoubtedly welcomed the easy availability of cheap chandu. Many remarks on the smuggling problem pointed to the high price of chandu as the chief reason for the success of the smuggling. A letter to the editor in the *Straits Times* noted that a smuggler could net $41,000 per chest of opium (the Singapore market price was between $520 and $560 per chest of raw opium) by underselling the farm price by 10¢ per chee.[55] Another article noted that chandu was actually being sold for more than the agreed ceiling in the licensed shops. The government had agreed to a price of $2.20 per tahil but the actual retail price was above $2.50.[56] Even the government's postmortem admitted a problem with the price and the general public image of the new farm: "The chief cause of the success of the conspiracy was that it was backed up by the general masses of Chinese, to whom cheap Chandu, smuggled or not, is a desideratum, and by whom the usual Farm army of unscrupulous Chintengs and informers is held in detestation."[57]

The fortunes of the farm appeared dismal. It was said that Chiu Sin Yong had lost one hundred thousand dollars during January 1883 alone. During the first week of February, sales were still 50 percent below the break-even point. It was at this time that Weld decided that extraordinary measures were going to be necessary and issued an order in Council on 5 February which forbade the export of opium to the Malay Peninsula and the Netherlands Indies except under special permit from the colonial secretary. This measure naturally brought immediate protests from the mercantile community, since it struck at the very heart of the free trade ideal and seemed calculated to drive away most of the small traders. The aim, of course, was to prevent the smugglers from exporting opium to Riau and Johor, processing it into chandu, and shipping it back into Singapore; but many wondered if it was necessary to forbid export to the entire Netherlands Indies.

In the Legislative Council debate of 28 February, Read described the impact of the trade stoppage:

> That trade is of considerable importance. To Netherlands India, the only parts for which I have returns, the exports have averaged about 300

55. Letter from "D," *ST,* 1 February 1883.
56. *ST,* 26 January 1883; see also "Market Reports" of *ST,* for 2 and 17 January, 1 and 13 February, and 31 March 1883, for the price of raw opium. The price was rising throughout this period, from $521 per chest on 2 January to $585 per chest on 31 March. By 13 February it was already up to $560. Thus, if the conspirators had purchased their opium during December 1882, when the price was lower, they would have had an additional profit margin over the farmer, who would be buying his opium at higher prices.
57. *Legco,* 1883, app. C., pp. 156–57.

chests per month for the last six months, of which 60 go to the Government of Batavia, and the rest, say 250 chests, to the other islands, from Bintang to Celebes. Now it is true that the Government gave permission to people to export Opium to these places if they asked permission and said where it was going to, but some of the traders complained to me that they were called upon to give security that the Opium would not be smuggled. Now this is very onerous, and, in consequence of it, one man told me he lost on sales in one week over $5,000.[58]

Weld's next move was to make use of another extraordinary provision of the excise ordinance to confiscate ships on which contraband chandu was found. One of the two vessels seized was the Dutch brig *Voorwaarts*, which was released when the governor learned that there would be a formal protest from the governor-general of the Netherlands Indies.[59] The other was the Singapore-registered steamer *Hong Ann*, which belonged to Wee Bin and Company, one of the major Chinese shipping firms in the colony. It was reported that two or three hundred dollars worth of chandu had been discovered aboard which belonged to the *chinchew*, or supercargo, of the vessel. He was apparently in the habit of buying a couple of balls of raw opium in Sulu (the ship had just come from Labuan), cooking it into chandu, and selling it to the crew during the voyage. If there was any left over, the chinchew sold it on his arrival in Singapore. The captain had forbidden the crew to use opium and selling the excess in Singapore was clearly illegal, but it was also a very small-scale operation and apparently unconnected with the big conspiracy. The supercargo and four other crewmen were arrested and fined. The ship was also seized, even though the ship's owners had nothing to do with the illicit chandu.[60] The government held the vessel for two weeks and finally returned it, but in the meantime, it had been used on government business to Melaka and back. In a letter to the editor in the *Straits Times*, Severo L. Cabreira, apparently a lawyer working for Wee Bin, attested to the high standing and integrity of the shipowner, Wee Boon Teck, and also pointed out that such an action could have ruined a less wealthy man.[61]

The police, primarily the inspector-general, Maj. S. Dunlop, and the protector of Chinese, William Pickering, conducted an investigation into the conspiracy—with difficulty because some witnesses claimed they had been threatened with violence. The arrest of Koeh Sun Chai, the head chinteng of the spirit farm, was apparently a breakthrough,

58. *ST,* 12 February 1883; *Legco,* 28 February 1883, p. 5.
59. *Legco,* 28 February 1883, pp. 11–12.
60. *ST,* 15 February 1883.
61. *ST,* 1 March 1883.

and he was pressured to give evidence against his employers. The police were also successful in getting the prominent Singapore merchant, Tan Kim Ching, to testify as to the nature of the conspiracy. The governor claimed he had received information confirming the existence of a conspiracy from Maharaja Abu Bakar.

The police decided there was evidence enough to show a conspiracy essentially led by the people involved in the former opium farm and the current spirit farm. Their prime suspects were Tan Keng Swee, Cheang Hong Lim, Tan Hiok Nee, and Tan Kim Fuan. Apparently Cheang and Tan Hiok Nee had decided to come out of retirement. The police also noted the involvement of a pepper and gambier merchant and former head of the Kongkek, Tan Eng Cheng. In addition to the high incidence of arrests, income from fines was way up, about nineteen thousand dollars during January alone. In most cases, police said, fines of five hundred to one thousand dollars had been paid immediately by otherwise impoverished coolies. People had been threatened, and violence had been used against the police and the revenue officers. The force behind the conspiracy was identified as the Seh Tan. In one case, a group of men, apparently members of the Seh Tan, had attacked a police station on Pulau Tekong and released some prisoners.

The police recommended that the governor banish Tan Eng Cheng, Tan Moh Yong, Tan Ah Choh, Tan Hock Seng, and Tan Hiok Nee. The banishment ordinance could not be used against Straits-born Chinese, so Tan Keng Swee and Cheang Hong Lim, who were also named as parties to the conspiracy, could not be banished; nor, since there was no direct evidence of their involvement in smuggling, could charges be filed against them.[62] Tan Moh Yong was named as the head of the Seh Tan in Singapore. He was said to be a relative of Tan Keng Swee and the holder of the Riau farms. The police claim to have received testimony from people who said they bought chandu from him. Tan Eng Cheng was the former head of the Kongkek and before this time enjoyed a reputation as a respectable merchant. One of the largest seizures of chandu (five hundred tins said to be worth ten thousand dollars) was traced to the Kongkek's headquarters. Witnesses testified in court that it was packed into boxes in the society's house. Eng Cheng was also said to have been one of Tan Keng Swee's closest acquaintances.[63]

62. The reasons for including Tan Hiok Nee are not clear. Nowhere in the evidence was his role in the conspiracy spelled out, nor did Johor seem to be used as a major smuggling base. There was no attempt to banish him either even though he was China born.
63. The police report is included as two enclosures with CO 273/1119b, G.D. No. 73, 26 February 1883, pp. 310–30.

Pickering reported that some of the conspirators had met with Chiu Sin Yong to see if he was ready to make a deal with them. The meeting was said to have been at a feast given by Lim Eng Bee, the pawnbroking farmer. Those present included Tan Keng Swee, Tan Moh Yong, Tan Eng Cheng, and "two of the present Opium Farmers." Cheang Hong Lim also sent his representative. According to the report, "The idea of amalgamation between the Farmers and the opposition was started, [sic] Hong Lim's representative refused to join. Keng Swee said that he would join if the Farm rent was reduced by $20,000 a month. This is commonly known in Town and was corroborated to-day by Tan Kim Ching."[64]

The other two deportees, Tan Hock Seng and Tan Ah Choh, were involved in the Kampong Glam Seh Tan, which was said to be independent of the Singapore town Seh Tan. No direct evidence was brought against these two. Each one was described as a "dangerous character at all times." Pickering and Dunlop said they had talked to people who claimed to have bought chandu from them but that none would testify in court for fear of retaliation.[65] No further mention has been found regarding action against Tan Hiok Nee in this matter. He was the only really prominent member of the accused group, and it can be assumed that he used his influence to get off the hook.

The newspaper report of the actions taken against the other four was somewhat different from the official record. It reported that one of the banishees was the head of the Ghee Hin and that the other was the head of the Hai San. In any case, one of them got away to Hong Kong, where he was later arrested, and the other escaped to Karimun. Only two of the four, Tan Eng Cheng and Tan Ah Choh, were actually apprehended in Singapore. Both gave statements in their defense. Eng Cheng claimed he knew nothing about anything. "Goes to his business every day and only minds that. Has heard nothing whatever about any acts of violence or intimidation or smuggling."[66]

The governor was surprised that Eng Cheng denied not only involvement in the conspiracy but also knowing one existed or even being aware of smuggling. There is also a hint in the Legislative Council debate as well as in the Governor's Despatches that Eng Cheng himself was the object of a conspiracy. Two members of the Legislative Council questioned his banishment. J. Graham suggested

64. Ibid., pp. 328–29.
65. The quotation, used several times in the various accounts, was " 'Why', said one of them, 'what is the good of your $10,000 reward, when so-and-so or some other may pay a man $500 to stick a knife into me?' " *Legco*, 28 February 1883, p. 10.
66. *ST*, 19 February 1883; CO 273/119b, G.D. No. 73, 26 February 1883, pp. 334.

that some business associates might gain from his deportation, and Gulland alluded to some difficulty between Eng Cheng and the maharaja of Johor.[67] This, and a few other loose ends, suggest more at stake than meets the eye.

Weld had made extraordinary use of the deportation power. The ordinance had never before been used in an excise case. Its purpose was to get rid of secret society leaders who threatened to cause riots. For this reason Legislative Council members asked for a special session to discuss the crisis. The record of their debate is a major source for this account. Despite their questions and a few objections, most of the European unofficial members of the Legislative Council supported Weld's action. Weld forcefully presented his case, stressing the need to suppress a "terrorist" conspiracy:

> We have not acted as upon a revenue question simply. It is not a revenue question, it is the question whether a powerful conspiracy should establish an opium ring—a ring as bad as any New York ring—and dictate to the Government. . . . It is a question who shall be supreme in this country, and a state of things which at any moment may lead to riot and bloodshed. We have been almost upon the eve of that, and I should think I had not done my duty in preserving the peace committed to me by the Queen.[68]

He got a big round of applause. Even though it was apparent that the really wealthy men behind the conspiracy would not be deported, including Tan Hiok Nee, Weld spoke decisively to the Legislative Council on the treatment the conspirators would receive from government in the future. He spoke of the future of the farm under Chiu Sin Yong: "Even were he ruined, one thing will never take place; he no doubt is always at liberty to strengthen his hands by taking into partnership even men who have been his rivals, as a private arrangement, but the Farm will never be transferred from him to the hands of those who have plotted against him. If he were broken tomorrow morning, those men should never have it, never, *never*! [Much applause]."[69]

---

67. *Legco*, 28 February 1883, p. 7. Gulland's remark is somewhat cryptic and there may have been a copying error. The passage reads: "Sir, I take it that, in deporting these men, you have reasonable proof of their guilt. I know the Maharaja of Johor has against Eng Cheng; and, if such is the case, should you, as some say, have stretched your powers in so doing, then I can merely say I congratulate the Colony upon your Excellency's having done so."
68. Ibid., p. 10.
69. Ibid., p. 11.

A careful reading shows that Weld had left himself an out. The final solution was, in fact, to take the conspirators into partnership. Weld reported to the Colonial Office on 10 April on the new arrangement for the farms, which apparently had been put together with assistance from Abu Bakar. He noted that the Singapore farmer Chiu Sin Yong and Lee Chin Tuan (apparently the Johor opium farmer) had formed a partnership with Tan Keng Swee and Lim Cheng Wha (presumably the Johor spirit farmer). Their agreement was to be guaranteed by the governor: "Damage in case of illegal ill faith to be decided by the Governor—his decision to be under a Rule of the Supreme Court. No fresh partners to be admitted without consent of Governor in writing. Losses already incurred up to $100,000 as well as future expected profits, are accepted by the new partners. It will be shown that Cheang Hong Lim and Tan Hiok Nee, who were really the principal ring-leaders of the conspiracy, are excluded from any participation in the farm."[70]

The Colonial Office administrators who received Weld's dispatch were not very impressed. One of them, R. Meade, wrote comments on Weld's letter that he was not satisfied that it "was as great a triumph over the conspirators as the Governor represents." He noted that Tan Keng Swee had gotten out of the "scrape" altogether by going into partnership with the opium farmers, "so that it is an open question whether the Victory is not a surrender."[71]

Aside from the four men who were actually banished, Cheang Hong Lim seems to have come off the worse for the whole affair. He was apparently stripped of his justice of the peace office and ended up having to write a rather abject apology to the governor, which was published in the newspaper. In addition to making a "public submission," he promised not to join any conspiracies and offered to make over his shares in the revenue farms of the Netherlands Indies— presumably Riau—to the Singapore opium farmer.[72] On the other hand, Hong Lim's submission included no admission of guilt, and in his own defense he sued James Carmichael and Mahomed Eusoff, the publishers of the *Straits Intelligence,* for accusing him of being involved in the conspiracy. The suit was filed on 6 March, but since no

70. CO 273/119, G.D. No. 81, 4 March 1883, pp. 354–55. Lee Chin Tuan and Lim Cheng Wha were not mentioned as being part of the conspiracy.
71. Ibid., p. 349. This is the second of the three handwritten memos at the beginning of this document.
72. *ST,* 20 April 1883; CO 237/120, G.D. No. 142, 6 April 1883. The letter was printed and placarded in the Chinese quarter of the town, but it does not say if it was translated into Chinese.

more was heard about it thereafter, one assumes it was ultimately dropped.[73]

Despite this fall from grace, Cheang Hong Lim appeared to suffer little long-term damage to his reputation. According to Song, Hong Lim died a very wealthy and respected man in 1893 and was recognized as a public benefactor who organized his own fire brigade and performed many other acts of philanthropy, and of course today his name continues to grace buildings, streets, and shopping centers in Singapore. Much the same can be said of his coconspirator, Tan Hiok Nee, who never made any public submission.[74]

Internationalization of Chinese Capital

The difficulty over the Singapore opium farm arose at this time as a result of the colonial government's intention to extend its control, not only over the farm, but also over Chinese society in general. Weld faced resistance from the company that had come to control the farms almost as a feudal privilege. The aim of the colonial government was to eliminate feudalistic remnants, meaning in this case the control of territory or a privilege by means of personal gangs and loyalties. The government also struck at the Chinese oligarchy who controlled the opium monopoly, a group that had really been created, or at least elevated, by the laissez-faire policies of earlier colonial governments.

If Weld was to accomplish his aim, he had to do two things, break the internal power structure of Chinese society and fully rationalize the relationship between the state and its contractors. The takeover of the farms, first by Koh Seang Tat in 1879, and then by Chiu Sin Yong in 1883, demonstrated that it was, in fact, possible to come in from outside the Chinese power structure with little more than money and buy a monopoly that had heretofore depended on a local socioeconomic infrastructure. Their victories were, in some respects, hollow; neither made much money nor founded enduring companies to hold the farms. Their names do not appear in the lists of partners in the Singapore farms in later years. Yet the monopoly power of the great syndicate seems to have been broken. In the long run the government

73. *ST*, 7 March 1883. No copies of the *Straits Intelligence* appear to have survived, but the text of the article was printed in the *Straits Times* together with the report of the court case.

74. Song, pp. 168–70.

benefited because its ability to confer and withdraw the monopoly was reaffirmed.

Actually, this opening up of monopolies to outsiders became a general phenomenon. If, in 1879, Koh Seang Tat could come down from Pinang and buy the Singapore farms, so too could Cheang Hong Lim go up and buy the Hong Kong farms.[75] Indications are that he and his partners were no more successful in Hong Kong than were their rivals in Singapore. In the midst of the Singapore smuggling crisis, the *Straits Times* carried a long notice from the Hong Kong government announcing that since the government had not "received what it considered a sufficient offer for the opium farm, [it] has taken the business under its own management."[76] The fact that the bids were all low suggests a combination controlled by local Chinese in Hong Kong and also that the previous farmer (Cheang Hong Lim) had lost money. The home advantage still counted for something. Yet raising the capital for farms seems also to have demanded outside contributions.

The Hong Kong government was unable to hold the farm on its own, and by 1886 the farms were back in private hands. Surprisingly, they were taken by Lee Keng Yam, who by then was also the holder of the Singapore farm. Lee was descended from a well-established Melaka family and a part of the Straits Chinese network of families.[77] From then on, Singapore Chinese capital began to move off shore and circulate freely throughout the colonial world of Southeast Asia and the China coast. The records show that Singaporeans were involved not only in the Hong Kong farms but also in farms in Shanghai, Batavia, Deli, Bangkok, and Saigon. It also became more and more common for outsiders from all over Southeast Asia and China to hold shares and sometimes even controlling interests in the Singapore farms.

The success of an internationalized system depended on two factors: the increasing size of the urban markets for opium and the weakness of secret societies in the face of money. During the 1870s, as already noted, the urban area of Singapore was where most of the secret society activity was. If it were possible for a Pinang firm to come to

---

75. *STOJ*, 1 February 1879. Hong Lim's partners were listed as "Gan Swee and Keng Ho."
76. *ST*, 1 March 1883.
77. Song, pp. 241–42; Khoo, 1972, p. 64. Lee Keng Yam was the son of Lee Qui Lim, who had moved to Singapore from Melaka. The Lees were linked to Tan Kim Seng's family, and Lee Keng Yam had worked in the Shanghai branch of Kim Seng and Company for thirteen years before coming back to Singapore to take the farms in 1885.

Singapore and take the local farms, then the combination that had heretofore operated between opium farming and pepper and gambier financing had to be much less necessary. But if it was not always necessary to have a monopoly hold on the local economy in order to successfully hold the farms, it still helped.

Not just anyone could come in and buy the farms; it still took money and organization. In fact, the farms had become so large in many of these cities that it was necessary to bring in capital from as many sources as possible. During the 1880s, it became possible to hold the farm without having to already control the loyalty of the triads, or some organization such as a surname group. Henceforth, a wealthy person could simply buy the protection of one or two local gangs. Most subsequent farmers had secret society or kongsi connections someplace, but that was usually on a frontier and not in the colonial cities, where relatively effective colonial police forces had been created.

The weakening of the secret societies which accompanied this development eroded some of the most important connections within Chinese society. Mak has a convincing argument regarding the Chinese mercantile elite's withdrawal from the secret societies between 1882 and 1889: In an earlier period this elite, particularly the excise farmers, had grown rich with the assistance of the secret societies. The societies, for their own benefit, needed the mercantile elite to serve as a link with legitimate society and, as in the case of people like Tan Seng Poh, to put them in contact with the much more abundant legitimate resources of society. With the withdrawal of these "double-role players," the secret societies were left to depend on lower-class leadership and cut off from the primary sources of wealth and influence in society at large.[78] One of the most successful of what Mak calls "double-role players" in Singapore was Tan Kim Ching, who was Pickering's informant on the opium-smuggling conspiracy.

Another result of these events was the resurgence of the old Straits Chinese families, many of whom were based in Melaka or Pinang. Between 1848 and 1886, no Melaka Chinese were involved as major holders of the Singapore revenue farms. Tan Kim Ching's evidence created suspicion and ill-feeling between the pepper and gambier clique and the British government. This led to a crack in the power base of the Singapore syndicate and thus, intended or not, opened the way for Straits Chinese to control the farms again. While the lists of the farm partnerships after 1886 are not complete, those available

78. Mak, 1981, pp. 107–8.

show the presence of at least one or two members of the old Keng Tek Hui, perhaps the most exclusive club in the Straits, which was composed primarily of Melaka families.[79] Several later syndicates were also organized by well-established Pinang families.

Perhaps the most telling long-term impact of the decline of the societies was the erosion of social and economic bonds that had formerly linked the elite to working-class organizations. Workers' societies, which is what the secret societies had originally been, had already yielded much of their power to the mercantile leaders by the mid-1860s. The 1870s and 1880s saw the abandonment of the societies by their leaders, at least in the urban areas controlled by colonial governments. The leaders sought official respectability at the cost of popular power. The police and the state then came between the triads and the upper levels of colonial society.

After the collapse of the farm conspiracy in 1883, what remained of the secret societies, although declining in importance, appeared, for a while at least, as almost legitimate organizations. Secret society festivals were mentioned in the *Straits Times* as part of the local "color." The paper in November 1883 described the Chinggay festival of the Hokkien Toh Peh Kong as well as the Teochew procession.[80] In 1886 there was a description of the Sembayang Hantu put on by the Ghee Hock, the opium and spirit farmers, and the Hokkien Ghee Hin on successive nights between Wednesday, 25 August, and Saturday the 28th. There were many Chinese and European visitors. "Preparations were quickly made and a goodly row of tables extending a considerable distance in front of both farms loaded with choice viands and fruits and very tastefully and expensively decorated were put up." There were no less than twenty-one separate wayangs at a cost of three thousand dollars. Mr. Gun Kum Lian, the "genial headman" of the Hokkien Ghee Hin, received many visitors at the kongsi house.[81] This was certainly a different aspect of the Ghee Hin that had dominated Singapore for so many years. The association with the Ghee Hock and the opium and spirit farmers is also significant: they had all gained a degree of respectability.

The events surrounding the great opium conspiracy of 1883 help to bring into focus the changes taking place in the Chinese society and economy of Singapore. The orientation of Chinese community leadership was undergoing a major change. They were becoming less and less

79. Song, p. 29.
80. *ST,* 1 November 1883.
81. *STWI,* 2 September 1886.

dependent on the local structure of the community and moving closer to the colonialist power structure. As opium farmers, however, they still had considerable influence in the administration of the colonial state because they remained the major source of tax revenue. Having separated them from their mass bases, the next step for the government was to eliminate them altogether.

7　The Demise of
the Farming System

The 1890s saw the beginning of major changes in the economy and society of Singapore and indeed of all of Malaya. This era marked the inception of a much more intensive variety of colonialism characterized by the shift in the global economy from commercial to industrial capitalism. The improvements in communications and transportation had placed the European metropolis not only within instantaneous reach by telegram but within economic reach of bulk commodities via steamers. Thus, politically, economically, and socially, Malaya came to be more closely integrated into the imperial economy and subject to the demands of the "home" market. At the same time, the Malayan economy was more open than ever before to the intrusion of European capital.

This was also the end of the opium farming system. The continuing shocks of the global commodity markets struck at Singapore through the opium farm. With international finance capital available, potential farmers were able to offer exceptionally high bids for control of the farms. If the economy then went into a recession, the revenue system collapsed with it. These collapses were felt more widely within the European administrative structure than previously because the colonial governments had come to depend on opium revenues for such a large share of their expenses. The opium farm had always contributed the lion's share of the revenues in the Straits Settlements, but in the earlier years of the century, the colonial government was so limited in its functions that the impact of an economic collapse was not devastating to the state. After the 1880s, colonial states began to contract large debts for development projects and make considerable investments in

183

the infrastructure. The idea of basing their calculations for these expenses on expected revenues from the opium farmer began to seem foolish, particularly when the farms began to collapse on a regular basis. Such undependable revenues did not make for rational budgeting.

At the same time, international pressures to end the opium trade had been growing since the 1880s. In 1893, the Society for the Suppression of the Opium Trade had prevailed on the House of Commons to organize a royal commission to study the opium trade and, along with it, the farming system. While pro-opium forces were successful then in staving off attempts to end or restrict either aspect of the system, it was only a matter of time. By the first decade of the twentieth century, economic concerns had given force to moral reservations, and the pressures to restrict drug trafficking had become institutionalized. In 1909 all of these forces came together.

Much of the financial power in the Singapore farming syndicates had come to be wielded by the Pinang families that had developed economic bases in the tin-mining states of Malaya's West Coast. Between 1890 and 1910 the revenue farms of Singapore were always held by syndicates that either included or were dominated by Pinang taukehs. Nonetheless, the farming syndicates that held the farms after Chiu Sin Yong show that compromises were reached among the members of other financial groups in Singapore. The long-term advantage in opium farming continued to lie with those who had major investments in labor-intensive industries organized around kongsi groups. There had been a shift in the economic center of gravity in the Malay world: a slow-down in the old gambier and general agricultural base of the Singapore taukehs and a tilt toward the more volatile and rapidly expanding financial base of the tin fields. In essence, those who commanded the largest labor force commanded the farms, simply because the laborers were always the major consumers of opium.

Thus we seek the causes of the demise of the farming system in the overall economy and particularly in labor organization. The general decline of kongsis, whether controlled by laborers, taukehs, or secret societies, was evidence of a crucial shift; for the growing influence of the Chinese Protectorate extended to policing the labor market. This erosion of the opium farmers' and the tin and gambier taukehs' labor monopoly, while not the perfect solution to European investors' labor demands, did free up the labor market to a considerable extent during the 1880s and 1890s, so that even European firms could engage in direct hiring without going through secret societies and coolie brokers.

This shift in labor control gradually eroded the economic base of the revenue farms. By the early years of the twentieth century, although the farming syndicates appeared to be flourishing, they were like old trees that had rotted from within—ready to be toppled by the next strong wind. It came in the years between 1907 and 1909, in the form of a series of global economic crises that hit the commodity markets to which Singapore exported. The fact that these crises coincided with an upsurge in the global anti-opium movement created the context for restrictive action by colonial authorities.

Socially and politically, Singapore had become a very different place. The triads still existed but as little more than extortion operations, squeezing protection money from petty traders and organizing gambling and illegal lotteries. Singapore had become a coolie town, of slums and row-house tenements like those described by James Warren.[1] They were inhabited by rickshaw pullers and coal heavers. If the kongsis had ceased to defend their interests, they were now open to new political messages coming out of China from refugee revolutionaries and nationalists and were being organized into labor unions. With the emigration of Chinese women, more and more Chinese were settling down and establishing families in the Straits.

Shifts in the Singapore Economy

The new openness of the Malayan economy is illustrated by the changes in the pepper and gambier business and the tin industry. Through the nineteenth century, as I have said, agricultural and mining enterprises—in fact all forms of primary production—had been beyond the reach of direct European investment. James Jackson, in *Planters and Speculators*, has told the sad story of the many failures of European agriculture in Malaya before the advent of rubber in the 1890s.[2] Europeans tried spices, sugar, coffee, tea (James Guthrie even tried pepper and gambier), all to no avail. The most spectacular failure was perhaps the American, James Balestier, who invested a great deal in a sugar estate in Singapore; by 1848 his estate was advertised for auction.[3]

This economic impenetrability had largely to do with labor and economies of scale.[4] In the economic and technological environment of the Straits Settlements before the 1890s, the development of pro-

---

1. Warren, *Rickshaw Coolie* (1986).
2. James C. Jackson, 1968.
3. Buckley, p. 483.
4. Trocki, 1979, pp. 197–98.

ductive and profitable enterprises in the Malayan rain forest could only be done by Chinese. Using their own systems of organization, finance, and management, they could make pepper and gambier agriculture pay. Much the same could be said of tin mining for the same period. These Chinese systems of production relied on the organization of the kongsi, the secret society, the debt structure, the coolie-brokering system, and the revenue-farming system. They were only accessible to those who could command loyalty based on the bonds of some form of brotherhood. It was only with the erosion of these systems and the creation of a new economic environment that direct European investment in primary production could be successful.

To a certain extent, the environment had been changed by the very Chinese systems that were becoming obsolete in the 1890s. The essential task of clearing and planting large stretches of primary rain forest and of making it accessible and productive had been the economic task of the pepper and gambier society. This economic zone had been integrated into the global commercial economy by free trade. The 1890s saw the end of free trade, however. Once the colonialists established control over real dominions, such as the Malay states, and the tin industry began to develop, a new age of imperial and industrial mercantilism was also born. The changes in the international economic environment, together with those effected by the Chinese, had opened Malaya to the steam dredge, the railroad, the Indian laborer, and corporate finance capital directly from the West. This new economy was rapidly taking hold in the West Coast states of Malaya under British Residents, and with the advent of rubber, that area produced a great economic bonanza during the opening years of the twentieth century.

Pepper and gambier, however, continued to be strong through these same years. Although little of either were grown in Singapore in the 1890s, and even the plantations in south Johor were being abandoned, the cultivation was still spreading outward, an expanding frontier of Chinese agriculture, as James Jackson has described it. Prices remained stable throughout the 1880s and 1890s despite temporary peaks of over $8.00 a pikul for gambier in 1889 and 1890 and again in 1895. Normally they fluctuated between $5.50 and $6.50 per pikul (table 4). Demand remained relatively strong and essentially stable because gambier had become an accepted and necessary resource for the leather-tanning industries, particularly in the United Kingdom and the United States (table 6).[5] Together the two countries accounted for

5. The U.S. leather-tanning industry seems to have been using virtually all the gambier imported into the United States. In 1900, the only year for which comparable figures exist,

Table 6. Gambier exports from Singapore to the United States and United Kingdom, 1900–1905 (Straits dollars)

Year	Total exports (pikuls)	Total value	United Kingdom	United States
1900	—	—	1,844,551	1,697,792
1901	—	—	2,500,109	2,008,225
1902	693,000	10,575,180	2,397,630	4,091,565
1903	648,000	9,039,660*	2,092,437	3,814,403
1904	637,000	8,886,150	1,590,754	2,313,475
1905	618,000	8,621,100	—	—

Source: SSADR, 1904, pp. 553–71; SSADR, 1907, p. 318.
*The values given for 1903–5 are based on the average value of gambier for the period 1902–6, which was $13.95 per pikul. The exact prices for each year are unavailable.

about 60 percent of Malaya's gambier market. The *Straits Settlements Annual Departmental Report* for 1904, which listed sixteen gambier-importing countries, did not list China;[6] the country that had been the original market for gambier had ceased to import it.

It goes without saying that by the end of the nineteenth century, the Malayan economy had diversified. Tin was the most important money maker. Not only had production increased, but the demand had risen even faster with the development of the canning industry in the West. By the 1890s, Malaya was producing nearly 75 percent of the world's supply. Likewise, coffee, sago, tapioca, pineapples, and finally rubber were beginning to account for increasing portions of Malayan exports. Despite this broadening of the commercial agricultural base, the economy remained tied to the production of primary products and to the health of the global economy. The economy depended on the availability of capital, which was tied to the European money market. The Malayan economy thus expanded and contracted with the international economy.

The two decades between 1885 and 1905 saw two sizable troughs in the economic cycles. Between 1885 and 1891 there was a general expansion, characterized by growth, rising prices, and an availability of capital. In 1891 and 1892 a recession hit and the prices of most Malayan commodities dropped. Gambier, for instance, which had

---

that industry used 128,428 bales of gambier for a value of US$890,066. (Unfortunately, the sources do not indicate the size or weight of a "bale," nor have I been able to determine the relative values of U.S. and Straits dollars. See U.S. Department of the Interior, Census Office, *Twelfth Census of the United States 1900* [1905]). This represented roughly a doubling of U.S. gambier consumption, so far as value was concerned (from US$410,580) but over a 400% increase in volume (from 28,387 bales) since 1890. Cf. U.S. Department of the Interior, Census Office, *Report on the Manufacturing Industries of the United States* (1895), p. 712.

6. SSADR, 1904, pp. 553–71.

Table 7. Singapore opium farm annual rent as a percentage of total revenue, 1883–1914 (Spanish dollars)

Year	Rent	Total revenue	Percentage
1883	960,000	1,774,548	54.1
1884	960,000	2,067,000	46.4
1885	960,000	2,015,403	47.6
1886	1,032,000	—	—
1887	1,032,000	—	—
1888	1,032,000	—	—
1889	1,350,000	—	—
1890	1,296,000	2,327,795	55.7
1891	1,115,000	2,187,698	51.0
1892	1,417,000*	2,022,852	70.0
1893	1,368,000*	2,083,578	65.7
1894	1,368,000*	—	—
1895	1,080,000	—	—
1896	1,080,000	—	—
1897	1,080,000	—	—
1898	1,458,000	—	—
1899	1,458,000	3,072,528	47.5
1900	1,458,000	—	—
1901	2,400,000	—	—
1902	2,400,000	—	—
1903	2,400,000	—	—
1904	4,245,000	6,786,596	62.5
1905	3,540,400	6,556,816	54.0
1906	3,420,000	5,969,311	57.3
1907	2,930,000	5,949,181	49.3
1908	2,985,000	5,621,048	53.1
1909	2,507,500	—	—
1910**	1,785,387	—	—
1911**	3,040,716	—	—
1912**	3,741,349	—	—
1913**	4,448,415	—	—
1914**	5,321,480	8,019,090	66.4

Source: Straits Settlements Blue Books; Annual Departmental Reports.
*These figures seem a bit high and may in fact be the value of all revenue farms, or at least of the opium and spirit farms combined.
**Government monopoly net profit, a figure comparable to the farm rent since it represents government profits after expenses including opium purchases, manufacturing equipment, personnel, and preventive services.

been selling for $8.25 per pikul in January 1890, dropped to $5.80 per pikul within a year. Prices did not climb back over $6.00 per pikul until early 1893. Pepper prices were even more erratic. The war in Aceh in the late 1880s and early 1890s had caused the price to rise to over $21.00 per pikul in 1888. By 1892, however, it too had fallen to under $9.00 (table 4).

The economy picked up in 1893 and went into a cycle of growth and expansion for the next decade. The gambier export figures in table 6

Table 8. Bankruptcies and liabilities in Singapore and the Straits Settlements, 1899–1909 (Spanish dollars)

| Year | Bankruptcies | | Liabilities | |
	Singapore	Total	Singapore	Total
1899	40	48	284,580	310,837
1900	25	28	148,456	173,075
1901	38	45	321,057	376,083
1902	34	42	683,589	1,025,727
1903	46	58	803,100	897,366
1904	84	97	1,293,982	1,522,517
1905	92	105	1,865,450	2,504,217
1906	76	84	2,017,200	2,228,467
1907	93	115	1,872,070	1,987,839
1908	100	132	5,186,332	6,344,388
1909	62	—	775,679	—

Source: SSADR, 1908, app. I, p. 32.

together with the values of the opium farm rent in table 7 are as good as any other economic indicator. They show this cycle of growth and expansion peaking around 1903, after which the economy went into a serious depression, much deeper and longer lasting than in 1893. Although gambier exports remained relatively steady at above six hundred thousand pikuls per year between 1903 and 1907, prices fell from a high of $15.26 per pikul in 1902 to $7.96 in 1907.[7] During the same period, other Straits' staples fell precipitously in price. Gutta percha, for instance, dropped from $184.23 to $54.18 per pikul, and pepper fell from $33.65 per pikul to $17.69. Between 1904 and 1908 an average of one hundred traders per year went bankrupt in Singapore, with steadily mounting liabilities (table 8). The worst year was 1908, when liabilities, which had been around a yearly total of just under two million dollars for 1905–7, suddenly jumped to over five million dollars in 1908.

The same period saw shifts in the value of the currency as well. For the entire nineteenth century most of the world had been on the gold standard. The rate of exchange between the Spanish (later the Mexican and finally the Straits) silver dollar and Sterling was relatively stable at $4.60 to $4.30 per £1, or at about 4s. 1d. to the dollar. Then in 1900, Britain went off the gold standard, and this caused an immediate dislocation of the Straits dollar, which fell to 1s. 8d. by 1902. Thus the apparent rise in the price of gambier between 1899 and 1902, from $6.50 per pikul to $13.95, was largely inflation (table 4). The cur-

7. *SSADR,* 1907, p. 306.

rency, however, continued to fluctuate, and between 1902 and 1906 the dollar rose back to 2s. 4d., where it was fixed on 29 January 1906. This rise in value of the dollar hurt dealers in Straits produce who had made contracts when the dollar was cheaper and then had to deliver when it had risen.[8] The shift in the currency values caused many of the bankruptcies.

The economic difficulties of this period were more than the simple cyclical changes in the economy. They indicated major shifts in the global economy and in that of the colony. After 1903 gambier exports began to decline steadily in quantity. At the same time, the gambier-producing areas that had served Singapore were declining at an even faster rate. Johor, for instance, saw its exports to Singapore drop from a high of over fifteen million dollars in 1903 to under nine million dollars in 1906.[9] Prices of many traditional exports from the Straits were falling. Those that were rising included some of the new growth crops such as rubber.[10] It was rubber that finally reversed the slumping economy in 1909, when bankruptcies dropped to only sixty-two in Singapore, with liabilities of only about $775,679. While the rise in rubber was a boost for the Malayan economy, this new crop lent itself to different forms of business management and a different sort of labor organization. In particular, it permitted capitalization by Western corporations more readily than the other crops that had served as Malay's staples since 1819. It required a substantial investment to clear and plant land and then wait six years for a return. British rubber planters had also begun the practice of bringing in Indian laborers, mostly Tamils, to work their plantations. This was one more blow to the revenue farmers and the kongsi-based economies of the Malay states. While the shift to rubber did not shut out the smaller producers—in fact it could be done rather painlessly by simply interplanting[11]—it did introduce competitors and new systems of labor organization and control to the traditional Chinese agricultural systems.

The Decline of the Farms

The history of the farms between 1885 and 1910 is not exactly a transparent succession of events. Information on the farm holders

8. SSADR, 1906, p. 96.
9. SSADR, 1906, p. 319.
10. SSADR, 1906, p. 297.
11. Yap, p. 14; see also James C. Jackson, 1968, pp. 223–32.

after the great conspiracy is rather haphazard despite the general increase in record keeping. It has not been possible to identify the major holders of the farms for all periods. The absence of information suggests a lack of perceived problems with the farms so far as the colonial government was concerned. Usually, no news was good news; but there were problems. Contrasts with the period before 1880 are obvious. For one thing, most of the chief figures in the farms were from Pinang. Even though individuals such as Koh Seang Tat and Chiu Sin Yong, once having been burned, did not try to come back and take the farms again, their experience did not stop other Pinang taukehs from trying their luck in Singapore (fig. 7). In addition to Pinang merchants, there were, however, also financiers from Melaka who attempted to take the Singapore farms. These inroads by people from outside suggest that substantial amounts of·capital were being generated from investments in different fields, mostly tin. The farms always tempted capital. As ever, drugs seemed to draw liquid cash.

The 1886–89 farming syndicate came into being in the midst of considerable readjustment in the Singapore administration. In 1885, Maharaja Abu Bakar of Johor and Governor Weld had traveled to London, and with the Colonial Office, negotiated a new treaty regulating Johor-British relations. Weld believed the treaty would enable him to place a Resident in Johor, but Abu Bakar had sufficiently watered down the wording so that no Resident came to Johor until twenty-five years later. At the same time, the Colonial Office recognized Abu Bakar as sultan of the State and Territory of Johor.[12]

In the middle of these negotiations, Abu Bakar or his secretary, Abdul Rahman bin Andak, suggested another treaty to formalize the relationship between the opium farms of Singapore and Johor. A draft treaty was prepared which would have arranged for the letting of the Singapore and Johor farms as one. The amount tendered would then be split according to a formula based on a population census. Initially, the division between Johor and Singapore was to be fixed at five-fourteenths for Johor and nine-fourteenths for Singapore.

Cecil Clementi-Smith, the acting governor in Weld's absence, received a copy of the treaty through unofficial channels from Abu Bakar's legal advisors in Singapore, Rodyk and Davidson. He telegraphed London in August protesting to the Colonial Office for attempting to arrange a revenue farm treaty without advice from the local authorities. He detailed his objections in a dispatch: The terms

12. Trocki, 1979, pp. 187–91.

Figure 7. Opium-farming syndicates, 1886–1909

1886–1888

Singapore, Johor, Melaka, & Riau opium & spirit farms

Lee Keng Yam & Wee Kim Yam   (Johor)
    Seah Ling Chai
    Seah Jim Kui
    Dato Mentri Ja'afar bin Haji Mohamed

1889–1891

Pinang Syndicate: Singapore, Johor, Melaka, Riau, & Negri Sembilan opium & spirit farms

Manager: Gan Gnoh Bee, with chops Ban Kee Bee, Ban Ban Bee, Ban Seng Bee, Goh Quan Beng, & Hock Hin & Co.

1892–1894   No data

1895–1897

Pinang Syndicate:
Farmer: Gan Gnoh Bee

Singapore	Pinang
Chen Kok	Lim Kek Chuan
Choo Yew	Khaw Joo Choe
	Yeoh Wee Gark
	Ho Teang Wan
	Thio Tiauw Siat

1898–1900

Singapore & Pinang Syndicate (territory uncertain)

Farmers:

Seah Song Seah	Tan Joo Chin	Koo Thean Poh
Seet Tiang Lim	Wee Kay Seang	Ng Pak San
Seah Pek Seah	Wang Ah Yeam	Khoo Teng Tay
Seah Eng Keat	Lim Leng Cheak	Cheah Toon Haw
Low Cheang Yee	Khoo Hun Yeang	Cheang Jim Hean

Partners:

Tan Eng Cheng	Khoo Hun Yeang	
Cheah Eng Kee	Lee Hay Thio	
Principal directors:	Seah Song Seah	Lim Leng Cheak
Principal managers:	Seet Tiang Lim	Tan Eng Cheng
	Khoo Teng Thay	Khoo Hun Yeang
Spirit dept. managers:	Ng Pak San	Khoo Hun Yeam

1901–1903

Singapore and affiliated opium & spirit farms		
Chop Chin Ho Bee		
General director:	Khoo Hun Yeang	
Managers:	Cheah Teow Eang	Tan Kheam Hock
	Chee Quee Bong	Khoo Sian Tan

1904–1906

Singapore and affiliated opium & spirit farms (to 31 August 1904)		
Khoo Hun Yeang	Khoo Thean Poh	Lim Cheng Tek
Khoo Hun Yeam	Tan Kheam Hock	Lee Toon Tok
Khaw Joo Choe	Yeoh Heng Keat	Lim Tian Hoon
Cheah Eng Kee	Cheah Eng Swee	Cheah Teow Eang
Cheah Eu Ghee	Goh Eu Kiong	Lee Hai Thye
Chean Guan Chee		
	Reorganized 1 September 1904	
Khaw Joo Choe	Khoo Sian Tan	Khoo Teck Seong
Joseph William Cashin	Lim Tian Hoon	Khoo Thean Poh
Cheah Teow Eang	Chew Guan Chee	Lee Toon Tok
Chee Kwee Bong	Lee Hai Thye	Lim Thong Seang
Tan Kheam Hock	Lim Cheng Tek	

1907–1909

Singapore and affiliated farms
Head: Khaw Joo Choe
(Membership of syndicate not certain, but probably the same as previous syndicate)

Sources: Lena Cheng U Wen, 1960, pp. 85–86, and CO 273/300, G.D. No. 363, 11 November 1904.

were not fair to Singapore. A split based on population alone would not take into account the "condition and prosperity" of the populations in the two countries. Furthermore, no census had ever been taken of Johor, and it would be expensive to take one. Lastly, he had already advertised for the 1886–88 farms, and kongsis had already been formed on the basis of the original conditions. A change of rules at this point would "disturb" their calculations and possibly cause the value of the farms to fall.[13]

Clementi-Smith's major objection was to Abu Bakar's attempt to finesse this arrangement through London, bypassing the local admin-

13. CO 273/135, G.D. No. 302, 1 August 1885.

istration. In his view, a treaty with the Colonial Office could only greatly reduce the flexibility of the Straits authorities in dealing with the sultan and the Chinese. The secretary of state in the Colonial Office was, on the contrary, convinced that such a treaty would help avoid the kind of difficulties that had caused the smuggling conspiracy in 1883. Clementi-Smith's objections finally carried the day, and the treaty was never signed.[14]

There appeared to be some difficulty with the bidding for the farms in that year. One of the parties submitting tenders was a European, P. J. Seth, which was quite unusual. There is no record of a European being involved in the farms since a couple of Europeans held the Pinang farms in 1806–7.[15] Clementi-Smith turned him down, but not without a certain amount of questionable dealing. Seth protested, claiming that the governor had accepted his tender, opened it, and then asked for others. He had also bid only for the Singapore farms and not the Johor farm. Clementi-Smith said he refused Seth's bid because Seth was "not a man of substance" and was simply acting as an agent for "certain Chinese who do not wish, for manifest reasons, to put themselves forward."[16] The Chinese are not identified, but it is possible that Cheang Hong Lim and Tan Hiok Nee and other members of the late great syndicate were involved. Other possibilities would be Tan Keng Swee and Lim Kwee Eng, neither one of whom appeared as members in any succeeding farming syndicates. There is, however, no hard evidence one way or the other. Clementi-Smith's remarks are indicative of the problems one faces when trying to understand the farms. There were obviously important undercurrents in many cases, but colonial administrators were extremely reluctant to name names or to be forthcoming with details.

The farmers in the 1886–88 syndicate were a strange mix. The head of the farms was Lee Keng Yam, who was the son of an old Melaka family. He had, until 1885, spent most of his working life in Shanghai, where he had worked for Kim Seng and Company.[17] Coming from outside the old pepper and gambier syndicate, he too had to find local partners and sought them among the pepper and gambier interests. Song mentions that Wee Kim Yam, the son of Wee Ah Hood, a major Teochew pepper and gambier dealer, was a partner in the 1886–88 farms.[18] Lee Keng Yam may have had the pieces of another large

14. Tong, 1953, pp. 22–24.
15. Wong Lin Ken, 1964–65, app. C, p. 122.
16. CO 273/135, G.D. No. 365, 16 September 1885.
17. Song, p. 242.
18. Song, p. 103.

syndicate; Song reports that he had also held "some Dutch farms," which probably meant Riau. In July 1888 he had also followed in Cheang Hong Lim's footsteps and purchased the Hong Kong opium farm. Unfortunately, he died at the relatively young age of forty-six in September 1888.[19] This apparently left the way open for another Pinang syndicate to come back and take the farms.

A different group emerged in Johor to take shares in their side of the farms in 1886. Documents from the Johor Archives record that Seah Ling Chai had an interest in the farms. He was the son of a former kapitan China of Johor, the Sekudai kangchu, Seah Tye Heng. At the same time, Ling Chai was also the Johor manager of the Kongkek. His partner was Seah Jim Kui (no relation). They bought sixty shares of the joint Singapore-Johor farms. They then sold twenty-one of these shares to Dato Mentri Ja'afar bin Haji Mohamed, the chief minister of Johor. The shares at this time were worth one thousand dollars each, but there is no record of the total number of shares in the joint farm.[20] Using the treaty formula of five-fourteenths as a guideline for the Johor farm, then the capital in the Singapore farm might have been about ninety-six thousand dollars. A local organization, tied to the pepper and gambier kongsi group and to the Malay administration, must have run the operation on the ground in Johor.

There is no report of the bidding or transference of the farm in 1888 for the 1889–91 farm contract, but when problems later began to arise, information about the identity of the farmer and the configuration of the syndicate did come out. The farmer began to run into trouble with the sagging economy almost immediately. By the end of 1889 it was apparent to the Straits' authorities that the farm contracts for both Singapore and Pinang would not be fulfilled. Clementi-Smith, still the acting governor, said he thought the tenders for 1888 had been too high. He wrote to the Colonial Office in mid-1891, explaining the problems: the economy had been depressed because of the state of the money market in London; local banks had refused to grant advances owing to orders from home; there had been substantial opium smuggling; and finally, Chinese immigration into the Straits had been dropping off. All these difficulties adversely affected the farmers, whom Clementi-Smith described as men of the "highest character," whom he had known for many years.

The manager of the Singapore farm was, at this time, Gan Gnoh Bee,

19. Song, p. 242.
20. Trocki, 1979, pp. 177–78; see also Johor Archives, *KSSSU*, S. 30, S. 31, S. 32, dated 30 and 31 March 1886.

who was a native of Pinang. The other partners in the farm were not listed by name, with the possible exception of Goh Quan Beng. The rest were listed by their *chops* (or trademarks): Ban Kee Bee,[21] Ban Ban Bee, Ban Seng Bee, and Hock Hin & Co. The scope of, or area covered by, this farming syndicate was somewhat larger than former ones. In addition to holding the opium and spirit farms for Singapore, the kongsi also held the farms for Johor, Riau, Melaka, and Negri Sembilan. The Pinang farm was then held by the former Singapore farmer Chiu Sin Yong, together with Chan Ley Kam, Khoo Thean Tek, and Chang Keng Kui. Chang was the kapitan China for Larut. The Pinang farmers also held the Kedah farms and most probably those for the rest of Perak beyond Larut.

Because of the depression during 1890 and 1891, both the Pinang and Singapore syndicates had suffered considerable losses, and the governor was willing to make allowances in both cases. As of June 1891 the Pinang farm was $589,000 in arrears in its payments and had already posted losses of $450,000. The governor had twice granted the Pinang farmers remissions on their rent. In the first instance he had forgiven $18,000 of a $95,050 debt in 1890; then in 1892 he had reduced the rent by $20,000 per month and extended the contract at the same rate for another three years, through the end of 1894. The Singapore farmer had done a little better, but Gan Gnoh Bee's losses amounted to $364,002 as of 1892. He, too, was given a reduction of rent and benefited from the extension of his contract.[22] Gan kept the Singapore farms for the 1892–94 period as well; for the Royal Commission listed him as the Singapore opium farmer when it interviewed him in December 1893.[23] Gan's rent for this period was reduced from $1,351,000 to $1,111,000 per year. A newspaper article describing these arrangements suggested that he would seek the partnership of "new men of capital."[24]

Gan managed to hang on to the farms for yet another term and was listed by Lena Cheng U Wen as the farmer for both Singapore and Pinang in 1895–97. His partners in Singapore were Chen Kok and

21. Chop Ban Kee Bee was the well-known wine and spirits distilleries of Cheah Kee Ee, a wealthy Pinang tin miner and, later, rubber planter. Most of his Malayan holdings were in Perak. It thus seems that Cheah Kee Ee was one of Gan Gnoh Bee's partners. Cf. Feldwick, *Present Day Impressions of the Far East* (1917), p. 862. It has not been possible to identify the other chops. There are also inconsistencies in the sources regarding the spelling of Gan's middle name; most give it as "Gnoh" but some others as "Ngoh." The latter *sounds* more correct, but I have followed the more prevalent usage.
22. CO 273/162, G.D. Confidential, CO No. 24027, 16 November 1889; CO 273/173, G.D. No. 264, 23 June 1891.
23. *Roycom*, vol. 5, *Straits Settlements*, app. 25, pp. 154–55.
24. *STWI*, 31 December 1890.

Choo Yew, and his Pinang partners included Lim Kek Chuan, Khaw Joo Choe (who would later try his luck in Singapore), and Thio Tiauw Siat (Chang Pi-shih), the wealthy revenue farmer from the Netherlands East Indies who had already made a fortune through farms in Java and was also the Chinese kapitan of Deli in Sumatra and founder of the Deli Bank, the first bank in Sumatra. He later moved to Singapore and became the Chinese consul to the Straits Settlements.[25] Song mentions that See Kee Ann held the Melaka farms in 1897. He was the son of Melaka merchant See Moh Guan, who was a partner with his brother in the Singapore firm of Eng-wat Moh-guan and Brothers. See Kee Ann was involved in tapioca and pepper and gambier planting, but he had no business activities himself in Singapore. It is probable that he had some connection with the syndicate that held the Singapore farms, but it is impossible to say.[26]

In 1899 and 1900 a large syndicate took over the Singapore farms. The *Singapore and Straits Directory* listed the names of eighteen people who were either "farmers" or "partners" (or both) of the farming syndicate for 1900 (fig. 7). The names are a virtual who's who of Chinese in Singapore. The leaders of this syndicate were Singapore men, the two sons of Seah Eu Chin, Seah Song Seah and Seah Pek Seah. They were joined by a third member of the clan, their nephew, Seah Eng Keat (or Kiat), the son of Seah Cheo Seah. By this time, all four were leading members of the Straits-born Chinese community of Singapore and apparently represented both Singapore and the pepper and gambier interests that had once been the charge of their uncle, Tan Seng Poh, and his son, Tan Keng Swee.[27] Another descendant of the former great opium syndicate in this group was Cheang Jim Hean, the son of Cheang Hong Lim. Song reports that Hong Lim died in 1893.[28]

Another Singapore Teochew in the 1900 syndicate was Low Cheang Yee. He was also Straits born and was the son of Low Ah Jit. His half-brother, Low How Kim, had been a chief assistant in the opium farm in 1877 with Cheang Hong Lim, Tan Seng Poh, and Tan Hiok Nee. The Lows were another long-standing Singapore pepper and gambier family. Low Cheang Yee was the father of Low Peng Yam, who later became one of the directors and largest shareholder of the Four Seas Bank (Sze Hai Tong), the major Teochew bank in Singapore.[29]

25. Lena Cheng U Wen, "British Opium Policy" (1960), p. 85; Godley, 1981, pp. 9–12.
26. Song, pp. 104–5. Cheng U Wen, 1960 (p. 85), lists Chi Eng Cheng, Chi Kwi Beng, and Li Keng Liet as the Melaka farmers for 1895–97.
27. Song, pp. 21–22, 259, 304, 372.
28. Song, p. 326.
29. Song, pp. 191, 141–42.

The backgrounds and the business and family connections of most of these people tie this particular syndicate to the great syndicate of the 1870s, which was essentially a Singapore and pepper and gambier group. Perhaps the most intriguing name on this list is that of Tan Eng Cheng. We cannot be certain, but it seems that this is the very person who was banished in the suppression of the smuggling conspiracy of 1883. There is no evidence of his return, but Chinese names are rarely duplicated.

The remaining names on the list are less easy to identify. Certain ones appear to be associated with different areas. Seet Tiang Lim, for instance, was descended from a Melaka family and was the grandson of See Boon Tiong, a tapioca planter in Linggi who had also been in business in Singapore and Melaka since 1825. Song lists See Boon Tiong as one of the members of the Keng Tek Hue. The See family had considerable landed property both in Singapore and Melaka.[30] Khoo Hun Yeang was the proprietor of the Singapore firm Chop Khoo Chin Hong Company and was the son of Khoo Thean Teck, one of the most powerful men in Pinang.[31]

The last member of this particular farming syndicate for whom any information is available is Ng Pak San. He also appears in the same issue of the *Straits Directory* as a partner of Loke Chow Kit in Chow Kit and Company. Loke Chow Kit, at the same time, was also the manager of the Selangor Revenue farm under the very wealthy Selangor merchant Loke Yew. Thus, there was probably a connection between Loke Yew and the Singapore farming syndicate of 1900, even though his name is not listed among the partners.[32]

Of the remaining names on the list, nothing certain can be said. Possibly Khoo Thean Poh was related to Khoo Tiong Poh, who had been a member of the farms in 1880 and had controlled the ship-owning firm of Bun Hin in Singapore and Pinang, but there is no available evidence to connect the two.[33] Likewise, Tan Joo Chin may have been related to Tan Joo Tiam, who was an important pepper and gambier merchant and served as a vice-president of the Kongkek in 1896–1900, but again, this is only speculation.[34]

30. Song, pp. 29, 70.
31. Wynne, pp. 251–56, 326. *SSD* (1910), 167.
32. "Selangor," *SSD* (1899), 268.
33. Khoo Tiong Poh was listed in another Singapore Chinese firm at this time (*SSD* [1878], 97), as a coproprietor of the first Ann Bee and Company along with Cheong Ann Bee, Syed Md. bin Ahmat Alsagof, Lee Peh Boon, Lee Boon Beng, Lim Eng Keng, and Lee Teck Loch. Song notes that he had opened Bun Hin in 1874 in partnership with Rajah Wichit from "Phya Puket" (p. 176). By 1882 Bun Hin had branches in Pinang, Hong Kong, Xiamen, and Shantou (*SSD* [1882], 87).
34. Song, p. 38; *SSTP* (Johor), no. 30, 5 May 1896. The only reason for suggesting a

This 1898–1900 syndicate marks the last appearance of Singapore's old pepper and gambier interests in the revenue farms. After 1900, there appears to have been another shift in the overall orientation of the farms. The succeeding syndicate, or syndicates, seem to have been composed of relative newcomers, some of whom were Singapore residents but most of whom had close relations to a couple major Pinang families. Judging by the subsequent history of the farm, the Seahs of Singapore and their friends got out in timely fashion.

I found no actual list of the 1901–3 syndicate and two slightly different lists for the 1904 opium-farming kongsi. The relationship of the two syndicates seems to have been quite close; the *Straits Directory* listed the head of the 1904 syndicate as Khoo Hun Yeang, who had also been a member of the 1900 syndicate.[35] The Colonial Office records contain a contract made by the members of this syndicate when they were forced to reorganize it—Khoo's syndicate collapsed when the crash of 1903 hit. The documents on the reorganization show many more participants in the kongsi than were listed in the *Straits Directory*.[36]

A person named on both the original contract and the new one ultimately emerged as the head of the farm. This was Khaw Joo Choe, who was connected to an important Chinese family in northern Malaya and southern Siam. Khaw Joo Choe was the nephew of the governor of Ranong and founder of the Eastern Shipping Company of Pinang, Khaw Sim Bee (Quah Beng Kee).[37] Actually, it appears that Khaw Joo Choe was the head of the last three syndicates (e.g., 1901–3, 1904–6, and 1907–9). The *Free Press* noted in 1903 that "the old farmer, Chop Chin Ho Bee, has secured the farm." Chop Chin Ho Bee was listed as the head of the farm for 1901, and this shows that the syndicate was considered to be in the same hands for 1904 through 1907.[38]

This syndicate must have done quite well initially. Little difficulty

---

connection here is the presence of the element "Poh" in both of the Khoos and of "Joo" for the two Tans.

35. *SSD* (1904), 176. The *SSD* also listed Cheah Teow Eang, Chee Quee Bong, Khoo Sian Tan, and Tan Kheam Hock as managers of the Singapore farm and Chew Guan Chee as the assistant manager for Johor.

36. CO 273/300, CO No. 41171, p. 289, enclosed with G.D. No. 363, 11 November 1904. Strangely enough, Chee Quee Bong and Khoo Sian Tan, who were on the *SSD* list, are not listed here.

37. Cushman, "Khaw Group" (1986); see also, by the same author, "Marriage of Convenience" (1984).

38. *SFP*, Wednesday, 22 July 1903. I am grateful to Jennifer Cushman for bringing this reference to my attention and for pointing out to me that Chin Ho Bee was Khaw Joo Choe's chop.

had arisen during the years of their first contract. Although economic data shows that the depression was already setting in by 1903, it does not seem to have discouraged the bidding for the 1904–6 contract for the farms.[39] Frank Swettenham, who was then governor of the Straits Settlements, held the auction for the 1904–6 farms in July 1903. He was able to get very high bids for all the farms of the three settlements. His superiors in the Colonial Office were rather surprised when he telegraphed them reporting that he had sold the farms for an increase of $4,000,000.[40] Even though he meant the opium and spirit farms of all three settlements, the increase was spectacular. Comparable figures for earlier years had been $2,957,400 for 1898–1900 and $4,580,000 for 1901–3. Swettenham had received bids as high as $8,556,000 for the 1904–6 contract. For the Singapore opium farm, the rise between the two triennial periods was over 100 percent: from $2,340,000 to $5,040,000 per annum.

This rosy prospect was marred only by a difficulty with Johor. Abdul Rahman bin Andak had offered the Johor farms for auction separately, since no treaty linking the two farms had ever been signed. Swettenham reported that Johor had "squeezed" the Singapore farmer for more money. The same farmer who held the Singapore farms also had held the Johor farm for 1901–3, presumably Khoo Hun Yeang. During that period he had paid $63,000 per month, or $756,000 per year. In 1903 he had offered $78,000 per month, but the Johor government reported that there were two higher bids, one for $85,000 per month and the other for $90,000. The latter bid was said to be from a "Johor Chinese" who had been banished from Singapore as a gambler. The banishment order had recently been canceled, however. The Singapore farmer complained, saying that the Johor farms were not worth even $80,000 but that he would give $85,000. He told Swettenham that if, however, he did not get the Johor farm, he would refuse to take the Singapore farm. The Johor people, for their part, said they had to give the contract to the highest bidder. Swettenham finally had to pay the extra $5,000 per month out of the Singapore treasury, in order to save

39. CO No. 41171, Anderson to Colonial Office, (with CO 273/300, G.D. No. 363, 10 November 1904). An enclosure is a revenue farm contract showing a reorganization of the syndicate. Apparently the syndicate that took the Singapore farms in January 1904 was composed as shown in figure 7. Eight of those in the top list dropped out in September 1904, and six new members joined, including a European, Joseph William Cashin. At that time, Khaw Joo Choe seems to have taken over as the head, and Khoo Hun Yeang stepped down. This being the case, it is probable that Khoo was the head of the 1901–3 Singapore opium farm.
40. CO 273/291, Telegram, 16 July 1903, CO No. 26197.

Table 9. Estimated monthly costs and sales of selected Malayan opium farms, 1903 (Straits dollars)

	Singapore	Pinang	Melaka	Johor	Kedah
Estimated Chinese population	164,000	98,000	19,000	150,000*	39,000
Estimated chandu sales (tahils)	140,000	74,337	11,000	80,000	28,000
Gross chandu sales	$433,740	$230,432	$33,000	$140,000	$76,000
Estimated costs	$138,540	$66,749	$9,150	$58,600	$30,200
Opium farm rent	$215,000	$172,000	$26,000	$80,000	$43,000**
Spirit farm rent	$50,000	$45,000	$5,000	$10,000	
Net profit or loss	$30,200	$−53,317	$−7,150	$−9,000	$2,800

Source: CO 273/291; G.D. No. 399, 17 September 1903, CO No. 37549.
*This figure was thought to be "greatly overestimated."
**This figure is the combined opium and spirit farm rent.

the original contract. As soon as word of this deal got out, Kedah demanded a similar increase from the Pinang farmer, Gan Gnoh Bee. Swettenham was, nonetheless, quite satisfied with his accomplishment. He wrote, boasting, to his superiors in the Colonial Office: "It is cause for congratulation that the Colony had not only obtained such a large increase, but that for the next three years, the farms are in the hands of the men best qualified to hold them—the men who have held them for the last three years with satisfaction to the Governments and the Chinese community and that they are protected against the most serious dangers to which they are liable by holding the Farms of Johore and Kedah in their own hands."[41]

Swettenham was particularly proud that in addition to obtaining such a large increase in the rent, he had also convinced the farmers to accept a new set of revenue regulations. The new rules gave the government substantial oversight in the working of the farms. From 1904 onward, it was possible for the protector of Chinese to have access to the books of the farmer and to monitor the finances of the syndicate. In the months before the bidding in July 1903, G. T. Hare, the assistant protector of Chinese, had been collecting data on the farms (table 9). Swettenham reported to the Colonial Office that in the future, "the Government will have over the new Farmers and their business a control such as it has never before attempted."[42]

According to the figures Hare collected (table 9), the Singapore farmer could expect to net $30,200 per month, which does not seem

41. CO 273/291, G.D. No. 341, 17 August 1903, CO No. 34273.
42. Ibid.

very lucrative. It would have been less than .7 percent of the gross. The table does not indicate whether the monthly costs included interest on capital and payments to shareholders. If interest and dividends were included in the costs, it is unclear how the $30,200 was to be divided among the fifteen or so syndicate members. At the time Swettenham sent these statistics to the Colonial Office, he remained sanguine about the prospects of the farm and the new level of control the government had attained: "From January next [the excise farms] will give more than two-thirds of the total revenue, no individual and no Department had [heretofore] made any study of the question and there is no one with experience to whom to appeal for advice on the subject . . . it can hardly be right that it should be no one's concern to understand the details of a revenue of $8,000,000 per annum raised by a Chinese Syndicate."[43]

The correspondence reveals no inkling of a problem with a profit margin of less than 10 percent of gross. By September 1904, however, Swettenham had left Malaya and moved on to other things. John Anderson was the governor when it was discovered that the Singapore farmers were bankrupt and stood to lose $3,135,000 by 1906 if the rent were not reduced. This revelation destroyed Khoo Hun Yeang, who was forced to turn over management of the farms to Khaw Joo Choe but continued to stand security. The farming kongsi had to be reorganized, and new capital was brought in (fig. 7).

Although the farming contract stipulated severe measures for failure to meet the terms, the government could not enforce its sanctions. By law, the government could confiscate the farmers' securities, which were usually property deeds, resell the farms, and hold the original farmer responsible for any loss to the government. Anderson said that if he tried to find a new syndicate to take the farms, the Chinese would combine to obtain a huge reduction. Besides that, he pointed out that total failure of the farms would have repercussions throughout the community: "These farms for many years have made large profits and many people outside the business itself have taken shares in them, and perhaps the bulk of the capital is found by people of moderate wealth who invest a few thousands of dollars a piece. If such people were to lose their capital by the complete collapse of a farm, it is likely that tenderers would in future be few and confined to men of great wealth."[44] In the final analysis, no matter how much the government knew about

43. CO 273/292, Confidential, 9 October 1903, CO No. 40854.
44. CO 273/300, G.D. No. 363, 10 November 1904, CO No. 41171 with enclosure.

the farms, they remained very much at the mercy of the farmers. There was so much capital tied up in the syndicates that all business would suffer from a fall. The farm had come to be a kind of bank or stock exchange for much of the Chinese community. It was perhaps the key vehicle for Chinese capital accumulation in its time.

The sources are not clear on the amount of the reduction given in 1904. According to the contract, the farmers should have paid $5,040,000, but the *Annual Departmental Report* shows a return from the Singapore opium farm of only $4,245,000. In 1905 the farms paid $990,600 less than in 1904, and in 1906 they obtained a further reduction of $244,400.[45] Based on the original contract, the shortfall by the end of 1906 was thus $3,020,600 (table 7).

The real problem, of course, was the general trade depression. Speculation in the currency coupled with the drop in prices and orders for Straits produce, particularly pepper and gambier, had been disastrous for the farms. Their collapse was all the more spectacular for the enormous increases the farmers had promised to pay. There was, at the same time, a rise of nearly 11 percent in the cost of raw opium in 1904.[46] This, together with the rise in chandu prices helped to further cut consumption at a time when consumers were facing economic difficulties.

At the same time, there was a reported increase in smuggling, but there were no accusations of a conspiracy. The most serious problem, so far as the government was concerned, was the appearance of new drugs. Around the turn of the century, morphine and cocaine began to find their way into the Straits Settlements. Although they were immediately recognized as a threat to the farms, no legislation was effective against them until 1907. In the meantime, between 1903 and 1907, morphine gained considerable popularity among the poorest of former opium users; for injections only cost about four cents. In Singapore the farmer took steps to prevent its introduction, but in Pinang the farmer, Gan Gnoh Bee, began to import it himself.[47]

Given the poor state of the economy in 1906, the farms were auctioned at considerable reductions below what was paid in the prior

45. *SSADR*, 1905, pp. 442–43; *SSADR*, 1906, pp. 168–69.
46. *SSADR*, 1904, p. 494. In 1903 Benares opium was selling for $1,014.50 per chest; during 1904 it rose to $1,124.50 per chest. The rise did not continue, however, and by 1905 the price had fallen back down to $987: *SSADR*, 1905, p. 278.
47. Warren D. Barnes, "Memorandum upon the Effect on the Consumption of Opium in the Straits Settlements of the Increase in Retail Price Effected in 1904," 25 February 1907, CO 273/327, CO No. 10841. This memo (Barnes memo no. 2) gives a good summary of the conditions surrounding the collapse of the 1904–6 farming syndicate.

term. For the 1907–9 contract, the high bid for the Singapore farms was only a little more than $2.9 million, and in 1909 the actual return was just above $2.5 million. By 1907 the Khoos were bankrupt, and a few of the other major backers of the kongsi were in court. Song mentions the failure of Khoo Teck Seong and his brother in particular. And before the end of the contract, Khaw Joo Choe was likewise bankrupt.[48] Even if there had been no anti-opium movement, it is difficult to see how the government could continue to allow the revenue to be determined by a Chinese syndicate. When the 1909 contract expired, the farms were abolished, and the sale of opium was placed under a government-run monopoly.

The Anti-Opium Movement

Cynical as it might seem to suggest that the anti-opium movement had virtually no influence on the final formulation of British colonial opium policy, one is hard pressed to find evidence of an impact. According to the numbers, one major result of the abolition of the farming system was an almost immediate increase in government revenues. Although the net profit from the sale of opium under the government monopoly was just under $1.8 million in 1910, by 1911 it was over $3 million, and by 1914 the government was netting over $5 million annually on opium sales in Singapore alone. This is scant evidence of moral reform. Nevertheless, at the time of the decision to abolish the farms, colonial officials formulating policy seemed to be responding to the pressures of the anti-opium movement. Like so many colonial bureaucrats, they claimed to be doing good when, in fact, they were doing very well.

There is no question, though, that the anti-opium movement, both in England and eventually in Malaya, did attempt to put pressure on the government to restrict and ultimately abolish the opium trade. As early as 1807 the Pinang Grand Jury had attempted to forbid opium usage in the Straits.[49] William Gladstone, speaking against Britain's involvement in the Opium War against China in 1839, called the trade "morally indefensible," and in the 1840s and 1850s voices continued to be raised against the use of opium in the Straits.[50] But these early attempts to restrict the trade and the farming system had little effect.

48. Song, pp. 102, 444–45.
49. Wright, *East India Economic Problems* (1961), pp. 167–68.
50. Owen, pp. 177–78; Little; Braddell.

The 1870s marked a change. After 1874 the Society for the Suppression of the Opium Trade, organized in London, began an intensive campaign to stop the cultivation of the drug in India and to end the trade to China. The movement gained support from missionary groups operating in China and from the Quakers in England.

Throughout the entire nineteenth century, Indian interests and most commercial interests involved in Asian trade kept Parliament from taking any steps that would prejudice the substantial revenues the colonial states derived from opium.[51] But as early as 1863 an editorial in the *Straits Times* pointed with some alarm to the growing anti-opium movement in England and warned that the Straits' revenues would become subject to closer scrutiny once the Settlements were transferred to the Colonial Office. The editorial spoke of a group it termed "the Exeter Hall party" in England which had "shown itself particularly ingenious in ferreting out what they term the political immoralities of the more distant outlying possessions of England." The article suggested that parties in the Straits "ought to take all measures in our power to counteract the extreme views of any such party." It also suggested a certain "moderation" in regulating the trade: "Indeed the only practical way of checking opium smoking is to render it expensive—to take it beyond the reach of the poorer and industrious classes, and to render its limited indulgence a necessary economy even with the better circumstanced portion of the Chinese inhabitants. If our thus adding to the expense of the vice, at the same time adds to our revenue, it should be a matter of congratulation with us, and not of superstitious aversion."[52] These words, which probably reflect the thoughts of John Cameron, then editor of the *Straits Times,* expressed the general feeling of the most influential parties in the Straits throughout the nineteenth century. The substantial economic interests that depended on the opium revenues in India, the trade to China, and the farms in the other colonies put up a long and successful holding action. As a *Straits Times Overland Journal* editorial pointed out in 1881, "Fortunately the anti-opium fanatics at home . . . are not likely to succeed. India's interests in the matter are exactly identical with our own. She cannot afford to sacrifice an annual revenue of eight millions sterling at the bidding of sentimental fanatics and spurious philanthropy based on imaginary facts and false argumentation."

51. A good summary of the literature on the anti-opium movement can be found in Owen. Perhaps the most recent treatment of the movement is Johnson, "Righteousness before Revenue" (1975), pp. 304–26.
52. *ST,* 24 October 1863; *STOJ,* 2 June 1881.

It was not until 1893 that the Liberals, swept into power by a strong anti-opium vote, found themselves confronted with the prospect of depriving the empire of one of its major financial assets. A royal commission to study the opium problem in India was proposed. Gladstone, by this time much older and far less idealistic, sufficiently limited the scope of the commission's inquiry so that it would not endanger the revenue. According to Lena Cheng U Wen, "The anti-opium faction had called for a commission to examine *how* the Indian opium traffic should be suppressed. Gladstone's amendment provided for a commission that would simply inquire *whether* the traffic should be suppressed, and would investigate the probable financial consequences of prohibition."[53]

The proceedings of the Royal Commission on Opium occupy seven thick quarto volumes printed in double columns of newspaper type. It runs to well over fifteen hundred pages, most of which is testimony taken in India and China together with an enormous amount of statistical data on the trade throughout the century. Little of it refers to the Straits Settlements. The commission did not visit the Straits; it only sent written questionnaires to forty-three prominent citizens of the colony, of whom only thirty-five responded. The responses, together with a summary, occupy only about thirty-eight pages.[54] Although among those questioned were missionaries and doctors, there were no opium smokers, nor, as Tong Tek Ing has pointed out, was there any effort to determine how many opium smokers there were in the Straits Settlements, or any place else. Those questioned simply gave their best guesses. The estimates given by thirty-one interviewees in the Straits varied between 7 percent and 85 percent of the Chinese population. Three of the four Chinese who responded to the questionnaire (Gan Gnoh Bee, Chiu Sin Yong, and Koh Seang Tat) were then, or had been, opium farmers. Their estimates were quite low. Chiu said that 20 percent of the adult males used opium, Gan said one-third, and Koh refused to guess.[55]

What impresses one about this study, at least insofar as the Straits Settlements were concerned, is that most of the data was simply opinion. Outside of the opium farmers, those questioned had virtually no direct knowledge of opium usage on which to base their answers as to how many smokers there were; the effects of the drug, both long and short term; what kind of people smoked; what might happen if the supply of Indian opium were cut off; and how the revenue would be

53. Cheng U Wen, 1961, p. 73.
54. *Roycom*, vol. 5, *Straits Settlements*, app. 25, pp. 145–84.
55. Ibid., pp. 154, 157, 158.

made up. Most of the interviewees were hardly objective; they fell into two categories: those like the missionaries and doctors, who were opposed to the trade, and all the rest, who were reluctant to sacrifice the revenue. Most merchants and officials defended the use and taxation of the drug, and given the circumstances, one might defend the idea that it offered certain benefits. According to the merchant (not the governor) John Anderson:

> I have travelled on both sides of the Malay Peninsula, over tin mining districts, and have seen thousands and thousands of Chinese miners working in swarms at tin mines, displaying physical energy and endurance that the white man, under similar conditions, could not have and apply, and at the same time keep his full health. . . . And when I have seen these Chinamen after working all but naked for hours together in water up to their knees, go back to their quarters, and either before or after their meal, or both, smoke a pipe or pipes of opium apparently without prejudicial effect, I have marvelled at the arbitrary inconsistency of some people in Britain who, with no true knowledge of the matter . . . would say to [a Chinese] 'Opium you shall not have.'[56]

Obviously he did not track these miners over time to see just how well their bodies tolerated that level of physical abuse. At the same time, nobody visited the hospitals, prisons, or paupers' refuges to see what happened to people who maintained the levels of use noted above over a ten-year period.

The real concern was revenue. J. Y. Kennedy, a Pinang merchant, pointed out that the colony was dependent on the opium revenue so abolition would cause injury to the trade and industry of the colony and discontent among the people. He said that people "would think the Government mad to abolish it."[57] In contrast, the American missionary W. G. Shellabear was quite sanguine about the prospects of doing without the opium revenue. He simply pointed out that "the deficit could undoubtedly be made up, the wealth of Singapore being very great." He cautioned, however, that the wealthy people would object to the abolition of the opium revenue for fear that they *would* have to make up the deficit: "The wealthy Chinese bewail the demoralization of their fellow countrymen, and kinsmen, . . . but in spite of this some . . . will uphold opium revenue rather than submit to taxation."[58]

Most people, whether civil servants, merchants, or missionaries,

56. Ibid., p. 175.
57. Ibid., p. 170.
58. Ibid., p. 167.

were of the opinion that the economy of the Straits Settlements, and of British Malaya in general, depended on opium. While certain persons such as Shellabear and Koh Seang Tat believed the colony could in fact find some reasonable way to eliminate opium without a catastrophe, most questionnaire respondents predicted dire consequences from the abandonment of the opium revenue, including riots, mass outmigration of Chinese, a crime wave of smuggling, and general financial collapse.

In 1848 Dr. R. Little projected an idyllic life for the Chinese in the Straits Settlements without opium:

> How different would be the condition of the people of this island if instead of spending on Opium $417,884 yearly, they knew not the vice; that money hardly and honestly toiled for would be spent on clothes, in food and better houses, the men could afford to marry, a taste would be formed for finery, and something more would be required, than bare rice, the necessary of life . . . instead of 40 or 50 living under one roof, too often a mass of iniquity, a man and his family, or one or two single individuals could afford to live in a house of their own.

The best life he could imagine for them was something approximating his own idea of the life of the lower middle-class Briton. Very possibly the Chinese would have chosen something different. Life in the Borneo kongsi of Montrado perhaps most closely resembled what the life of the working-class Chinese in the Malay world might have been like without opium. But that would also have been a world without British imperialism and without capitalism. Perhaps Wang Tai Peng's ideal of a native Chinese brand of democracy, rooted in the traditions of brotherhood, could have taken hold in Singapore. That, however, was the path not taken. A few years later, Thomas Braddell could remark cynically, "In a state of society where so large a proportion of the public revenue is derived from the encouragement of opium and baang smoking and the drinking of spirits, the public does not expect perfection."[59]

The 1893 Royal Commission on Opium had almost no impact. A disappointed SSOT could only continue its pressure both at home and abroad until a combination of factors brought a new wave of disapprobation of opium, some fifteen years later. For several years after 1894 the Indian government tried to maintain a low profile on opium and in fact had already been slowly decreasing production. In 1901 the

59. Little, pp. 73–74; Braddell, p. 78.

standard provision (for export) was set at forty-eight thousand chests, and the government professed its intention to regulate cultivation; but as Lena Cheng pointed out, "Though it had become more sensitive to criticism, and 'had determined in the future to give as little offence as possible', there was no intention of discouraging the trade or relinquishing any of the opium revenue."[60] Somewhat the same attitude prevailed in the Straits and in Malaya, but there was, on the whole, less sensitivity to criticism and little serious thought on the idea that the opium revenue might be any cause for embarrassment.

In 1893 the *Straits Times Weekly Intelligence* commented on the foolishness of the Victorian Legislature in Australia which had passed an "Opium Restriction Bill." The bill, it said, would "simply disturb but not destroy the opium trade in Australia. Victoria will not benefit in the least by this measure, but on the contrary lose a revenue of some 20,000 a year without checking, as was expected from the sale of the drug. Wise in their generation, the New South Wales colonists have refused to join in the anti-opium cry."[61] There were, however, some problems and "misunderstandings." In 1893 Chia Tek Soon and Chiu Sin Yong, both Pinang opium farmers at the time, were nominated for appointments as justices of the peace. These appointments were questioned by Lord Ripon, then secretary of state for the colonies. He pointed out that in India, the keepers of opium shops were prevented from holding public office. The Straits' authorities tried to show that there was a difference between opium shopkeepers and opium farmers: the farmers were "respectable" men. Lord Ripon was not convinced, and the two appointments did not go forward.[62] Later, the Straits government apparently was able to put such appointments through; in 1914, one-time farmer Gan Gnoh Bee was listed as a justice of the peace in Pinang, although it is uncertain whether he was still an opium farmer when appointed.

In 1903 the U.S. Congress had appointed a commission to study the opium question in the Philippines. D. E. Owen states that its report, although much shorter, avoided the shortcomings of the British report: "Whereas the British seemed befogged by a cloud of witnesses and pressed for time, the Americans pursued their inquiry in a fashion leisurely enough to enable them to assimilate the evidence as it was received." The committee spent five months touring the East and took "infinite pains" to interview as many different people as possible. The

60. Cheng U Wen, 1961, p. 37.
61. *STWI*, 26 December 1893.
62. Tong, p. 29; also CO 273/191, CO No. 5056, H/C, 28 March 1893.

report offered a reasonably balanced view of the trade but also had an influence the British report did not. One result was the total prohibition of opium in the Philippines in 1906. In fact, 1906 was the key year for the turn of the tide against the opium trade. Owen described the chain of events as "fortuitous." A series of negotiations between Great Britain and China over the status of Tibet almost accidentally led to a reopening of talks on suppressing the opium trade between India and China. By 1906 both sides had reached an agreement. Essentially, China would take steps to eradicate opium cultivation inside China. An imperial decree was issued in September 1906: opium cultivation and use would be eliminated within ten years. The Indian government would, at the same time, cut exports to China by 10 percent per year, eliminating them altogether at the end of that period, provided the Chinese were successful with their aims. At the same time, the forces of reform in Britain had swept into Parliament once again, and no less than 250 of the newly elected members of the House of Commons were committed to the anti-opium cause. On 30 May 1906 the same sixty-year-old resolution was introduced into Parliament condemning the opium trade as "morally indefensible" and passed without division.[63]

Within a month of the announcement of the imperial decree in China, anti-opium forces in the Straits Settlements and Malaya began organizing to suppress opium usage in British Malaya. At the forefront of the movement were a number of foreign-educated Chinese. The first result was the organization of the Opium Refuge in Singapore by Dr. Yin Suat Chuan and Dr. Lim Boon Keng in the beginning of 1906. A few months later, Dr. Goh Lean Tuck (also known as Wu Lien-Tieh), a physician from Pinang, and Dr. Chen So Lan began organizing in Pinang and Kuala Lumpur.[64]

On 20 October 1906 Wu held a meeting in Pinang, attended by about two thousand people (all Chinese), which was addressed by J. G. Alexander, the honorary secretary of the SSOT. The meeting unanimously passed a resolution against the opium-farming system in Malaya. It pointed to the recent agreement between Great Britain and China and called attention to the parliamentary resolution condemning the India-China opium trade as "morally indefensible":

63. Owen, pp. 327, 329–39.
64. Lena Cheng U Wen, 1961, pp. 56–60. It seems that Goh Lean Tuck's surname should be "Goh," but in correspondence with the government he signed himself "G. L. Tuck, M.D": Petition to the Earl of Elgin, 31 October 1906, pp. 260–61, CO 273/324. Cheng reports that he was engaged in bacteriologic research at the Liverpool School of Tropical Medicine. He returned to the Straits in 1903. After arousing the opposition of the colonial regime in Malaya, he went to China and won fame fighting the plague; cf. Wu (1959).

This meeting, considering that the system at present enforced in the Straits Settlements of farming out opium licenses is also morally indefensible, in as much as it gives to the opium farmers a strong inducement to increase their profits by increasing the sales of a pernicious drug, and lends the sanction of Government to a degrading and vicious habit, respectfully urges His Majesty's Government to substitute for the existing system legislation similar to that in force throughout New Zealand and the Australian Commonwealth, by which the sale, use and possession of opium for other than medicinal purposes are strictly prohibited.

It also asked for temporary provision of the drug for addicted users, until they could be cured. On 31 October, Dr. Chen So Lan, then a member of the Selangor State Council, organized the Anti-Opium Society in Kuala Lumpur. The first meeting was attended by about two thousand people, and a similar resolution was passed.[65]

The Straits government reported Wu's meeting to London, forwarding a copy of the petition. The cover letter expressed skepticism as to the seriousness of the situation. It noted that Dr. Wu was said to be a Queen's Scholar, had been educated in the United Kingdom, was "very much occidentalized and is one of the school which advocates the amputation of the pig tail. If the rest of the meeting were of the same school, it probably did not properly represent Chinese feeling."[66]

A speech given by a Dr. R. M. Connolly in Ipoh in March 1907 provoked much deeper concern. The meeting was a gathering of representatives of all the anti-opium societies in British Malaya. Connolly was elected president of the conference. In the opening of his speech he suggested that if the Straits Settlements and the Federated States possessed the same powers of self-government as did Australia and New Zealand, and if the opinion of the populations were truly polled in Malaya, then a majority would support the abolition of opium usage. He further noted, "We do not wish to state that the British Officials in Malaya favor the Opium Trade or the unrestrained use of Opium amongst the Chinese."[67]

The minutes and handwritten comments on the copy of the speech sent to Colonial Office show the status of the debate in London over the opium question. The covering minute, signed by "R.E.S.," took issue with Connolly's statement: "Dr. Connolly apparently said or implied that the C.O. was standing in the way of reform in opposition to the desires and advice of its own officers. It is almost unnecessary to

65. CO 273/324, pp. 260–61; CO 273/324, CO No. 4445, 7 November 1906.
66. CO 273/324, CO No. 43288, 31 October 1906.
67. CO 273/334, CO No. 29251, received 15 August 1907, p. 154.

point out that there is not a word of truth in this suggestion." He went on to note that a commission had been appointed and until some word was received of its findings, it seemed "rather a waste of labor to go into details." He did, however, add a defense of the farming system: "The Farm system has been shown by experience to be the least troublesome and costly to work. A system of licenses was substituted in Hong Kong in the early '80s but it was found necessary to revert to the farm system. The great difficulty in the Straits and Hong Kong is that there is no customs staff and therefore to attempt to check import will necessitate the establishment of such a staff. At present the Farmer takes this work off our hands." He also raised the question of a substitute for the opium revenue and cautioned against the imposition of a customs duty; for such a move would "transfer Singapore trade to Sabang Bay" (presumably Sebong Bay in Riau). Although this outcome was virtually unthinkable in 1907, Straits officials and merchants had been raising that bugaboo for nearly ninety years.[68]

Another comment on the same minute, apparently by Sir F. Hopwood, the undersecretary of state for the colonies, was more critical. He said that the subject would be brought forward in Parliament and added, "Our position is little short of scandalous." In a responding comment, the earl of Elgin laid out the Colonial Office's position:

> I do not agree in imputing anything scandalous. We have just seen a very remarkable change in the position regarding opium. Hitherto, it had been assumed, practically without contradiction, that the Chinaman desired opium: and so long as that assumption was acted upon, the object of reformers was to check excess. We now find a movement in China for prohibition rather than restriction. It is rather soon to judge—but if this movement is genuine—not merely an official move—and I certainly hope it is genuine, certainly we should not fall behind in our colonies.

The upshot of these developments was the appointment of the Malayan Opium Commission in July 1907. The commission was composed of six members, all prominent citizens of the Straits: John Anderson, head of Guthrie and Company; Tan Jiak Kim; Dr. J. Galloway; Bishop W. F. Oldham; W. R. C. Middleton; and E. F. H. Edlin. A majority could probably be considered pro-opium; only Tan and Oldham were known to favor suppression. The tasks with which the commission was charged reflect the orientation of the inquiry: to determine the extent to which "excessive indulgence" in opium smok-

68. Ibid., pp. 150–79.

ing prevailed in Malaya; to find out whether opium smoking, either in moderation or excess, had increased; and finally, to determine "the steps that should be taken by Government to minimize and eventually *eradicate the evils arising from* the smoking of opium in our said Settlements" [italics added]. Nothing was said about eradicating opium smoking as such.[69]

The commission interviewed seventy-four persons and collected considerable statistical data but, like the royal commission, did not attempt a census and tried to finish its work within six months. The report of its findings occupies three volumes totaling 1,352 pages. A full analysis of this report would be the work of yet another book. Some study of it has been undertaken by Cheng.[70] Her findings and the actual results of the commission demonstrate how severely limited the entire inquiry really was. The basic outcome of the commission was the recommendation that the system of farming the opium revenue be abolished and replaced with a government-run monopoly. According to Cheng, the commission rejected the testimony of several doctors simply because they were known to hold anti-opium views. The commission refused to recommend a rise in the price of chandu, even though this had been shown to decrease smoking. Great care was taken not to incur any additional expense for government; thus the establishment of a government-run refuge for opium smokers was rejected on the grounds that it might be abused and that it would only benefit a small section of the community. The registration of smokers was likewise rejected.

The main concern of the commission, in the final analysis, was, as in earlier official moves regarding opium in Malaya and elsewhere, the safeguarding of the revenue. Cheng suggests the main reason for abolishing the farming system was the removal of the "chinteng menace." It was considered an annoyance to travelers that the chintengs came around and searched their effects. A second reason was the fact that the farms had simply not been performing very well. Since 1903 they had been losing money, and the revenue had been declining. As she sees it, the purpose of the policy was bureaucratic rationalization rather than moral reform:

The Report was mainly concerned with justifying and safeguarding the opium revenue, and where it was convenient, a few restrictive measures

69. CO 273/328, G.D. No. 308, 24 July 1907, CO No. 29672.
70. Cheng U Wen, 1961, pp. 65–73.

were introduced, provided that these did not jeopardize the revenue. Such measures were not calculated to decrease the consumption of opium. The Opium Commission Report appears to be the first step in the elimination of opium in the Straits Settlements, but it would be more correct to look upon it as a last desperate effort to justify the Government's policy of collecting revenue from opium.[71]

A look at the opium revenue statistics after the establishment of the government monopoly demonstrates that the "last desperate attempt" was not really so desperate at all; rather, it was highly successful. As the figures in table 7 show, revenues had been declining since 1904 owing to the depression and general difficulties with the farm. During 1910, the first year of the operation of the government monopoly, the new service made less than the previous year's rent. That was the only year that such low profits were obtained. Thereafter, profits from opium sales by the government monopoly began to rise rapidly. By 1913 the monopoly was yielding more than the farm had ever paid, and profits continued to rise for the next decade. It was not until 1920 that the Malayan government began to take steps to actually *reduce* opium consumption. Actual sales of chandu seem, on the basis of incomplete data, to have fluctuated between 1.1 million and 1.8 million tahils per year for the first three decades of the twentieth century. In 1920 total chandu consumption in the Straits Settlements was over 1.8 million tahils.

The monopoly's efforts at limiting consumption were confined to raising the price of chandu. The monopoly began in January 1910, selling chandu at the same price as the farm, $3.00 per tahil. In April it raised the price to $4.36, in 1912 to $5, and then in 1913 to $6. By October 1919 the base price was $12.00 per tahil.[72] The peak year for opium sales appears to have been 1920, when the net profit from the monopoly nearly reached twenty million dollars for the Straits Settlements. After 1920 both the number of tahils sold annually and the overall profits of the monopoly began to fall steadily. By 1925 net opium revenues only constituted 39 percent of the total Straits Settlements revenues.

As opium revenues fell between 1920 and 1930, however, total revenues fell as well, and much of the decline can be attributed to the generally deteriorating Straits economic situation as well as to the overall changes taking place within the Chinese community: the rising

71. Ibid., p. 73.
72. *SSADR*, 1919, p. 418.

percentage of women in the total population, the general settling down of many Chinese in the Straits, and a real decline in migration. With the onset of the worldwide Depression in 1929, opium revenues plunged, falling from nearly $14 million in 1928 to $9.7 million in 1929 and to $8.8 million in 1930. They fell steadily until 1942, when the Japanese invaded. Nevertheless, in 1929 it was estimated that there were over three hundred thousand opium addicts in British Malaya out of a total adult population of three million. Chen So Lan calculated that one in four Chinese was an addict.[73]

It was only in 1943, by which time the Japanese occupation forces had total control of Malaya, that the British government followed suit and prohibited opium smoking as well. Writing with what can only be termed the "seamless hypocrisy" of the imperial bureaucrat, Victor Purcell has summed up the history of Malayan opium policy in the twentieth century as if it were somehow a triumph of Christian morality, rather than simple greed and administrative expediency:

> All that need be stated here is that in 1907 a Commission on Opium was appointed which made its report the following year, that at midnight on 31 December 1909 the opium farms in Singapore, Penang and Malacca suspended business and the Government Monopolies Department entered into possession of the premises and reopened them for business as usual the following day; that a policy of gradual suppression of opium-smoking was followed for many years, and that His Majesty's Government on 10 November 1943 adopted a policy of total prohibition in British and British-protected territories in the Far East then in enemy occupation.[74]

Chinese Society after the Farms

Purcell's comments seem to skip over most of the questionable issues regarding the farms and the colonial government's policies toward opium use and taxation in Malaya. They are, in fact, nothing more than a thin and threadbare carpet under which a large and unsightly lump has been swept. My purpose here, however, is not to needle twentieth century Britons about the deeds of their predecessors. Rather, I wish to look closely at the farms because therein lies one of the few institutional remains of nineteenth-century Chinese society. The end of

73. Chen, "Opium Problem in British Malaya" (1935).
74. Purcell, 1965, p. 275.

the farming system was not just a matter of administrative rationalism or embarrassment about a blatantly exploitative system. It signaled a substantive change in the fundamental relations of the Chinese community. The essence of that change was the separation of political relations from economic relations within Malayan and Singaporean Chinese society.

One of the key variables determining control of the revenue-farming syndicates, it seems, was capital control of the largest labor-intensive industries. That is to say, whoever dominated the flow of capital in the large commodity-producing enterprises in the Malay world was also in a position to dominate the opium revenue farms. The taukehs who dominated the farms had to have links into the kongsis and secret societies. Even after the commercialization that began in the 1880s, within each revenue-farming syndicate there was someone with links back to the kongsis in the jungle. Power in Singapore had just shifted from the pepper and gambier taukehs to tin mining taukehs.

Originally, those in Singapore who controlled the capital flows into the production of pepper and gambier—the industry that occupied the largest number of kongsi-based laborers therefore the greatest number of opium consumers—also controlled the farms. This meant that pepper and gambier taukehs controlled not only the farms but much of the public life of the Chinese community during the middle and later years of the nineteenth century. Then in the 1880s the spectacular growth of the tin industry in the West Coast states gave unprecedented advantages to the Pinang families that had invested in it. Their domination of capital flows into an industry that absorbed thousands of laborers gave them the edge in bidding for farms, not only in Pinang and the West Coast states, but also in Sumatra and Singapore. In the mining industry of the West Coast, capital and labor continued to be mobilized within kongsis, giving the clear advantage to taukehs who were a part of, or in fact dominated, the brotherhoods.

Of particular importance were the clique (or cliques) of taukehs related to the Hai San secret society group dominated in the 1860s and 1870s by Khoo Thean Teck. During the 1880s and 1890s, it was persons from this group who managed to keep control of the Singapore farms. They may not always have been connected among themselves, but they all seem to have had some link to the Khoo group. They included Koh Seang Tat, Chiu Sin Yong, and Gan Gnoh Bee. The appearance of Khoo Hun Yeang (Thean Teck's son) in later syndicates in the 1890s and in the twentieth century reinforces this conclusion. What they all had in common was their connection to industries that employed large labor forces organized into kongsis and engaged in the production of export commodities.

The pepper and gambier taukehs of Singapore were challenged by this group of interlopers but were never completely dislodged from the farming syndicates until the twentieth century. Because pepper and gambier agriculture continued to employ opium-consuming coolies, its taukehs were able to maintain political and economic links to the labor force. As long as they held the strings of those networks, the Singapore taukehs had a financial empire with a popular base in the Malay states. The inheritors of this empire were the sons of Seah Eu Chin, who succeeded to the management of their father's holdings after the death of their elder uncle, Tan Seng Poh. Although Tan Keng Swee (Seng Poh's son) and Lim Kwee Eng (son-in-law of Cheang Hong Lim) had dropped out of sight by the mid-1880s, Cheang Jim Hean's name appeared with those of the Seah group, representing the Hokkien side of the old pepper and gambier kongsi. This continuing connection between labor forces, commodity production, and opium consumption formed the economic foundation of the Chinese communities in Malaya and Singapore. The dynamics of Singapore's history in the nineteenth century is to be found in the changes within these interlocked relationships.

There was a fourth element in this combination that divided capital from capital. Although it is difficult to get at the heart of Chinese families and family-based social institutions, it seems that only those families that had successfully established family kongsis stayed on top in the changing economic environment. The Seahs, the Khoos, the Cheangs, and finally the Khaws all maintained tightly linked family groups that, through marriage links and business partnerships, kept their wealth concentrated. These family networks ultimately returned control to the Straits Chinese, since they were the only ones with deep roots and the capability of marrying potential competitors. In the end, it was not enough to simply have access to the kongsis that dominated the commodity-producing labor force; capital itself had to be consolidated with a family kongsi.

Cushman's study of the last surviving family clique in the Malayan revenue farms, the Khaws of Pinang and Ranong, is most illuminating in this respect. Through a combination of marriages, business partnerships, and astute political relationships, the Khaws put together a complex of insurance companies, steamship companies, tin mines, tin smelters, steam dredges, and revenue farms that stretched from Bangkok to Sydney. In fact, the Singapore revenue farm syndicate of Khaw

Joo Choe that collapsed between 1907 and 1909 was just one piece of a much larger complex of revenue farm holdings. Between 1907 and 1909 the Khaw group had succeeded in taking control of the revenue farms of Pinang, Kedah, Perak, Johor, Bangkok, and Singapore. Ian George Brown's study of the Siamese Ministry of Finance indicates that the Khaw Joo Choe-Cheah Choo Yew syndicate's holdings in Siam included almost the entire kingdom.[75]

The Khaw connection with Siam is instructive. By the end of the nineteenth century, the only places where kongsi-like institutions could flourish were in environments that remained beyond the reach of colonial bureaucratic rationalization and Western corporate enterprise. Cushman's discussion of the Khaw group stresses that these were the two major enemies of the expansion of Chinese business groups. Thus the Malay states and Siam were the last refuges of these "traditional" institutions, but their successes—their footholds in these places—were only temporary and sufficed only so long as the area remained a frontier.

The Khaws, like the Seahs, the Cheangs, the Khoos, and Tan Seng Poh, were not, however, of the frontier; they simply managed it. All these groups lived on the margin between Western colonial capitalism and the precommercial Asian world. Most of them established economic bases in the colonial enclaves and, wherever possible, obtained European subject status, which gave them a large degree of legal immunity in the "native states." One way or another, they were part of the colonial apparatus, the frontiersmen of global capitalism. Through the revenue farms, they captured the Chinese kongsis of the Malay world and brought them into the global economy, and at the same time they facilitated the extension of colonial political controls. Their relationships with the Chinese coolies were both economic and political, but the expansion of the colonial political agenda meant the erosion of these "traditional" political linkages.

Once those political links were broken, and the British administration, through the Chinese Protectorate, could establish its own system of police control over the Chinese masses, the forces of the secret societies and revenue farm chintengs were unnecessary. Not only could

75. Cushman, 1986. Her table of the Khaw group's holdings ca. 1907–10 show that the membership of the interlocking revenue farm syndicates included Khaw Joo Tok, Khaw Joo Choe (Singapore), Khaw Joo Ghee, Foo Choo Choon (Pinang), Cheah Choo Yew (Bangkok), Chung Thye Phin (Perak), Goh Boon Keng (Pinang), Lim Kek Chuan (Pinang), Ng Boo Bee, and Yeo Wee Gark (Pinang); Brown, pp. 272–75.

governments collect their own taxes on opium, but European corporate enterprises could gain access to supplies of "free" Asian labor to hire as employees. This could not happen until the Chinese had been stripped of the protection of their native social institutions, the kongsis and the traditions of Chinese brotherhood.

8 Opium and the Political Economy
of Colonial Singapore

I have tried to define, or perhaps to redefine, the historical context of the Singapore Chinese and to describe the process of historical development in Singapore. I need now to show how the historical context and evolution of colonial Chinese society helps us understand Chinese society as it exists today in Singapore and, to some extent, in Malaysia.

While most would agree that Singapore Chinese society evolved in a context of struggle, the explanations of that conflict are usually flawed. British colonial writers have tended to reject the conflict model and sought to explain away outbreaks of violence rather than understand them as evidence of the historical process. This tendency applies particularly to the secret societies but also to difficulties encountered with the revenue farmers, the Malay chiefs, and indigenous social and political institutions. In contrast, I have focused on economic struggle; for virtually everyone who came to Singapore came for economic reasons. I have identified and described four groups of actors in the struggle: the Chinese kongsis, or brotherhoods; the Chinese merchants and revenue farmers; the Malay chiefs; and the British, both merchants and officials. All parties, one way or another, were seeking wealth and power, more often the former than the latter. And all, with the possible exception of the Malays, intended to return "home" with their winnings. Finally I have shown how wider global forces affected the purposes and decisions of the actors. Most important was the expansion of the global market communicated to Singapore through the major trades: opium, capital, and manufactures from India and the West. Pepper, gambier, tin, and the other major commodity flows

220

generated in Southeast Asia originally moved with the Western trade, to China. The shift in the global balance of payments that opium brought about at the beginning of the nineteenth century affected all these currents of world commerce. In addition to redirecting the commodity flows to the West, the shift created a vast demographic eruption. It was as if the current of wealth flowing out of China began to pull with it the Chinese people themselves. Singapore came into being as a result of these global forces, and they continued to affect the development of the city and its society throughout the nineteenth century.

The process of historical development really began in the eighteenth century, when the Chinese kongsi brotherhoods established the commodity-producing industries. The Chinese laborers came out of China with the Nanyang junk traders in the eighteenth century to produce gambier, pepper, sugar, tin, sago, gold, and other products to send back to China. These products were the foundation of Singapore's economy. With opium the British were able to open the door for themselves, into not only the kongsi economy but all the economies of monsoon Asia. It is difficult to see how the British could have taken control of the commerce of India, China, and Southeast Asia in less than a half century without opium. It was the major form of economic leverage.

From the Chinese viewpoint, the kongsi as an institutional form served as the basis for Singapore's economic order and thus also as the essential framework for social and political order in the colonial environment. Britain seized the island and declared it a free port but offered little by way of a social contract. The two communities were essentially on their own, which was the way things had always been in such places—a situation into which laissez-faire fit very comfortably.

Wang Tai Peng offers the best framework for describing the development of kongsis in overseas Chinese society. In his view, the kongsi form of organization was one of the most important pieces of cultural baggage the Chinese, both laborers and merchants, brought with them when they emigrated to the Nanyang. The kongsi was an eminently flexible type of organization. It enabled groups of Chinese to pool labor and capital on a quantifiable basis to pursue economic tasks. At the same time, the concepts of brotherhood upon which it was based provided an ideological component that facilitated the generation of institutions sufficient to accomplish the political and economic tasks of the community. Whether or not we accept Wang's idealistic pronouncements about their democratic nature, it is true that the kongsis provided a vehicle through which leadership based on popular support could arise and through which the masses of society could be mobilized and led.

It was in the most isolated and frontierlike situations that the kongsi came fully into its own as a foundation for self-government. The kongsis of Borneo in the eighteenth century and those of Bangka and Riau show some of the permutations. Similar cultural assumptions underlay the organization and functional success of groups like Ngee Heng in Singapore and Johor in the 1840s and 1850s and the Ghee Hin and Hai San kongsis in Perak and Selangor in the 1860s. Whether we find the term *triad, hui, kongsi,* or *secret society,* they all represent minor variations of the same fundamental social institution.

If what Wang has identified as a native Chinese form of democracy was honored more in the breach than in the practice, the kongsis did, at crucial periods, function as agents of the popular will. While it may be incorrect to view the kongsis as socially progressive, some of the secret society wars of the nineteenth century seemed to have approached class conflict. As a representative of the Chinese working masses, the kongsi could never have been anything but a threat to the colonial social and economic order.

The second group of actors, Chinese merchants (really two groups, China merchants and Straits merchants), were crucial to the exercise of British authority. The Singapore colonial authorities were continually forced to rely on the merchants as spokesmen for Chinese laborers. As a result, those Chinese gained status, which was reinforced by their control of the societies and the debt structure. Freedman notes that the conditions of rule in colonial Singapore "produced a structure of control in which the relation between employer and employee and between creditor and debtor were likely to be political as well as economic. Moreover, these political and economic relations might be expressed in the setting of voluntary associations, so that various forms of ritual and secular solidarity could enter into the ties between men unequally balanced in wealth and status."[1] Chinese of wealth and status needed to be able to function in both worlds, that of the British administrators and that of the kongsis. The farmers, in particular, who were charged with providing their own police power in order to control their monopoly and were thus forced to rely on the societies, were major practitioners of the art of double-role playing.

It was the Chinese businessmen, already involved in the small-scale

1. Maurice Freedman, "Immigrants and Associations in Nineteenth Century Singapore" (1960), p. 29.

archipelago trade, that brought Europeans into contact with the society and economy of the kongsis. Europeans had always dealt in Straits produce to a certain extent, but this part of the commerce began to expand at a disproportionate rate after 1840 because of new demand in the industrializing West for certain tropical products. The trades that eventually developed in pepper, tapioca, sago, sugar, gutta percha, gambier, and tin all depended on the rise of industrial production in Europe and the United States. Singapore's agency houses needed access to those goods. The only sure means of tapping into the kongsi economies was opium capital.

The Chinese laborers who produced these goods became a captive market, first for opium and later for European manufactures. While it is true that these scattered settlements of coolies never approached in size the potential market that beckoned in China, they were, nonetheless, nearby and penetrable. Few Europeans got rich quickly in this branch of commerce, but its profits managed to cover overhead expenses, for individual firms and certainly for the colonial state. The Chinese who got rich were those who allied themselves with the British in effecting these connections. This working relationship between British merchants and Chinese middlemen and between British administrators and Chinese revenue farmers was the foundation of the colonial state.

Both relationships pivoted on opium. The study of Chinese society in nineteenth-century Singapore thus cannot be separated from that of opium. The two may already have been joined before the foundation of the British entrepôt—the kongsi-based economies of the region seem to have been infected by opium from at least the 1780s—but the founding of Singapore and the growth of its population of pepper and gambier planters brought all the actors into close proximity.

Opium offers a unique lens through which to observe the formation of Chinese society in this particular environment. Opium, whether as an item of consumption, trade, speculation, control, or taxation, allows the student of nineteenth-century British Malaya to focus on the key events that shaped the emerging colonial society. The overwhelming importance of the drug to the financial security of the British Empire in Asia made it a major variable in the historical development of the entire region. Singapore would have been a very different place without opium. As a source of excise revenue, it made it possible to run Singapore as a free port. Opium paid for free trade; without it, Raffles's "broad and liberal principles" would have been only so many words.

Raffles has been given far more credit than he deserves for the success of Singapore. The actual construction of a workable administration was none of his doing. John Crawfurd, who established the first workable revenue farms and cut expenses, understood that economic success lay with the Chinese. According to Turnbull, "Crawfurd was even more ardent in promoting free trade and restraining government expenditure than Raffles himself. He was convinced that the key to economic success lay in British leadership combined with the energy of Chinese settlers, untrammeled by official economic shackles."[2] This decision by Crawfurd was no doubt based on his calculus of "one Chinaman," as both producer and consumer, being worth two Indians and four Malays in value to the state.[3] It was also based on Crawfurd's supreme confidence in "British leadership." The combination, then, of British rule and Chinese energy provided the dynamic of Singapore's history. More accurately, the combination was British opium and Chinese social and economic institutions.

A hundred and twenty years after Farquhar established the first opium revenue farm, R. N. Walling wrote a brief essay, "House of Tiny Tim Tubes," on the Singapore government's opium monopoly packing plant at Pasir Panjang. It produced a million tahils of chandu a year. He described in some detail the modern machinery designed for the task of efficiently mass producing daily some 450,000 two-hoon tin tubes of chandu, one inch long and a half an inch wide: "The machines which do this are beautiful, highly technical and impossible for me as a layman to describe. After sealing, they [the tubes] are weighed by delicate, automatic, weighing machines, and packed small boxes, two hundred at a time. They rest there like miniature Sainsbury's cooking eggs!"[4]

Perhaps Purcell was sincere in believing that the government he served had pursued a policy of gradual suppression, but it certainly took a very long time to work. In the meantime, the society that had come into being in Singapore was born with opium in its very blood. The results of over a century of living with the drug were not to be erased by the stroke of a pen. The long struggle between the British administrators and the Chinese opium farmers and secret society headmen had established the basic pattern of social and economic relations in the British colony. The effects of that struggle and the colonial policy that emerged from it have left permanent marks on the body politic of Singapore that remain to this day.

2. Turnbull, 1975, p. 109.
3. "I entertain so high an opinion of the industry, skill and *capacity of consumption* of the Chinese, that I consider one Chinaman equal in value to the state to *two* natives of the Coromandel Coast and to four Malays at least": John Crawfurd, quoted in *JIAEA* 10 (1854), 410.
4. Walling, *Singapura Sorrows* (1931), pp. 33–36.

From the viewpoint of British economic interests, Singapore was a continually changing experiment. Initially the port was intended to serve the China trade and to provide a staging area for the distribution of Indian opium. These trade interests led to the founding of the settlement and the realization of the free trade philosophy. But would traders have come to Singapore for opium even if there *were* duties and port charges? After all, even though there was theoretically free trade in opium, the British and Americans did exercise a practical monopoly on the trade between India and the Straits. So long as they brought their opium to Singapore, other traders were certain to follow. I believe that opium was more important than free trade.

Monopoly went naturally with the opium trade. The conditions of its production in India and of its distribution in China lent the opium traffic, in the long run, to total monopoly. The period of free trade in the drug between the early nineteenth century and the first Opium War notwithstanding, it was only a matter of time before the carrying trade was rationalized. First the Jardines, Mathesons, and Dents took over the Calcutta-to-Canton trade, and then the Sassoons, who had monopolized the Malwa trade of Bombay, took over the entire trade. While Europeans in Singapore continued to deal in opium after the crash of 1837, the warning was clear. There was no room for "men of small capital" once the Sassoons had established their vertical monopoly stretching from Bombay to Shanghai. By the 1880s, according to Gulland, the trade was in the hands of "Jews and Armenians," not to mention the Chinese.

The monopoly in the drug trade created more difficulties for those merchants dealing in British manufactures. While the opium trade forced open the door of the Chinese Empire, it blocked it as well. This is not to say that there would not have been difficulty anyway selling the Chinese things they neither wanted nor needed. Penetration of the market by British manufactures was a very slow process, and in the long run this too was largely the work of Chinese middlemen. Singapore's European merchants were forced to lower their sights from the China market to the one in and around Singapore. Dealing with Chinese speculators, who took British goods on credit in exchange for a promise of "native produce" within three months, became their mode of business.

The Process of Struggle

The essence of the evolutionary process of the colonial social order has been struggle. Lee Poh Ping's proposition of a dialectical relationship between the free trade society of the British port and the pepper and gambier society of the Chinese settled in the hinterlands needs modification. If we take the dichotomy to have been between the Chinese kongsis on the one hand and the British agency houses and the colonial state on the other, his distinction makes sense. The two societies had grown from separate origins. Each was organized around its own priorities, controlled by its own internally generated rules, and focused on its own economic goals. Each was wrapped in its own cocoon of culture and language. More important, each functioned around very different socioeconomic ethics. Between the two societies were the Chinese merchants, the taukehs, who had to move in both worlds, and there were more gradations of allegiance among this group than Lee suggests. Some merchants were part of the kongsis; others, of the colonial entrepôt economy.

Initially, the free trade society of the port, its merchants working in close association with Europeans, coexisted with the pepper and gambier kongsi society of the countryside. The latter grew as a result of more-or-less continuous migration from Riau and China. It was only sporadically, when major crises struck, such as the drastic fall in gambier prices in the late 1820s and early 1830s that led to unemployed Chinese planters engaging in gang robbery, that the two societies came into contact. That changed with the entry of European capital, channeled through Chinese hands into the pepper and gambier agriculture, bringing the two societies into sustained and intimate contact. Each was forced to readjust to the changed situation.

Throughout this early period of contact and adjustment, the revenue farms were dominated by Melaka Chinese, or certainly by those Chinese who had the confidence of the British. Choa Chong Long, Tay Eng Long, Tay Han Long, Kiong Kong Tuan, and other early revenue farmers were all of Melaka or Straits families. They managed to collect some kind of opium tax from the Chinese pepper and gambier planters, probably by limiting their sales to outlets inside the town and by simply dealing with specific headmen and allowing them to carry on their own business with the Chinese in the interior. Thus the Teochew pepper and gambier shopkeepers and their kangchus in the countryside controlled the opium distribution networks and retail sales to their coolies.

The farms were the mechanism of government, so controlling them was not merely a competitive exercise to be taken with the highest bid. A potential farmer needed downward links to the Chinese laborers as well as upward ones to the European hierarchy. These links always made losing bidders a destabilizing force, no matter how well assimilated or capitalist they happened to be. The link between opium and labor made the farms something more than a business proposition. Lee, obviously, did not extend his hypothesis of conflict to the revenue farms, a major weakness in his argument. I believe the societal conflict can only be properly understood with the opium farming syndicates as a primary element.

Also important are the secret societies; for the brotherhoods originally functioned as the only agency of authority in the rural areas. The secret societies, at least the Ngee Heng, did not follow the planters from Riau into the hinterland of Singapore and then into Johor. On the contrary, a study of the actual sequence of events suggests that the society *led* the Chinese planters into these areas and governed relations among them. The societies settled disputes, parceled out the various preserves, and administered justice, very often in their own way. John Cameron spoke of their "courts":

> At the time these societies possessed great power among the Chinese; and though there was no direct evidence of the fact, it was strongly suspected that at the courts they were known to hold, they frequently awarded and carried out the sentence of death. Many murdered bodies were found about the country, each mutilated in a peculiar manner: generally with either the right or left hand chopped up into a certain number of parts, left hanging together by the skin; and in these cases Chinamen never were the informants, nor could they ever be induced to give evidence.[5]

According to Lee's hypothesis, as the forces of the free trade economy and the administrative machinery of the European state began to extend into the hinterland, conflict arose with the kongsi that had populated the interior. Capitalist enterprises, apparently financed with new infusions of European support and probably led by such persons as Seah Eu Chin, began to move into the pepper and gambier business. He seems to have done so without much backing or cooperation from the old kongsi leadership. Through the 1830s and early 1840s, as the agriculture expanded to meet rising world demand and fill the untouched jungles of Singapore, it soaked up the excess labor and probably drew new immigrants, this time many more Hokkiens than before. So long as the economy continued to expand, disputes were few; when the bottom dropped out of the economy and more and more immigrants began to chase declining prices on less land, tempers began to flare.

Then in the mid-1840s two events signaled change. A group of

5. Cameron, p. 265.

Teochew merchants moved to break the Baba/Hokkien monopoly on connections with the British. At the same time, the Hokkien merchants, probably in association with the Melaka Chinese, attempted to break the Teochew/Ngee Heng monopoly on connections with the pepper and gambier planters in the hinterlands of Singapore (which included Riau). The first serious clashes between the two societies were those stemming from the Chinese Funeral Riots of 1846 and the associated collapse of the gambier prices and the concurrent crisis in the revenue farms that accompanied the opening of Johor. The economic crisis thus brought conflict at both the mass and the elite levels. The appearance of a new Hokkien secret society, the Quan Tek hui, or the Toh Peh Kong, to rival the Ngee Heng coincided precisely with the emergence of a powerful Teochew mercantile faction that challenged the Hokkiens and their Straits Chinese allies in their control of the revenue farms and thus in their relationship with the colonial state and the European mercantile community.

The events of 1846 are crucial to understanding the realignment of social and economic forces within Singapore's Chinese society. The Chinese Funeral Riots, the struggle over the revenue farms, the opening of Johor, events in Riau, and the founding of the Ngee Ann Kongsi all suggest a crisis in the old order and a new alliance of mercantile and secret society factions. The victorious groups here were the Teochew interests led by Seah Eu Chin within the Ngee Ann Kongsi and the Hokkien, Ch'ang T'ai group led by Cheang Sam Teo. Affiliated with them were the Ngee Heng Kongsi and the coalition of pepper and gambier taukehs associated with it as well as the ruler of the state of Johor.

This does not seem to have been an absolute amalgamation of territories and functions, but rather a complex of working arrangements between more-or-less autonomous networks. All the allies perhaps agreed to work within the same revenue-farming coalition so long as the leading taukehs in each were permitted to hold shares as members of the syndicate. At the same time, each group held their own plantations within their own debtor/creditor networks (e.g., shops, kangkars, plantations) and probably agreed not to poach on those of their allies, or to violate their debt arrangements. That is, they were to buy opium from the farm at farm prices and not smuggle or purchase from smugglers; also, they were not to steal, entice coolies from other plantations, compete with other merchants, or undercut their debt networks. To some degree, the colonial state was a part of this coalition. At least for a time it acquiesced in its operation and in fact depended on the successful monopolization of the economic complex represented by pepper and gambier in and around Singapore.

The coalition was a fragile one at best. Ethnic tensions, hard economic conditions and the steady stream of opium, coolies and the vast stretches of unsettled land all eroded the stability of such monopoly arrangements. Nevertheless, at certain times it could act with ruthless effectiveness against interlopers. The campaign against the Roman Catholic hongkahs seems to confirm the power that the alliance was able to mobilize.

On the other hand, things were never entirely smooth, if only because the alliance itself was dominated by economic interests that could not prosper unless the coolies were both immobilized on their plantations and impoverished as a result of opium consumption. In addition, the umbrella of the monopoly was never big enough to include all the aspiring taukehs. There were always hungry entrepreneurs and always unhappy and unattached coolies willing to join them.

Economic realities, exploitation, and the market itself corroded the ties of brotherhood which gave the triads their power to mobilize the loyalties of the membership. If the trend was for successful secret society leaders to gravitate to the urban complex and ultimately to be coopted and become merchants, the other side of the coin was for the coolies to become alienated, if not from the triad itself, at least from the established leadership. At the same time, the triad leaders who had a certain charisma but were not good businessmen found themselves coming up short. Moreover, the rhetoric of the triad was a continuing appeal to the Chinese laborers, especially to the warriors. These disaffected coolies and local leaders found it easy to make common cause with the new group of refugee triad warriors who arrived in Singapore in the early months of 1854.

The Hokkien-Teochew riots of 1854 comprised a very complex series of events and we do not clearly understand the forces, factions, and underlying issues in the struggle. It contained elements of ethnic conflict, economic competition, a triad fight, and, I suggest, class conflict. One element was missing, however. Although the security of the revenue-farming monopoly was frequently compromised during the mid- and late 1850s, it is clear that no new syndicate emerged from the fights. If anything, the monopoly was affirmed.

If any particular group lost the struggle, it seems to have been the activist elements within Ngee Heng itself. Henceforth the Ngee Heng became more completely the tool of taukeh-sponsored groups within it, especially the seh, or surname groups. Those ex-triad fighters from the Xiao Dao hui who joined forces with the newly emerged Ghee Hock are somewhat problematic. They appear to have remained outside the main action, an excluded opposition operating on the fringes. One consistent element was the opposition between the Seh Tan and the Ghee Hock, between Chua Moh Choon and Tan Seng Poh, that persisted from the appearance of the Ghee Hock through the 1870s. It is possible that this group found support from those Teochews who had always been disaffected from the Ngee Ann Kongsi, as Yen Ching-hwang suggests. In the absence of more specific information, the best analysis of the events of 1851 and 1854 must be based on the observable results. These are simply that disaffected elements among the lower classes could appeal to outsiders at the top, and the same process could work in reverse.

Chinese society contained within itself sufficient causes for division, but it is clear that outside forces continually worked to exacerbate these. Market forces were perhaps beyond the control of any individual or faction, as were the pressures of continuing immigration. The relationship between Chinese shopkeepers and European merchants personified market forces. When European trading ventures failed, it was because many smaller Chinese firms had gone under before them. When market pressures hit, Europeans swallowed up as many of their Chinese debtors as they could catch before they themselves were swept away.

If there was such a thing as a free-trade society, it was actualized in the European merchant community, and the economic principles that governed it were communicated to the Chinese merchant groups. These were in conflict with the egalitarian and redistributive ideals of the triads and the kongsis. European influence did not turn taukehs into raving free-trade liberals, nor did Chinese merchants need lessons in how to exploit their laborers, but they did have to create new relationships of a very different sort with the men who constituted their source of capital.

The colonial state had interests of its own which further muddied the waters. Monopoly promised a certain level of social peace that it did not really deliver. On the other hand, the monopolists got wealthy at the expense of the state. Eventually, the colonial governors saw that it was in their interests to encourage competition among the revenue farmers, even if it meant destabilizing comfortable arrangements. Thus, the state too had an impact in creating social and economic conflict among the Chinese of Singapore.

With the aging of the Lau Joon Tek/Cheang Sam Teo syndicate in 1859 and 1860, the accommodation that had gradually been hammered out by the disparate elements of Singapore's Chinese communities came apart. The renewed conflicts of the early 1860s, coupled with the shift in population from Singapore Island to Johor, once again pitted Hokkien taukeh against Teochew taukeh. The new ruler of Johor, Abu Bakar, became active on his own behalf. The continuing conflict between Tan Seng Poh and the Cheangs, between Abu Bakar and Cavanagh, nearly nine years long, demonstrated the difficulties faced by the British administration in dealing with the revenue farmers and the Asian power structure in general. Yet even though relations were not always smooth, the government received its regular rent and, despite the difficulties of the farmers, was not forced to grant large rent remissions.

Concurrent with the long seesaw battle between the Hokkien and Teochew syndicates were battles between their secret society allies, the Ghee Hock and the Seh Tan. The stakes in the struggle were not just the revenue farms, but also the pepper and gambier agriculture itself. Over the long run, it proved necessary to form a syndicate that would dominate the farms for an area coterminous with the geographic extent of the agriculture, in this case, Singapore Island, Johor, Melaka, and the fourteen Riau islands. This task was accomplished by the great syndicate, which was, in the final analysis, peculiarly and intimately connected with the internal dynamics of Singapore Chinese society, the pepper and gambier agriculture, and the Singapore political order.

The rise and fall of the great syndicate is central to this story. Its leaders cannot be classed as free traders or pepper and gambier merchants. They operated in both societies, but their actions worked to the benefit of the capitalist advance. The European mercantile and administrative groups gained from Tan's control of the farming syndicates. The farms were the mechanism through which the administration of the Chinese community took place. Until then, so far as the British were concerned, the functions of government barely extended beyond taxation and the exercise of the most rudimentary police powers—just enough to keep the Chinese from trying to take over the place themselves.

For the whole of the 1870s the farm came to seem a veritable part of the government. The heads of the farm were justices of the peace and municipal commissioners and were able to expand their interests into a wide range of activities. Chinese society came to be organized around the structures controlled by the Cheangs, the Tans, and the Seahs. The farm enterprise was not simply a revenue-farming kongsi but an agricultural industry, a debt structure, a social and political hierarchy, all stabilized by its own system of law enforcement. It was the epitome of laissez-faire government and perhaps the real accomplishment of British leadership and Chinese energy.

So far as the kongsis were concerned, the social gap had increased. Those brotherhoods that had managed to ally themselves with the revenue farmers survived and prospered, most importantly the Seh Tan, which seems in fact not even to have been a part of the triad organization. Groups like the Ghee Hock and branches of the Ghee Hin may still have managed to control the coolie trade, but most brotherhoods were sliding down the social scale during the 1870s. More and more they became the preserve of "criminal" elements and limited to controlling "illegitimate" vices, such as gambling and prostitution. Newcomers arriving from the wars and rebellions in China found the most profitable enterprises already firmly under the control of local Chinese authorities—the revenue farmers—and the kongsi no longer an avenue of mobility. Thus the secret society conflicts of the 1870s were between haves and have nots, between the incipient brotherhoods and the well-entrenched monopoly of the great syndicate.

Wynne's interpretation of these conflicts, dismissed by most other scholars, is the only one that recognized the durability of conflict among the Chinese and sought a comprehensive explanation. His delineation of two opposing mercantile factions, both in Pinang and Singapore, struggling for control of the revenue farms and at the same time linked to opposing secret societies, is correct. Neither Comber, Purcell, nor Blythe has really grappled with this circumstance. But Wynne's determination that the conflict was the result of fundamental ideological opposition within the secret societies was incorrect. He may have confused cause with effect and assumed that the secret societies controlled and directed the mercantile factions. I believe that the opposite was closer to the truth. Even when conflict arose between two specific secret societies, its fundamental causes were usually to be found in the economic struggle.

Both the merchants and the secret societies were at the mercy of economic forces generated outside their own spheres of influence. Revenue farm crises as well as triad riots regularly coincided with periodic economic dislocations. It is thus possible to see both elite conflicts and mass struggles as linked to the expansion of the global capitalist economy. The great syndicate thus fell when its economic foundations eroded: The filling up of the gambier frontier in Johor and

Riau limited the growth potential of the agricultural system. New fortunes spawned by the rapidly expanding tin-mining industry of the West Coast Malay states gave the financial edge to the Straits Chinese taukehs allied with Tan Kim Ching. While the sources of Singapore's capital had certainly not dried up, the new age was one of highly mobile capital, which need not be tied to any one production system. Moreover a substantial portion of Singapore's opium-consuming public was now urban rather than rural. And there was the brevity of human existence. Even economic systems must be replicated if they are to persist from generation to generation. Thus the failure of the great syndicate came not only with economic changes but also with the aging of its leadership and the generational change that took place in 1879 and 1880. The fact that this change occurred when the style of colonial rule was also changing made the syndicate all the more vulnerable.

The 1880s also marked a real change in the exercise of colonial control in Malaya. As Sadka has shown, even though British residents were taking charge of the Protected Malay States (Perak, Negri Sembilan, Selangor) since the early 1870s, rationalized administrative control did not really take shape until the 1880s. The new breed of colonial civil servant now coming to Malaya was less likely to tolerate systems of informal control such as those characterized by the great syndicate and by revenue farming in general. They were even less likely to accept the notion of sharing power with revenue farmers, secret society kapitans, and double-role players. The arrival in Singapore of people like Frederick Weld, with his reputation for killing Maoris in New Zealand and his company of Sikh riflemen, was clearly a surprise for the old leadership of the great syndicate. His ruthless suppression of the opium-smuggling conspiracy in 1883 was a rude reminder to the Chinese taukehs of where the real power lay. From Weld to Swettenham, Singapore's Chinese had to deal with governors who were deeply dedicated to the expansion and intensification of British power and who were, moreover, convinced of the racial and cultural superiority of the Anglo-Saxon race.

While Weld's victory over the great syndicate in 1883 may have been less than complete, the door had been opened. From the 1880s to the demise of the farms themselves, the farms were increasingly available to whomever had the money and whomever controlled the labor force. Although success in running the farms was largely dependent on the world market for Malaya's primary products, those Chinese who had moved into the Protected States before the British and who were able to take advantage of the new trends were the most likely to succeed. There were, however, other avenues now opening to Chinese capital. Ex-revenue farmers tended to move into real estate, shipping, and banking, once they had made fortunes in opium. The importance of finance capital gave renewed prominence to the old Pinang and Melaka families of Straits Chinese, who regained a measure of economic and social control by the end of the century. Their networks expanded and became interconnected to link nearly all of British Malaya under one vast syndicate. At the same time, they reached to the Netherlands Indies, Siam, Hong Kong, and even China. This expansion of Chinese capital posed a serious threat to the imperial order. Its final elimination was thus a bureaucratic imperative.

The final failure of the farms was clearly not the result of an attack of philanthropic morality, nor of the inability of the state to collect a tax on opium consumption. It was, rather, the result of the continuing trend toward bureaucratic rationalization. From the time that Swettenham began to investigate the farmers' books and bought the premises of the farm, the movement of the government seems clear. Even without prodding from the Chinese and American reformers and the local anti-opium movement, the demands of administrative efficiency would soon have made it necessary for the government to take full control of its own taxation system. The economic collapse of 1904–8 simply provided an immediate situation in which the farmers' vulnerability was painfully apparent. Coming fortuitously in the midst of a reforming movement, the failure justified the formation of the government monopoly in 1910. The fact that the government nearly tripled its revenue from opium within four years after the formation of the monopoly confirms the influence of the bureaucratic imperative on the process.

The farms did not disappear simply because the British tired of dealing with semiautonomous Chinese leadership. The British had tired of that long before the middle of the nineteenth century. The farms survived as long as they did because they were necessary. The French in Indochina and the Dutch in the East Indies had replaced their farming systems with government monopolies long before the British moved to do likewise in Malaya. Were the French and Dutch more clever or more able colonial rulers than the British? No. Neither had such an enormous population of working-class Chinese. Because the Malayan and Straits Settlements farms were based on huge Chinese labor forces engaged in primary production, they represented the entire economic system upon which British financial stability depended.

The farming syndicates had weakened by 1909 because the economic enterprise upon which they relied had declined. Gambier was out and rubber was in. Tin mining was becoming less labor intensive and more capital intensive. Moreover, Europeans were finally finding ways to engage in primary production without Chinese labor. For rubber plantations, they could recruit Tamils from India; in the tin mines, much of the labor could be undertaken by steam dredges. For European estate and mine managers, those substitutions greatly reduced the headache of dealing with the alien expectations of working class Chinese.

The Legacy of Opium and Empire

The idea that the productive enterprises of the Southeast Asian Chinese were, in fact, kongsi based is an extension of a line of argument that can be traced back to the observations made by Maurice Freedman in the early 1960s. One of these comments has been a guiding principle of this book: "Singapore is so overwhelmingly a Chinese settlement that from one point of view it may be seen as an extension of China."[6] I have attempted to treat the history of Singapore as the continuing story of the institutional forms that the Chinese adapted to the environment of the Malay world. The focus on various aspects of the kongsi has made possible a reevaluation of the role of secret societies and the nature of conflict in nineteenth-century Singapore Chinese society. Freedman was one of the first European scholars to conceptualize the secret societies as anything other than criminal gangs. His suggestions stand in contrast to much of the earlier (and often later) writing on secret societies, which shows the administrative and police bias: that is, virtually everything written on the topic in Singapore and Malaya up to the midtwentieth century, including writings by Pickering, Wynne, Comber, Purcell, and Blythe. As far as these writers were concerned, at least publicly, the secret societies represented an *"imperium in imperio"* that sought, according to Purcell,

"to enjoy the benefits of British rule and, at the same time, to ignore any laws that did not suit their convenience". A large number of the members were criminals, the scourings of Canton and other Chinese cities. Furthermore, the people of the different provinces, and sometimes of the districts

6. Freedman, 1960, and "Overseas Chinese Associations: A Comment" (1961), p. 478. See also the (1979) collection of his essays, *The Study of Chinese Society*, edited by G. William Skinner.

of the same province, hated one another bitterly for generations and carried on bitter feuds. These ancestral feuds they brought with them to the Straits. Blackmail gathered from brothels, opium dens, and shop-keepers was a regular part of the income of the *hui*.[7]

This view was only natural for Europeans who came to the situation as administrators bent on establishing law and order over an alien population. They perceived the institutions of Chinese society which they could not manipulate as threats to their own authority. They were hardly predisposed to present the history of the kongsis in an objective light. Nevertheless, it is difficult to see how British authority could have been exercised at all during the nineteenth century without the societies. Freedman points out that the societies functioned in situations where British authority did not in fact exist. He notes that the secret societies "were for a long time the means by which control was exercised within the Chinese fold by Chinese and a way of regulating the contact between the mass of Chinese and the 'alien' administration." As a result, "the Singapore authorities found themselves making use of the secret societies as an instrument of government [because from 1826 to 1877] . . . there seems to have been no official institution for administrative contact between the government and the Chinese."[8]

Freedman's conception of the historical role of the societies was much closer to reality than those of Purcell, Blythe, and Wynne. Freedman drew attention to the economic elements in the organization of overseas Chinese society. But he placed no particular stress on the pepper and gambier business, nor did he attempt to integrate the opium-farming system into his conception.

No citizen of the world at the end of the twentieth century needs to be reminded of the virulent power that a drug trade can have on legitimate economic and political structures. There is, however, some-thing we can learn from the Asian experience of the nineteenth cen-tury, when Europeans inflicted opium upon the traditional polities of the region. Opium not only made possible the penetration of the Chinese market by European capitalism; it also eroded traditional economic structures in the regions where it was produced, the places where it was traded, and the countries where it was consumed. From Turkey to Tokyo, no place was unaffected. As one company official observed: "the opium trade carried all before it."[9]

7. Purcell, *Chinese in Malaya* (1967), p. 161.
8. Freedman, 1960, pp. 33–34.
9. Quoted in Pamela Nightengale, *Trade and Empire in Western India* (1970), p. 233.

Opium left whole societies vulnerable to commercial penetration, absorbing loose cash and creating a continuing demand for more cash. Nothing destroyed peasant self-sufficiency faster than the need for silver to feed a habit. Nothing kept a laborer working for a substandard wage more effectively than dependence on a drug. And if the supply of the drug was made a part of his wages, then he could be induced to produce for practically nothing. The cash flow created by a system like this could finance an empire, as was the case in colonial Malaya. In Malaya and Singapore, opium, or rather the opium-smoking coolies, financed free trade, paid for the accumulation of Chinese and European capital, and financed the state that oversaw their exploitation.

I have drawn attention, throughout this book, to the incredibly determined efforts by the Colonial Office, British officials in Malaya, and the British economic community in the colonies to oppose anything that might decrease the opium revenue or otherwise shift the tax burden. Any argument that the imperial system did not rely on opium and was not, in the pathogenic sense, systemically dependent on the drug is simply not in accordance with the facts. This was true not only of Malaya, but also of all India and virtually every place under British control east of Suez. Sir Cecil Beadon, commenting on Indian finances in 1871 when the Indian government was making £9,000,000 annually from opium, pointedly observed: "Indian finances are in this position that, in a majority of years, you have very serious deficits, and you are constantly borrowing. . . . Shall we sacrifice the whole or any portion of the opium duty? And it seems to me that the present state of the Indian finances is such as to prevent us giving any answer but one to that question—that we cannot give up any of the opium revenue; we cannot afford to do so."[10] This remained the situation until the end of the century. One might even make the argument that the decline of the empire really began when the British got out of the opium business.

More specifically, however, opium was at the heart of British Malaya, and its influence went beyond the financial realm. The opium system had remolded, in fact, created local Chinese society, and despite the demise of the opium syndicates, the century-old opium economy left its continuing stamp on that society. The farms, by providing an avenue for status and capital accumulation, facilitated the formation of a peculiar type of Chinese oligarchy throughout British Malaya. It was no accident that the oldest Straits-born families ultimately

10. Sir Cecil Beadon, "Report on East Indian Finances," *Papers Relating to the Opium Question* (1872), p. 10.

ended up in control of the farms; nor did ultimately losing the farms mean they lost their fortunes. Farming was only important so long as it was a part of economic production and investment; the demise of farming coincided with its separation. Opium revenue was no longer necessary to protect investments, and new opportunities were opening up for Chinese capital in banking, rubber, and European-style corporations.

Social control within a much more stabilized Chinese community was now possible through such organizations as the hui guans and surname groups as well as through institutions such as the Chinese Chamber of Commerce. These institutions were essentially conservative and mercantile in origin and orientation and closely bound to the colonial power structure. They were more appropriate to a social situation increasingly characterized by Chinese in family groups. These were not large, extended families because most Chinese coolies continued to live in grinding poverty. But brotherhood organizations, which had flourished in the "kongsi lines," could no longer maintain social and political influence once men no longer worked, lived, and socialized only with their coworkers. Chinese coolies had been urbanized and atomized.

The major casualty of opium, aside from the thousands of Chinese who fell victim to it, was the native democracy of the kongsis. The brotherhoods and secret societies had been criminalized except in Johor, where the Ngee Heng continued as the only legal society until it dissolved itself in 1916. This trend toward criminalization only deepened the social and economic gap between rich and poor. The delegitimation of the brotherhoods was a serious loss to Chinese society in the region; for it stripped the social fabric of institutions that might have represented popular aspirations. There was thus no legitimate social protection against the demands of an authoritarian state or against the pressure of an entrenched and unresponsive economic oligarchy. Although new rebels were already arriving in the Straits from the struggles in China and beginning to mobilize support for a new round of class struggle, they would be fighting at a disadvantage, and in the long run, attempts to organize popularly based democratic institutions were to meet with repeated failure.

From 1900 to 1950 there was no possibility of advancement for Chinese who were only leaders of men, or more correctly, political leaders. Not only did British colonialism criminalize the secret societies; all Chinese political activity was, by the definitions of the age, illegal. Sharon Carstens' study of the changing reputation of Yap Ah

Loy, the militant secret society leader who founded the city of Kuala Lumpur, traced the decline of charismatic, military leadership among the Malaysian Chinese.[11] In both Malaysia and Singapore it was the same. There was no longer room for heroes. The rise in importance of taukehs, of economic leadership, was not, in itself, a disadvantage; but the elimination of a path for charismatic and popular leadership seriously weakened the basis of community. Depoliticized communities are like AIDS victims, they have no host defense mechanisms against the political cancer of tyranny.

It is perhaps for this very reason that the Chinese of Johor continue to gather for their semiannual sacrifice to their ancestors of the Ngee Heng. Today, effective Chinese political activity is as likely to meet with approval from the established political authorities as it was a century ago. The identity of the community is more threatened that at any time in the past. It is perhaps a time when heroic leadership is needed. The only viable example of effective Chinese political leadership remains the old symbol of brotherhood that brought the Chinese into the Malayan jungles in the first place.

11. Sharon A. Carstens, "From Myth to History: Yap Ah Loy and the Heroic Past of Chinese Malaysians," (1988), pp. 206–7.

Glossary

BALL. Of raw opium. A ball weighed about 3 pounds and was wrapped in poppy petals at the EIC factories in Patna and Ghazipur.

BANGSAL. A pepper and gambier plantation, usually including the cauldron and shed for boiling gambier leaves and buildings for housing workers.

BHANG. A cannabis preparation usually sold to Indian laborers under the farming system in nineteenth-century Malaya and India.

CATTY (*kati*). A weight equivalent to 1⅓ pounds, or sixteen tahils (s.v.) (taels).

CHANDU. Opium prepared for smoking by dissolving raw opium in water and boiling it several times into a paste.

CHEE. A weight equivalent to one-tenth of a tahil (s.v.), usually used as a measure for chandu (s.v.).

CHEST. Of opium; made from mangowood; contained forty balls (s.v.) of raw opium packed into two levels and separated in pigeonholes. The entire chest weighed about 140 pounds or about one pikul (s.v.) and was wrapped in burlap and sewn shut. Cost depended on the Calcutta market if it was Benares (Ghazipur) or Patna opium.

CHINCHEW. A supercargo of a Chinese junk or Chinese-owned vessel.

CHINTENG. A private policeman in the employ of the revenue farmer, often known as a revenue peon.

CHOP. A trademark or trade name generally used by Chinese businesses, it served as the name of the firm.

CHUKANG. The headquarters of a kangkar (s.v.) village; sometimes included the surrounding pepper and gambier plantations as well; usually prefixed by the proper name of the settlement (Tan Chukang, Lim Chukang, Chan Chukang).

DOLLAR. The Spanish or Mexican silver dollar, standard commercial currency of Southeast Asia and the China coast in the colonial era; contains about one ounce of silver; worth about four shillings.

HOON. A weight, equivalent to one-tenth of a chee (s.v.); usually used as a measure for chandu (s.v.).

241

HUI. A society, possibly a secret society or triad (s.v.).

HUI GUAN. An association not usually a triad (s.v.).

KAMPONG. (Mal.) Village or settlement.

KANG. A port or river mouth.

KANGCHU. The head of a river mouth settlement of pepper and gambier planters in Singapore, Riau, or Johor.

KANGKAR. The seat of the kangchu (s.v.), usually a couple of rows of shop houses near a landing or dock. The shops included gambling and opium dens, a pawnbroker, a pig farm, a small temple or shrine, a couple of general provision shops, and a few residences.

KAPITAN. (Port.) The head of the Chinese community in a colonial city of Southeast Asia, usually appointed by the government.

KONGSI. A partnership, company, secret society, or other shareholding socioeconomic grouping.

NANYANG. The South Sea; a Chinese term for Southeast Asia.

ORANG LAUT. (Mal.) Sea people, usually boat dwellers.

PANG. A Chinese speech group or speech group organization (Hokkien, Hakka, Teochew, Cantonese, Hainanese, etc.).

PERANAKAN. (Mal.) Locally born.

PIKUL. A weight equivalent to 100 catties (s.v.), or 133 pounds.

PUKAT. A small Chinese-style junk used for local trade around Singapore and the coasts of the Malay Peninsula.

QUAN TECK (actually *Kien Teck*). The name of a secret society that appeared in Singapore in the 1840s to challenge the Ngee Heng.

RUPEE. The basic Indian unit of currency; worth approximately one-half of a Spanish or Mexican silver dollar (s.v.).

SAMSENG. A Chinese thug or ruffian.

SEH (Xing). A Chinese surname or surname organization.

SINKEH. (Chin.) Also "Hsin k'o," literally "new guest"; refers to a newly arrived Chinese immigrant.

SURAT SUNGAI. (Mal.) A river letter, usually the legal document, given by the ruler of Johor to the kangchu (s.v.), that authorized the latter to rule the kangkar (s.v.).

TAHIL (tael). A weight equivalent to 1.3 ounces, or one-sixteenth of a catty (s.v.).

TAUKEH (towkay). Literally, a head man or boss; used to refer to a merchant.

TEMENGGONG. (Mal.) Title of Malay court official, some of whom became territorial rulers in the eighteenth and nineteenth centuries.

TODDY. An alcoholic beverage made by fermenting the juice tapped from the flowers of the coconut palm; sold by farms or government monopolies in British Malaya.

TONGKANG. A type of boat, generally used as a lighter in the Singapore roads.

TRIAD. The union of heaven, earth, and man; the philosophical concept that underlies the Chinese secret societies or brotherhoods, often known as heaven and earth societies.

Bibliography

Archival Sources

Colonial Office Records (Great Britain)

Co 273 Series (Malaya).
Straits Settlements Annual Departmental Reports. Singapore.
Straits Settlements Blue Books. Singapore.
Straits Settlements Government Gazettes. Singapore.
Straits Settlements Legislative Council Proceedings. Singapore.

East India Company Records

Unless otherwise stated, these were consulted in the India Office.

General Collections

Accounts General Series.
Bengal Financial Consultations.
India Financial Consultations.
Letters, Political and Secret.
Separate Revenue Proceedings
Straits Settlements Factory Records. Penang Consultations.
Straits Settlements Factory Records. Singapore Diary.
Straits Settlements Records. Singapore.

Miscellaneous Documents

"An Account of the Revenues and Charges of the Bengal Presidency for Three
Years According to the Latest Advices with an Estimate of the Same for the

243

Preceeding Years." *Copies of Documents Drawn out for the Honorable Houses of Parliament: The Lords of His Majesty's Treasury and the Board of Control, May 1832–1836.* Her Majesty's Printing Office, London, 1837.
Administrative Reports of the Government of India. 1855–56. Pts. I and II. V/10/2 and V/10/4.
Administrative Reports of the Government of India, 1861–62. V/10/19.
"Collections Relating to Trade and Finance, 1811–1813." 262 pp. Ms. CPL.
"Financial and General Letters to the Court of Directors of the East India Company, 1812–1813." 325 pp. Ms. CPL.
"Financial Report to the Court of Directors from Lord Moira and the Council, 1814." 158 pp. Ms. CPL.
General Letters to the Court of Directors (from Minto, Colebrooke, Hewett), 1809–1812. 388 pp. Ms. CPL.
India, Financial Proceedings. Z/P/1259. Index for 1845.
Judicial and Revenue III, 1814, [12]. 552 pp. Ms. CPL.
"Manuscript and Printed Regulations etc. Concerning Salt and Opium, 1788–1850." 288 pp. CPL.
Memorandum of the Improvements in the Administration of India during the Last Thirty Years and the Petition of the East-India Company to Parliament. EIC, London, 1858.
"Public Letters from London to Bengal and Canton Detailing Changes due to the New Charter of 1813, 1813." Ms. CPL.
Seton-Kerr, W. S., C.S., (comp.). *Selections from the Calcutta Gazettes of the Years 1798, 1799, 1800, 1802, 1803, 1804, and 1805, Showing the Political and Social Conditions of the English in India Sixty Years Ago.* 4 vols. Calcutta, 1868. CPL.
Tabular Statements of the Commerce and Shipping of Singapore, Prince of Wales Island and Malacca for the Official Year 1862–63, 1863–64, 1864–65, 1865–66. Calcutta, 1867.

Johor Archives Records

Buku2 Daftar. Surat2 Jual, Beli, Pajak dan Hutang, 1284–1324 A.H. (Register of Bills of Sale and Concessions, 1867–1906). 5 vols.
Buku2 Daftar. Surat2 Keterangan Membuka Kebun, 1260–1325 A.H. (Register of Licenses to Open Plantations, 1844–1908).
Kumpulan Surat2 yang di-Simpan oleh Setia Usaha Kerajaan (Collection of Letters Kept by the Secretary to Government, 1843–1927).
"Letter Book of His Highness the Maharaja of Johore, 1855–1868" (JLB1).
Official Letterbook. 1885–1911 (JLB2). 5 vols.

Parliamentary Papers

Accounts Respecting the Annual Revenues and Disbursements, Trade and Sales of the East India Company for Three Years (1826/27)–(1827/28)–(1828/29)

According to the Latest Advices: Together with the Latest Estimate of the Same (1829/30). House of Commons, 1831.

Correspondence Relating to the Affairs of Certain Native States in the Malay Peninsula in the Neighborhood of the Straits Settlements, 1874–1916. Parliament, 1916.

Correspondence with the Superintendent of British Trade in China upon the Subject of Emigration from That Country. House of Commons, 1853.

Papers Relating to the Opium Question, Calcutta, 1870, with Supplement, 1872. House of Commons, 1872.

Papers Relating to the Opium Trade in China, 1842–1856. Parliament, 1857.

Returns of the Charges etc. to the East India Company Incurred in the Growth and Monopoly of Opium. House of Commons, 1857.

Returns of the Trade of the Various Ports of China for the Years 1847 and 1848. House of Commons, August 1849.

Returns Relating to the Trade of India and China from 1814 to 1855. Ordered by the House of Commons. Printed June 1859. Paper 38–11, vol. 23, 1859.

Statistical Tables Relating to the Colonial and other Possessions of the United Kingdom, Part I. Presented to Both Houses of Parliament. Eyre & Spottiswoode, London, 1856.

Articles

Blussé, Leonard. "Batavia, 1619–1740: The Rise and Fall of a Chinese Colonial Town." *JSEAS* 12 (March 1981), 159–78.

Blythe, Wilfred L. "Historical Sketch of Chinese Labour in Malaya." *JMBRAS* 20 (June 1947), 64–113.

Braddell, Thomas. "Gambling and Opium Smoking in the Straits of Malacca." *JIAEA,* n.s. 1 (1856), 66–83.

Butcher, John. "The Demise of the Revenue Farm System in the Federated Malay States." *Modern Asian Studies* 17 (1983), 387–412.

Carstens, Sharon A. "From Myth to History: Yap Ah Loy and the Heroic Past of Chinese Malaysians." *JSEAS* 19 (September 1988), 185–207.

Chen So Lan. "The Opium Problem in British Malaya" (pamphlet). Singapore Anti-Opium Society, 1 January 1935, p. 22.

Cheng, H. "The Network of Singapore Societies." *Journal of the South Seas* 6 (1950), 10–12.

Cheng U Wen, Lena. "British Opium Policy in the Straits Settlements 1867–1910." Academic Exercise, University of Malaya, Singapore, 1960.

———. "Opium in the Straits Settlements, 1867–1910." *JSEAH* 2 (March 1961), 52–75.

Chng, David K. Y. "On the Discovery of a Century-Old Grave of a Ngee Hin Headman, Chua Moh Choon" (in Chinese). In National Archives, *The Development of Nee Soon Community,* pp. 138–41. National Archives, Oral History Department, Grassroots Organisations of Nee Soon Community Publication, Singapore, 1987.

Coope, A. E. "The Kangchu System in Johore." *JMBRAS* 14:3 (1936), 247–63.

Crawfurd, John. "The Agriculture of Singapore." *JIAEA* 3 (1849), 508–11.

Cushman, Jennifer Wayne. "A Marriage of Convenience: Australian Mining Investment and Its Thai Sponsors in Early Twentieth Century Siam." In *Rural Thai Society: Development of the Thai Economy.* Chulalongkorn University, Thai Studies Program, Bangkok, 1984. Bound in a set of papers produced as vol. 1 of the proceedings of the International Conference on Thai Studies, 22–24 August 1984, 1–22.

———. "The Khaw Group: Chinese Business in Early Twentieth Century Penang." *JSEAS* 17 (March 1986), 58–79.

Dotty, E., and W. J. Pohlman. "Tour in Borneo from Sambas through Montrado to Pontianak . . . etc. during 1839." *Chinese Repository* vol. 8, pp. 283–310.

Earl, G. W. "Narrative of a Journey from Singapore to the West Coast of Borneo in the Schooner *Stamford* in the Year 1834, with an Account of a Journey to Montradoh, the Capital of a Chinese Colony in Possession of the Principal Gold Mines." *JRAS* 3:5 (1836), 1–24.

Fong, Peng Khuan. "Khoo Clan Temple of Penang." *Arts of Asia* 11 (January–February 1981), 105–11.

Forrest, Robert J. "Political Summary." *Commercial Reports, China, 1872,* no. 3 (1873), 104–5.

———. "The Chinese in Borneo." *China Review* 7 (1878–79), 1–11.

Freedman, Maurice. "Immigrants and Associations in Nineteenth Century Singapore." *CSSH* 3 (October 1960), 25–48.

———. "Overseas Chinese Associations: A Comment." *CSSH* 3 (July 1961), 478–80.

Hamilton, Gary G. "Nineteenth Century Chinese Merchant Associations: Conspiracy or Combination? The Case of the Swatow Opium Guild." *Ch'ing-shih wen-t'i* 3 (December 1977), 50–71.

Horsfield, Thomas. "Report on the Island of Banka." *JIAEA* 2 (June 1848), 299–397, 3 (1849), 796–824.

Hughes, George. "The Small Knife Rebels: An Unpublished Chapter of Amoy History." *China Review,* 1 (1872–73), 244–48.

Jackson, James C. "Mining in Eighteenth Century Bangka: The Pre-European Exploitation of a 'Tin Island.'" *Pacific Viewpoint* 10:2 (1969), 25–54.

Johnson, Bruce D. "Righteousness before Revenue: The Forgotten Moral Crusade against the Indo-Chinese Opium Trade." *Journal of Drug Issues* 4 (Fall 1975), 304–26.

Khoo Kay Kim. "Review of Lee Poh Ping, *Chinese Society in Nineteenth and Early Twentieth Century Singapore: A Socioeconomic Analysis.*" *JMBRAS* 51:2 (1978), 153–58.

Kramer, John C. "Speculations on the Nature and Pattern of Opium Smoking." *Journal of Drug Issues* 8 (Spring 1979), 247–56.

"Lan Fang Kungsi Chronicle." Reprinted in J. J. M. de Groot, *Het Konsiwezen Van Borneo,* pp. 39–54. The Hague, 1885.

Little, R. "On the Habitual Use of Opium in Singapore." *JIAEA* 2, (January 1848): 1–79.

Low Siew Chek. "Gambier and Pepper Planting in Singapore 1819–1860." B.A. thesis, University of Malaya, Singapore, 1955.

Mak Lau Fong. "The Forgotten and Rejected Community—A Sociological Study of Chinese Secret Societies in Singapore and West Malaysia." Dept. of Sociology, University of Singapore, 1978.

———. "Rigidity of System Boundary among Major Chinese Dialect Groups in Nineteenth Century Singapore: A Study of Inscription Data." *Modern Asian Studies* 14 (July 1980), 456–87.

Newbold, T. J. "The Chinese Secret Society of the Tien-Ti-Huih." *JRAS* 6 (1841), 120–58.

Ng Chin–keong. "Gentry-Merchant and Peasant-Peddlers: The Response of the South Fukienese to the Offshore Trading Opportunities in 1552–1566." *Nanyang Ta-hsueh-pao*, vol. 7, p. 167. Singapore, 1973.

O'Brien, J. Roderick. "Correspondence: The Use of 公 司 as a Translation of 'Company.'" *JMBRAS* 50, pt. 2 (1977), 171–74.

Pickering, W. A. "Chinese Secret Societies and Their Origin," *JSBRAS* 1 (1878), 63–84.

Pitt Kuan Wah. "From Plantations to New Town: The Story of Nee Soon." In National Archives, *The Development of Nee Soon Community*, pp. 193–225. National Archives, Oral History Department, Grassroots Organisations of Nee Soon Constituency Publication, Singapore, 1987.

Schlegel, G. "L'organisation des Kongsis a Borneo." *Revue Coloniale Internationale* 1 (1885), 448–65.

Siah U Chin (Seah Eu Chin). "Annual Remittances to China." *JIAEA* 1 (1847), 35–37.

———. "The Chinese of Singapore." *JIAEA* 2 (1848), 283–90.

Spence, Jonathan. "Opium Smoking in Ch'ing China." In Frederic Wakeman, Jr., and Carolyn Grant, eds., *Conflict and Control in Late Imperial China*, pp. 143–73. University of California Press, Berkeley and Los Angeles, 1975.

Thio Eunice. "The Singapore Chinese Protectorate: Events and Conditions Leading to Its Establishment." *JSSS* 16, pts. 1 and 2 (1960), 40–80.

Thomson, J. T. "A Glance at Rhio." *JIAEA* 1 (1847), 68–74.

———. "General Report on the Residency of Singapore. Drawn Up Principally with a View of Illustrating Its Agricultural Statistics." *JIAEA* 3 (1849), 618–28, 744–55, 6 (1850), 27–41, 102–6, 134–43, 206–19.

Tong Teck Ing. "Opium in the Straits Settlements, 1867–1909." B.A. Honours Academic Exercise, University of Malaya, Singapore, 1953.

Trocki, Carl A. "The Johor Archives and the Kangchu System, 1844–1910." *JMBRAS* 48:1 (1975), 1–41.

———. "The Origins of the Kangchu System, 1740–1860." *JMBRAS* 49:2 (1976), 132–55.

———. "The Rise of Singapore's Great Opium Syndicate, 1840–1886." *JSEAS* 18 (March 1987), 58–80.

Turnbull, C. M. "The Pepper and Gambier Trade in Johore in the Nineteenth Century." *JSSS* 15:1 (1959), 43–55.

Wang Tai Peng. "The Word *Kongsi*: A Note." *JMBRAS* 52:1 (1979), 102–5.

Ward, B. E. "A Hakka Kongsi in Borneo." *Journal of Oriental Studies* 1 (1954), 358–70.

Watt, G. "Papaver somniferum." In Sir George Allen, ed., *Dictionary of the Economic Products of India*, vol. 6, pp. 75–105. London, W. H. Allen, 1893.

Winstedt, R. O. "A History of Johor 1365–1895 A.D." *JMBRAS* 10:3 (December 1932), 1–167.

Wong, J. Y. "Monopoly in India and Equal Opportunities in China, 1830–33: An Examination of a Paradox." *South Asia: Journal of South Asian Studies* 5 (1982), 81–95.

Wong Lin Ken. "The Trade of Singapore, 1819–1869." *JMBRAS* 33:4 (1960), 1–315.

———. "The Revenue Farms of Prince of Wales Island, 1805–1830." *JSSS* (1964–65), 56–127.

———. "Review Article: The Chinese in Nineteenth Century Singapore." *JSEAS* 11 (March 1980), 151–86.

Yen Ching-hwang. "Early Chinese Clan Organization in Singapore and Malaya, 1819–1900." *JSEAS* 12 (March 1981), 62–92.

Yong Ching Fatt. "Chinese Leadership in Nineteenth Century Singapore." *Journal of the Island Society* 1 (December 1967), 1–18.

———. "Pang, Pang Organisations and Leadership in the Chinese Community of Singapore during the 1930s." *JSSS* 32, pts. 1 and 2 (1977).

Books

Allen, George Cyril, and Audrey Gladys Donnithorn. *Western Enterprise in Indonesia and Malaya*. Macmillan, New York, 1957.

Balasz, Etiene. *Chinese Civilization and Bureaucracy: Variations on a Theme*. Yale University Press, New Haven, Conn., 1964.

Begbie, P. J. *The Malayan Peninsula*, Oxford University Press, Kuala Lumpur, 1967. (First published, Madras, 1834.)

Blythe, Wilfred L. *The Impact of Chinese Secret Societies in Malaya: A Historical Study*. Oxford University Press, London, 1969.

Brown, Ian George. "The Ministry of Finance and the Early Development of Modern Financial Administration in Siam, 1885–1910." Ph.D. diss., University of London, 1975.

Buckley, Charles Burton. *An Anecdotal History of Old Times in Singapore*. London, 1903. Reprint, University of Malaya Press, Kuala Lumpur, 1965.

Cameron, John. *Our Tropical Possessions in Malayan India: Singapore, Penang, Province Wellesley, Malacca*. 1865. Reprint, Oxford University Press, Kuala Lumpur, 1965.

Chang Tsuen-kung. "Historical Geography of Chinese Settlement in the Malay Archipelago." Ph.D. diss., University of Nebraska, 1954.

Chesneaux, Jean, Fei-ling Davis, Nguyen Nguyet Ho. *Mouvements populaires et sociétés en Chine aux XIXe et XXe siècles*. Maspéro, Paris, 1970.

Chia, Felix. *The Babas*. Times Books International, Singapore, 1980.

Clammer, J. R. *Straits Chinese Society: Studies in the Sociology of the Baba*

Communities of Malaysia and Singapore. Singapore University Press, Singapore, 1980.

Comber, Leon. *Chinese Secret Societies in Malaya: A Survey of the Triad Society from 1800 to 1900.* Association of Asian Studies, New York, 1959.

Cushman, Jennifer Wayne. "Fields from the Sea: Chinese Junk Trade with Siam during the Late Eighteenth Century and Early Nineteenth Centuries." Ph.D. diss., Cornell University, Department of History, 1975.

Davis, Fei-ling. *Primitive Revolutionaries of China: A Study of Secret Societies in the Late Nineteenth Century.* University of Hawaii Press, Honolulu, 1971.

Feldwick, Edward W., ed. *Present Day Impressions of the Far East and Prominent and Progressive Chinese at Home and Abroad.* Globe Encyclopedia Co., London, 1917.

Freedman, Maurice. *The Study of Chinese Society: Essays by Maurice Freedman.* Ed. G. W. Skinner. Stanford University Press, Stanford, Calif., 1979.

Furber, Holden. *John Company at Work.* Yale University Press, New Haven, Conn. 1935.

Godley, Michael R. *Mandarin-Capitalists from Nanyang: Overseas Chinese Enterprise in the Modernization of China, 1893–1911.* Cambridge University Press, Cambridge, 1981.

Great Britain, Foreign Office. *The Opium Trade, 1910–1941.* Scholarly Resources, Wilmington, Del., 1974. Facsimile reproduction of Foreign Office Collection, F.O. 415.

Great Britain, Parliament. *First Report of the Royal Commission on Opium: With Minutes of Evidence and Appendices . . . etc.* 7 vols. Printed for H. M. Stationery Office. Eyre & Spottiswoode, London, 1894–95.

Historical Personalities of Penang, Penang Festival 1986, Historical Personalities of Penang Committee, Phoenix Press Sdn. Bhd., Penang, 1986.

Holloway, C. P. *The Tabular Statements of the Commerce of Singapore during the Years 1823–1824 to 1839–1840 Inclusive Shewing the Nature and Extent of the Trade Carried on with Each Country and State.* Comp. from official documents, Singapore, 1842.

Hong Lysa. *Thailand in the Nineteenth Century: The Evolution of Economy and Society.* Institute of Southeast Asian Studies, Singapore, 1984.

Jackson, James C. *Planters and Speculators: Chinese and European Agricultural Enterprise in Malaya, 1786–1921.* University of Malaya Press, Kuala Lumpur, 1968.

————. *Chinese in the West Borneo Goldfields: A Study in Cultural Geography.* Occasional Papers in Geography, No. 15. University of Hull, 1970.

Jackson, R. N. *Immigrant Labour and the Development of Malaya, 1776–1920: A Historical Monograph.* University of Malaya, Kuala Lumpur, 1961.

Khoo Kay Kim. *The Western Malay States, 1850–1873: The Effects of Commercial Development on Malay Politics.* Oxford University Press, Kuala Lumpur, 1972.

Lee Poh Ping. "Chinese Society in Nineteenth and Early Twentieth Century Singapore: A Socioeconomic Analysis." Ph.D. diss., Cornell University, 1974.

————. *Chinese Society in Nineteenth Century Singapore: A Socioeconomic Analysis.* Oxford University Press, Kuala Lumpur, 1978.

Le Fevour, Edward. *Western Enterprise in Late Ch'ing China: A Selective Survey of Jardine, Matheson and Company's Operations, 1842–1895.* Harvard East Asian Research Center, 1968.

Lim, Margaret Julia Beng Chu. "Britain and the Termination of the India-China Opium Trade, 1905–1913." Ph.D. diss., London School of Economics, 1969.

Lo Kuan-chung. *Three Kingdoms: China's Epic Drama.* Trans. and ed. Moss Roberts. Pantheon, New York, 1976.

Lovat, Lady Alice. *The Life of Sir Frederick Weld: A Pioneer of Empire.* John Murray, London, 1924.

Lubbock, Basil. *The Opium Clippers.* Brown, Son & Ferguson, Glasgow, 1933.

McNair, Major J. F. A., and W. D. Bayliss. *Prisoners Their Own Warders.* London, 1899.

Mak Lau Fong. *The Sociology of Secret Societies: A Study of Chinese Secret Societies in Singapore and Peninsular Malaysia.* Oxford University Press, Kuala Lumpur, 1981.

Marshall, P. J. *East Indian Fortunes: The British in Bengal in the Eighteenth Century.* Clarendon Press, Oxford University Press, Oxford, 1976.

Mukherjee, Ramkrishna. *The Rise and Fall of the East India Company: A Sociological Appraisal.* Monthly Review Press, New York, 1973.

National Archives. *Scholar, Banker, Gentleman Soldier: The Reminiscences of Dr. Yap Pheng Geck.* Times Books, Singapore, 1982.

——. *History of the Chinese Clan Associations in Singapore.* National Archives, Oral History Department, Singapore Federation of Chinese Clan Associations Publication. Singapore News & Publications, Singapore, 1986.

——. *The Development of Nee Soon Community.* National Archives, Oral History Department, Grassroots Organisations of Nee Soon Constituency Publication, Singapore, 1987.

——. *A Pictorial History of Nee Soon Community.* National Archives, Oral History Department, Grassroots Organisations of Nee Soon Constituency, Singapore, 1987.

Newbold, T. J. *Political and Statistical Account of the British Settlements in the Straits of Malacca.* 2 vols. London, 1836.

Ng Chin-keong. *Trade and Society: The Amoy Network on the China Coast, 1683–1735.* Singapore University Press, Singapore, 1983.

Nightengale, Pamela. *Trade and Empire in Western India, 1784–1806.* Cambridge South Asian Studies Series, Cambridge University Press, Cambridge, 1970.

Oliphant, Laurence. *Narrative of the Earl of Elgin's Mission to China and Japan in the Years 1857, '58, '59.* 2 vols. Blackwood, Edinburgh, 1859. Reprinted, in 1 vol., Kelley, New York, 1969.

Owen, David Edward. *British Opium Policy in India and China.* Yale University Press, New Haven, Conn., 1934.

Purcell, Victor. *The Chinese in Southeast Asia,* 2d ed. Oxford University Press, London, 1965.

——. *The Chinese in Malaya.* Oxford University Press, Kuala Lumpur, 1967.

Report of the Opium Commission (Singapore, 1908). Government Printing Office, Singapore, 1909 (vols. I and III published).

Rush, James R. *Opium to Java: Revenue Farming and Chinese Enterprise in Colonial Indonesia, 1860–1910*. Cornell University Press, Ithaca, N.Y., 1990.

Sadka, Emily. *The Protected Malay States, 1874–1895*. University of Malaya Press, Kuala Lumpur, 1968.

Scott, James C. *The Moral Economy of the Peasant: Rebellion and Subsistence in Southeast Asia*. New Haven, Conn., Yale University Press, 1976.

Skinner, G. William. *Chinese Society in Thailand: An Analytical History*. Cornell University Press, Ithaca, N.Y., 1957.

Song Ong Siang. *One Hundred Years History of the Chinese in Singapore*. University of Malaya Press, Singapore, 1967. Reprint.

Thio, Eunice. *British Policy in the Malay Peninsula, 1880–1910: The Southern Malay States*, vol 1. University of Malaya Press, Singapore, 1969.

Trocki, Carl A. *Prince of Pirates: The Temenggongs and the Development of Johor and Singapore, 1784–1885*. Singapore University Press, Singapore, 1979.

Turnbull, C. M. *The Straits Settlements: From Indian Presidency to Crown Colony, 1824–1867*. Oxford University Press, Singapore, 1975.

——. *A History of Singapore*. Oxford University Press, Kuala Lumpur, 1977.

U.S. Department of the Interior, Census Office. *Report on the Manufacturing Industries of the United States at the Eleventh Census, 1890*. Pt. 1, "Totals for States and Industries." Government Printing Office, 1895.

——. *Twelfth Census of the United States, 1900, IX: Census of Manufactures*, pt. 3, pp. 719–920. Special Reports: George C. Houghton, "Leather, Tanned, Curried and Finished." Government Printing Office, 1905.

Vaughan, J. D. *Manners and Customs of the Chinese in the Straits Settlements*. Singapore, Mission Press, 1879.

Walling, R. N. *Singapura Sorrows*. Singapore, Malaya Publishing House, 1931.

Wang Tai Peng. "The Origins of Chinese *Kongsi* with Special Reference to West Borneo." M.A. thesis, Australian National University, 1977.

Warren, James Francis. *Rickshaw Coolie: A People's History of Singapore (1880–1940)*. Singapore, Oxford University Press, 1986.

Wells, William S. *The Chinese Commercial Guide Containing Treaties, Tariffs, Regulations, Tables, etc. Useful in the Trade to China & Eastern Asia: With an Appendix of Sailing Directions for Those Seas and Coasts*. 5th ed. Shortrede, Hong Kong, 1863.

——. *The Middle Kingdom: A Survey of the Geography, Literature, Social Life, Arts and History of the Chinese Empire and Its Inhabitants*. Rev. ed., 2 vols. Scribners, New York, 1907.

Wong, C. S. *A Gallery of Chinese Kapitans*. Ministry of Culture, Singapore, 1963.

Wright, H. R. C. *East Indian Economic Problems in the Age of Cornwallis & Raffles*. Luzac, London, 1961.

Wu Lien-teh. *Plague Fighter*. W. Heffer & Sons Ltd., Cambridge, 1959.

Wynne, Mervyn Llwellyn. *Triad and Tabut: A Survey of the Origins and Diffusion of Chinese and Mohammedan Secret Societies in the Malay Peninsula, 1800–*

1935. Government Printing Office, 1941. (Released in 1957 with an introduction by Wilfred L. Blythe.)

Yap Pheng Geck. *Scholar, Banker, Gentleman Soldier: The Reminiscences of Dr. Yap Pheng Geck.* Times Books, Singapore, 1982.

Yen Ching-hwang. *A Social History of the Chinese in Singapore and Malaya 1800–1911.* Oxford University Press, Singapore, 1986.

Index

Library of Congress Cataloging-in-Publication Data

Trocki, Carl A.
  Opium and empire : Chinese society in Colonial Singapore / Carl Trocki.
    p.   cm.
  Includes bibliographical references.
  Includes index.
  ISBN 0-8014-2390-2 (alk. paper)
    1. Singapore—Social conditions. 2. Chinese—Singapore—History—19th century.
  3. Opium trade—Singapore—History—19th century. 4. Alien labor, Chinese—
  Singapore—History—19th century. I. Title.
  HN700.67.A8T76   1990
  306'.095957—dc20   90-55123